MOON

The True-Life Story of a Global Adventurer

POOL

MOON

The True-Life Story of a Global Adventurer

POOL

Jim Broman

MOON POOL
THE TRUE-LIFE STORY OF A GLOBAL ADVENTURER

iUniverse books may be ordered through booksellers or by contacting:

iUniverse
1663 Liberty Drive
Bloomington, IN 47403
www.iuniverse.com
1-800-Authors (1-800-288-4677)

ISBN: 978-1-4917-5039-1 (sc)
ISBN: 978-1-4917-5040-7 (hc)
ISBN: 978-1-4917-5041-4 (e)

Library of Congress Control Number: 2014918749

Printed in the United States of America.

iUniverse rev. date: 12/12/2014

You can't live from fear and *faith.*

CONTENTS

PART I
Moon Pool in Cyanide Creek— North Queensland, Australia

Over the course of time, I have come to see that life is a series of moon pools. I say this as both an experienced deep-water diver and a man who has sought and found lifelong adventure. My own life has been more exciting than even my wildest dreams, set against the backdrop of some of the most magnificent, exotic locales in the world: North Queensland, Australia (and various other parts of Australia too); Territory of Papua, New Guinea; Mozambique, Africa; Singapore; Japan; South Korea; Taiwan; Mexico; Southern California; and on and on. Always my experiences juxtaposed danger and deep beauty, excitement and tranquility—whether in the midst of African wildlife or immersed in the underwater mysteries of the Great Barrier Reef. I've led an incredible life.

Some of my moon pools have brought me to the face of death; others have shown me the true meaning of life. They've all been life-altering experiences, each in their own way: challenges, opportunities for growth or change or healing, incredible moments of varying duration that were nonetheless filled with deep and far-reaching significance. I've gone from one moon pool to another, always believing that the best moment was the one I was living in that very instant—because we never know how many moments we will have beyond that very instant. Relishing the preciousness of every single moment is the only way to live life to the fullest.

Those of you who are divers already know what I mean when I refer to moon pools. For you nondivers, a moon pool is an opening in a ship's hull (or in a specially designed platform or chamber) that allows access into the water. Marine technicians and researchers work with their tools and instruments in a sheltered environment by means of the moon pool. Moon pools offer protection from the elements; they are a safe harbor out on the open sea.

Early on in my career as a deep-water diver, I discovered the value of moon pools. Later in life, I came to see them as a metaphor for where we go internally to make our decisions and choices in life. The moon pool is the still, serene place within each of us. It is filled with wisdom and insight but only when that is what we seek. When we crave excitement and danger, the moon pool can be deceptively tranquil, as inviting, beautiful, and serene as a South Pacific lagoon—until we discover a raging whirlpool in its depths that threatens to pull us underwater and drown us. The surface of a moon pool may sparkle like diamonds or shimmer like pearls, but that gleaming, crystalline clarity is a mirage. Life is much the same: calm, untroubled times can become fraught with worry or stress or anguish or grief on the turn of a dime.

If only we could really go to an actual moon pool every time we encounter trouble or pain! Life would be so much simpler. But in our minds we can always access that center of serenity. This is the place where we each go to make our choices in life, whether we realize it or not. We each always have the power to choose which way to live, whether to go shallow or deep.

Moon pools are not always completely reliable sanctuaries for divers. Like any harbor, there are forces beyond the control of each moon pool. A moon pool may change at a moment's notice, with no warning, just as life can … and often does. Moon pools may suddenly become rougher, uglier, or murkier; they may suddenly turn dangerous, threatening, or dark. A clear moon pool can quickly develop zero-visibility conditions that will cause great harm.

What do you do in the midst of a suddenly dangerous moon pool? You always have the choice to abandon ship, to withdraw, or to hold the course and wait for calmer seas to return. It's the same way in life. It's always your choice where you go, in your actions, in your mind, in your heart, in your decisions. Things are always a mix of risks and rewards. You find yourself at the crossroads more often than not, and that is a moon pool too. Do you go where you have never been before, or do you play it safe and risk spending the rest of your life wondering, *what if?* You'll be tested through the choices you make in life, and the moon pool offers a way to prepare. Do you take the risk required to be courageous, or do you settle for being a coward? Do you stand up to speak the truth, to be a person of candor, dignity, and integrity, or do you take the easy way out, lying and manipulating to get what you want? Risk is always exciting; it's part of life, and courage and integrity are what you will carry with you until you draw your last breath. When you face your last enemy, death, wouldn't you rather say, "Go on and take me. I'm brave. I'm not afraid of you. I've lived full and well, so you don't scare me." When you say that, though, you have to mean it.

I invite you to journey with me now through the course of my life and its many moon pools—from nearly drowning in a flooded creek in North

Queensland, to fighting potentially fatal swells during deep-water dives in the Pacific, to winding up on life support as the result of a car crash. I'll give you a glimpse of one of my moon pools that was both actual and metaphorical. When I was the lead deep-water diver for an oil-drilling operation in Port Moresby, Territory of Papua, New Guinea, our contract was for the parameters of zero to five hundred feet. I entered the ocean through a moon pool—a thirty-by-thirty-foot opening in the center of the ship. It was a potential life-or-death situation, just as it would be for any hard-hat deep-water diver. Sitting on the edge of the moon pool in Southeast Asian Pacific waters, with swells bursting all around, it was truly the perfect storm. The seas were like the waves of Mavericks, California, during my youth.

I knew from the get-go that poisonous sea snakes swarmed in those waters, as did tiger sharks cruising to the ocean floor and looking for a meal. (They are second only to the great white in reported attacks on humans.) So the moon pool was my safe place but only relatively speaking. I hit the water, bounced up to the surface, dumped the air in my suit, and headed for the sea bottom through powerful currents so formidable that I could barely hang on to the guide wire that I clutched. (Guide wires are attached to the baseplate on the ocean floor, in this instance, 340 feet below the moon pool.)

The rest of this book will be like an exciting ride on a wave from Mavericks, California, as I share with you some significant moments from my journey through life. From a fifth-grader who brought a pickled octopus in a jar for show-and-tell, to a high-school dropout who joined the military tactical fighter squadron, to a deep-water diver, international entrepreneur, adventurer, wild man, and lover of women, I have pretty much done it all, seen it all, and lived it all. You will never forget my story because all I am about to tell you is absolutely true.

The Mistake—North Queensland, Australia (1975)

It was the wet season in North Queensland, Australia. Torrential rains had been pounding the area all day. Cyanide Creek had flooded, overflowing its banks. As I attempted to cross it in my Toyota Land Cruiser, I realized just what an out-of-control current it had become, as dangerous as any raging river. I had already committed to the crossing, so I had no choice but to go on. The problem was that the raging river had caught me off guard, which was not like me. Not like me at all.

Keep it together. You'll get through this, I told myself inwardly, drawing upon all the inner strength, resilience, and practiced calm that a life spent in extremely dangerous situations can give you. I took a deep breath, forcing myself to focus and stay calm.

Crossing the flooded creek was a situation of extreme danger, but, for once, it was not one that I had chosen. I had received a cable in my private mailbag (PMB 20) delivered to me by boat at the Cape, via Hayles Company, the same outfit that operated the cable ferry crossing the Daintree River. The cargo/passenger/mail boat left from Cairns and stopped in our cove. We would go out with our boat and get our mailbag and supplies at Cape Tribulation, and the supply boat would continue on to Cooktown. The supply boat would unload at Cooktown and leave for Cairns the following day. On its way to Cairns, the boat would briefly stop at the Cape again, this time to pick up our mailbag. This procedure occurred once every week.

Earlier that day, the supply boat had brought a cable. It was an emergency: I needed to call California immediately. This was serious enough for me to make the twenty-eight-mile trek through the rain forest to the Daintree River, take the cable ferry across, and drive to Mossman.

As a result of the call, I discovered that I needed to fly back to the States to take care of some urgent business related to property I owned along the California side of Lake Tahoe. (This is one of the most beautiful, crystal-clear mountain lakes in the world, and my property offered the most incredible views of the magnificent lake that anyone could imagine. Long story short, I risked my life to purchase that property, making dangerous deep-water dives for years in order to pay it off, and Governor Jerry Brown had put a moratorium on all building of properties along

South Lake Tahoe. Litigation ensued between the state government and the property owners. Although environmental issues were at stake, and certainly I supported the moves to prevent Nevada casinos from destroying the pristine lake and its environs, property owners who sought to live in natural beauty—and to preserve that beauty—should not have been penalized.) Suffice it to say, that was a heartbreaker. I was in a state of shock afterward, and on my way back to the Cape all I could do was think about that call. I wasn't really paying attention to the weather conditions.

As I started down the bank, with the emergency call to California still consuming my mind, it was pouring in sheets, but I was pretty oblivious. There was hardly any visibility, so I didn't realize the magnitude of the raging water in the creek. It was about to engulf the Land Cruiser with me in it; I would be a goner, just like that.

In the instant that I knew I had made a mistake attempting to cross, I also knew that I couldn't turn back. The bank was so steep and slippery from the incredible amount of rain coming down that I had no choice but to go down the bank and try to cross the creek. As soon as I hit the water, I knew I had to get out of the vehicle; otherwise, I would be trapped inside … I would drown in the creek that now was a savage, raging river.

As the vehicle was rolling underwater, I got out. The raging water turned the vehicle over multiple times, and I managed to get out on the passenger's side. I was underwater, under the vehicle, and then the current hurled me through the water.

For a split second I almost laughed, thinking I was really up a creek without a paddle. My deep-water experience, dangerous as it was, always came with top-notch equipment. Now I was at the mercy of the water. Huge boulders crashed into me, and I worried that they would crush me. The current sucked me under, but I fought to stay above water as much as I could. Somehow I managed to get to the bank without being crushed. I saw a tree root, grabbed it, and pulled myself up the bank. After what seemed like eternity, I lay exhausted on the rain forest floor.

* * * * * *

Meanwhile, my longtime girlfriend, Ali, was back at our place on the cove at the Cape. She was upset and very concerned because she knew I was out in the middle of this horrific storm, deep in the rain forest, on my way back to the Cape. Before long, she got on the remote radio to contact the Royal Flying Doctor Service (RFDS) that we belonged to, reporting that I had not yet arrived home from my trip to Mossman. (The RFDS is well known in rural and remote Australia as the provider of aero-medical retrieval and transport services, remote medical consultations, and RFDS medical chests. As members, we had a chest that contained a range of pharmaceutical and other items that provided us with the ability to administer health care in emergency situations. Aero-medical retrieval and transport services are able to respond to calls twenty-four hours a day, seven days a week. Cairns was one of eight bases in Queensland, and it was the one closest to us at remote Cape Tribulation.)

The thought of a saltwater crocodile attacking me terrified Ali; she knew that they came out during and after the big storms of the wet season in North Queensland. One of the most feared animals on earth, the saltwater crocodile has honed its hunting techniques for two hundred million years. No man is a match for this fearsome beast.

All these thoughts ran through Ali's mind while she waited for me to come home—or be brought home. I'm not a mind reader, so I couldn't have known it at the time, but she told me about it later. The weirdest part is that she couldn't have known how right she was to be afraid of my encountering a croc.

* * * * * *

As I was crossing the Daintree River on the ferry, on my way back from Mossman before the storm got so intense, the ferry operator had pointed to the Cape Tribulation side of the river where there was a huge croc close to the bank.

These crocs can grow up to eighteen feet in length in Northern Australia, and when they are that long, they weigh about two thousand pounds. They have been known to take down water buffalo, and they attack at least a couple of people every year. They are usually well camouflaged both underwater and on dry land, which is what makes them such efficient hunters; they strike at an amazing speed. The most powerful croc attack—the death roll—consists of grabbing the prey, rolling powerfully, and then dragging it under water until it dies. Don't confuse them with alligators; crocs are so much more aggressive and far more dangerous. They are cunning and smart and super quick. Although its jaws are the croc's weapon, its success depends on patience and the ability to ambush its prey. A crocodile will stalk a target for hours, even days if necessary, and an eighteen-foot, two-thousand-pound croc can hide in two feet of water and never give itself away. You can be close to shore and think you're safe, but you'll never see the attack coming. The crocodile explodes from the water, takes you under, and you're gone. It's over in seconds.

One almost took my good friend Wyatt, who'd bought close to three thousand acres in Bloomfield (farther north and up the coast from Cape Tribulation). I'll tell you more about Wyatt later. He lived on the property with his wife and children, in pretty much total isolation. It had been a really heavy wet season. He was and still is an expert fly fisherman, and there was a break in the heavy rains, so he headed out to one of the many streams flowing through his property. (These streams all flowed to the Bloomfield River and then on to the Coral Sea.) Fishing one of the streams, he caught a small trevally, and as he was bringing it in, a barramundi took it. There he was, with a barramundi hooked! He was thrilled because they are one of the primo sport fish in Australia.

The fish put up a savage battle, but he got it close to the bank. But then, from out of nowhere, a huge saltwater crocodile burst out of the stream, coming right at him. He told me it was no more than half an inch from his face, and he reckoned it was fifteen feet long or so. According to Wyatt, the bank behind him was about six feet high. He turned and scrambled up the bank as the croc lunged again, just missing his foot. As he kept on crawling, the croc's attention went to the barramundi still hooked and flapping on the beach. The croc devoured the barramundi. That was the only thing that saved Wyatt's life. There he was in remote North Queensland, with no neighbors for miles, and a fifteen-foot crocodile less than an inch from his face. He was still in shock when he told me about it, and I could relate.

I knew a lot about crocs because I had hunted them while living in Port Moresby (Territory of Papua, New Guinea) and later on in Darwin, Australia. My divers made extra money on their time off by hunting crocs and selling their skins for excellent money. After killing the first one, I stopped. I really didn't like killing animals. I had many opportunities in Africa, but I just photographed them. No killing for me except to protect myself and to provide food when necessary (like pig hunting for the Aborigines).

Wyatt's story stayed with me, and I guess it must have stayed with Ali too. There have been numerous reports of deaths in the Daintree River from crocodile attacks over the years, so I knew how important it was not to step close to the riverbank, to stay within the confines of boats, and to absolutely never swim in the river.

Mountains and deep valleys surround the river. Because of the climatic conditions of the area, the river is prone to quickly developing floods with little warning. Heavy rainfalls in the high mountain ranges (altitudes of 3,280 feet) around the catchment and the influence of the cyclonic forces in the adjacent Coral Sea all contribute to the river's propensity for flooding.

But never forget: crocodiles inhabit these waters. While Ali was worrying about my encountering a deadly croc, I caught a glimpse of one in the Daintree River—a little bit closer, I'd have been dinner. Soon after, I was fighting for my life in the torrent of the flooded creek and then lying exhausted on the rain forest floor. An extreme situation, to be sure, but a world apart from the magnificent rush of deep-water diving. It was more my jet-fighter training that got me through—that and the rescuers who answered Ali's radio call.

* * * * * *

I imagined my adventure reported by a radio announcer, broadcasting throughout Australia:

> A search party today left Cairns, North Queensland, Australia, for Cape Tribulation, a section of one of the most beautiful and exotic rain forests in the world. It is believed to be the oldest rain forest anywhere in the world, more than one hundred million years old, one of the only areas in the world where the rain forest meets the reef. This magnificent property, with its year-round warm climate, lush tropical rain forest, exquisite white-sand beaches, fringing coral reefs adjacent to the Great Barrier Reef, and pristine jungle

streams with tropical waterfalls that flow out to the Coral Sea, it is a true Australian treasure.

Upon reaching Cape Tribulation, you soon enter no-man's-land, exiting the main road and taking a ferry across the crocodile-infested Daintree River, then twenty-eight miles through the rain forest on a four-wheel-drive track, crossing jungle streams to the end of the track, which cuts Cape Tribulation off from civilization. The path is loaded with wild boar, the dangerous cassowary, and the even more dangerous saltwater crocodile.

Nevertheless, the drive to Cape Tribulation is stunning. A winding track meanders up and down, covered in dense rain forest. At various points, the foliage thins out, revealing views of white-sand beaches and the blue Coral Sea below.

A highly decorated, retired full-bird US Army colonel, David Hackworth, is personally leading the search party looking for his friend and fellow Californian, Jim Broman. The former owner of an elite deep-water diving company operating around the world, Broman now lives at Cape Tribulation permanently.

At one time, Colonel Hackworth was the most decorated soldier in the history of the United States. He was awarded a total of ninety-one medals, including two Distinguished Service Crosses, ten Silver Stars, eight Bronze Stars, eight Purple Hearts, a Distinguished Flying Cross, a Legion of Merit, and an Air Medal.

When he was just fifteen, Colonel Hackworth lied about his age in order to enlist in the army. He won a battlefield commission at the age of twenty, becoming the youngest captain in the Korean War. Later, during the Vietnam War, he became America's youngest full colonel.

He was in Cairns, North Queensland, when he first heard the news that his friend Jim Broman was missing. He was shocked. Before setting out on the search, Colonel

Hackworth made the statement that he didn't think Jim Broman was dead.

Nonetheless, Jim Broman's four-wheel-drive Toyota Land Cruiser had been found in Cyanide Creek. This creek is very slow and gentle in normal times, as compared to the other streams and creeks you cross on the way to the Cape. But it has a steep incline, and it can flow fast and furious during heavy rains, such as the storm that hit during Broman's journey from Mossman back to Cape Tribulation. Torrential downpours frequently hit North Queensland during the wet season. (The region gets some 250 to 300 inches of rain per year.) During the extremely violent storm that coincided with Broman's travel, Cyanide Creek had risen dramatically as huge amounts of water rapidly poured into its steep and narrow bed. Broman crossed the creek just as it turned into a raging river.

Locals say it was like an underwater avalanche, with huge boulders being pushed by the raging current, making it highly unlikely that any human could have survived it. This storm was unexpected and, again, extremely dangerous.

When the storm subsided, a local found Broman's wallet and passport. His Land Cruiser lay crumpled like a ragdoll—completely smashed, crushed, totaled, destroyed.

Locals say Broman had to have been mangled, mashed, and crushed, just like his Land Cruiser. His remains must have washed out to the Coral Sea, pulled by the massive torrent of water and the huge boulders pushed by the raging current. The vehicle had rolled and turned over many times.

By all reports, Broman was considered an excellent bushman who had made that trip many times. He had the best four-wheel-drive all-terrain vehicle available: a Toyota Land Cruiser, a brand-new flatbed. Broman was known to walk each of the many streams and creeks that you had to cross on the twenty-eight-mile track before getting to the Cape, so it was somewhat of mystery as to how he had been caught in that predicament.

Locals say it was one of the most savage, violent downpours that area has ever seen—at least in their lifetimes. They also say it was sad to see the once-powerful and capable Toyota Land Cruiser, the envy of the local populace for its customized flatbed that could be loaded with supplies, crushed, mangled, and made useless forever. And it was very sad indeed for Jim Broman, who had been so proud of that vehicle, who was considered an excellent bushman, and who had made that trip many times in similar storms. Welcome to the wet season in North Queensland, Australia.

* * * * * *

Meanwhile, Colonel David Hackworth remained convinced that I was alive, that I had survived—somehow. He was my friend, and he knew me. At the same moment, David Hackworth, Ali, and I all were praying for the same miracle.

On the trail where local residents had found my Toyota Land Cruiser lived a pair of conservationists, a beautiful Canadian girl and her boyfriend. To make a long story short, they talked to David Hackworth, telling him that they had seen me alive.

"At around two in the morning, a noise sounded in the middle of this savage storm. It scared us out of our wits," the girl told David.

That noise was me, Jim Broman.

In shock, I somehow made it back to the Cape. Ali was waiting for me. We were devastated by the loss of our beloved Land Cruiser. Ali explained that she had notified the RFDS, which in turn had alerted the authorities to start the search for me.

I decided to go by boat to Cyanide Creek to meet the search party. I wanted to meet them face-to-face to let them know I was alive.

I got a hold of Willem Rijker, whose place was the only one close enough to ours to make him really a neighbor. He and his elderly mother were just days away from moving, feeling that the area their family had settled in during the 1960s had since become too developed. (Keep in mind that this area still had no electricity, no telephone service, and no road, just a four-wheel-drive track through the dense rain forest.) Once the Rijkers left the Cape, Ali and I became the only permanent residents in the area.

I could have taken my bigger boat, but Willem's handmade teak boat was better to hug the coast. All the while, I was hoping he didn't wear his dress; it would be so embarrassing to pull up to meet the search party with Willem wearing a dress. But, sure enough, he was in a dress, a blue-and-pink number—thank God, it wasn't a mini! (I should add that Willem was a homeschooled mathematical genius convinced that wearing a dress made him feel "cooler" in the summertime. His brother tried to break him of the habit, to no avail.)

As I landed at the entrance to Cyanide Creek from the ocean, who was leading the search party but my good friend, Colonel David Hackworth. To his credit, as soon as he saw me coming in on the boat, he started shouting to the rest of the search party, "Here comes Jim Broman! I told you he wasn't dead!" He repeated this to me when I landed on the beach. "When I first heard the news in Cairns, I knew you weren't dead, Jim. I told everyone so."

It was so encouraging and heartening to know I had a friend like David. He was a true hero throughout his life. After we greeted each other, we hugged and laughed, and he teased me about Ali. He always flirted with her, and he had brought champagne to console her, in case he was wrong and I *was* dead. We laughed about that too.

David quickly dispersed the search party. They were all friends of his, so that was that.

We loaded up Rijker's handmade teak boat. It leaked, but we would bail with a can when the water in the boat started to be a problem. I put David on the bow, lying flat on his stomach on top of all the supplies he brought. And then we headed out through the gentle surf. David was a soldier, not a sailor, and I got a kick out of trying to scare him on the voyage back to Cape Tribulation.

To tell you a bit more about my great friend, David loved women, just like I did. He was a true hero, as I've said—on the battlefield and off. He was a born leader with great integrity. It was a privilege to know him and an honor to be called his friend.

Colonel David Hackworth and I originally met through a close friend of mine. David came up to the Cape especially to meet me; he'd heard about this American who had given up his international deep-water diving company and previous lifestyle in order to embrace the principles of the so-called hippie lifestyle. He had also joined the peace movement.

It was true that my company, Broman International, was the most efficient deep-water diving company at that time. As the owner of that type of company, David and I had a lot in common: the men who trusted us put their lives at stake every day. David's men stood on the front lines; the men who worked for me dived the ocean's depths. Both sets of circumstances were dangerous and potentially life threatening. More than most, David could understand why I would give up my previous glamorous lifestyle, drop out of the rat race, and choose tranquility instead.

When we met, that's exactly what I was doing: living this incredible lifestyle in the Australian rain forest, with my beautiful, dedicated girlfriend, and our wonder dog, Dee-fer. Ali and I were contributing members of the Kuranda Commune, doing our part in this exciting new era of "war" against the establishment and the old-time government.

At the time, I had no idea who this cool and powerful man was. But the moment he shook my hand, pronouncing, "I'm David Hackworth," I knew he was special. I also knew he was going to be my friend for life, my brother.

"What the hell are you doing this far from Redondo Beach?" David wanted to know.

I laughed at the reference to the town where I'd gone to grammar school in California. David was raised in nearby Santa Monica, a couple of beach towns away, before moving farther along the coast to Long Beach. Childhood and adolescence spent in California provided our first common denominator.

At that moment, David and I looked straight into each other's eyes, and then we both burst out laughing. Two adventurers who lived life to the fullest now sharing a moment together deep in the middle of the rain forest, giving each other mutual respect. I knew nothing about his military achievements then, but as I said, I knew just by his presence that he was an extra-special person. To put it simply, David and I clicked. From that initial meeting, we became fast friends, and we remained so.

David loved Cape Trib. He saw how organized I was on my property, and he respected the lifestyle. Cape Trib was remote and isolated; Ali and I lived with no electricity. We used lanterns for light, cooked with wood, ate vegetables and fruit from our magnificent garden and trees, ate fish and lobster from our little reef, and baked fresh bread every day in our camp ovens in the huge fireplace. We were like an ad in the *Whole Earth Catalog.* David thought it was great. He especially liked our hot baths. We heated the water in a copper tub over a fire every day; this was fresh, living water from the artesian spring next to our freshwater stream. The water came right into our kitchen. It was great; Ali and I loved those baths as much as David did.

Later a successful author and writer for *Newsweek,* David was very much in demand as a consultant. He eventually became a TV personality on Fox News. I did not learn until much later that his battlefield exploits were legendary; he was a powerhouse in the military.

"We were a wild bunch," David said in an interview with the *Los Angeles Times* in 1989.

He became more and more independent, even rebellious, over time, once threatening to take his troops to Canada if commanders persisted in talking about the use of nuclear weapons in Vietnam. He ran a bordello and a massage parlor in order to keep his men happy and relatively protected from a virulent strain of syphilis.

A true hero and a born leader, just like I said.

Having explained how I met Colonel David Hackworth at my paradise at Cape Trib in the Australian rain forest, my next story must center on how I came to Cape Tribulation in the first place.

Rosebud Farm—Kuranda, North Queensland, Australia (1974)

The commune's name was Rosebud Farm, but sometimes the locals called it the American Commune. It was a collective farm started by my friend Wyatt, who was the leader and financial backer. (This is the same Wyatt who nearly died battling a crocodile.) Two of his childhood schoolmates from Wilmington, Delaware, were his partners in Rosebud Farm.

Wyatt and I were kind of like the "hippie and the entrepreneur." As the owner of a worldwide deep-water diving company, Broman International, I was an entrepreneur from the "establishment." Wyatt was a self-proclaimed hippie. But in much the same way as I described what happened when I first met Colonel David Hackworth, Wyatt and I just clicked. I was completely captivated by this tall, lanky, East Coast young man, with hair to his shoulders, an earring in his ear, and either hiking boots or flip-flops on his feet. Wyatt and his two best friends lived in abandoned sheds or beneath the shade of any one of many canopy trees. (Incidentally, one of those friends was Charlie Dean, brother of politician Howard Dean. More about Charlie later.)

They were blue bloods, a family famous in Wilmington, Delaware. Wyatt's father was a former congressman and had also been mayor of Wilmington. Wyatt was a great guy, the oldest of eight children, and he rejected all that was offered to him. Eschewing power and prestige, Wyatt, his father's pride and joy, had become a hippie. Living out of a backpack, Wyatt had traveled around the world, from Africa to Australia. His extremely wealthy family owned valuable properties in the United States, and they were major stockholders in many blue-chip companies.

This East Coast scion was good at everything, but he didn't like school. He preferred to learn from experience, just like I did, which was part of the reason why we hit it off. Wyatt had a trust fund, so he could pretty much do whatever he wanted. It must have hurt his dad that his eldest son had hair down to his shoulders and an earring in his ear, that he smoked pot and was a free spirit. He was totally against the establishment, committed to his beliefs and to changing the world, and willing to risk it all. Of course, he did have his trust fund and wealthy family still behind him.

One day, Wyatt introduced me to Jack Duncan, the leader of the Cape Tribulation Commune who was visiting at the time. Duncan was one of the new messiahs, an ex-convict who had been buying property with the profits from his marijuana business. These properties were huge tracts of land, beautiful areas of the rain forest and cattle ranches farther north. Anyway, this leader of the Cape Tribulation Commune was extremely handsome, enormously powerful, and very confident. Arrogant would actually be a better way to describe him. In addition, he was radical and dangerous. Like Wyatt, Duncan wore his hair to his shoulders and had an earring in his ear, but, unlike my lanky friend, Duncan was powerfully built, lean, and muscular, and he talked like a messiah for the hippie movement. People on the commune would gather around him to listen intently to whatever he had to say. They called it a rave, but I thought he was just an enthusiastic rambler.

He soon showed me a baggie of his marijuana. It had a striking, eye-catching label, "Sunshine Marijuana," with an illustration of the sun bursting over a rainbow. The image was so attractive, so beautiful in color, it was impossible not to be drawn to it. They grew their crop on a patch, as they called it, way up in North Queensland, Australia, in the most remote part of the rain forest. I was very impressed.

Duncan rolled a joint, and we smoked. Man, did we get high; it was incredible dope. I was tripping at my friend's commune in the middle of the rain forest, just him and me and an ex-convict, in remote North Queensland, Australia.

The messiah then began to tell me about this property he owned, saying he was going to sell it and move farther up north, to another large tract of land that he owned. "The property I'm selling is where my commune is. It's called Cape Tribulation."

Remembering a conversation I'd had with my friend Charlie Dean about the same place, I was immediately intrigued. I'll share that conversation in full a bit later on. For now, suffice it to say that Charlie had called Cape Trib "magical." The name Cape Tribulation can be traced back to Lieutenant (later Captain) James Cook, who was trying to find a way through what he described as "the insane labyrinth," an "intricate combination of reefs in which it was difficult to find one's way or to reach the exit"—this maze, network, web, complicated arrangement, that was and still is the Great Barrier Reef. Cook's ship ran into Endeavour Reef, north-northeast of Cape Tribulation. He wrote: "I name this point Cape Tribulation, because here began all my troubles." And that's how Cape Trib got its name.

Willem Rijker explained the history of Cape Trib to me. The Rijkers had arrived in the early 1960s. This Dutch family floated up the coast on a raft and went ashore on Cape Tribulation Beach, where they laid claim to virtually the whole bay, as well as the beaches and forests in the hills behind it. To say that they were independent-minded people is quite an understatement. Local legend has it that when the father died, the family put him on a big pile of firewood on the beach to cremate him. A big landowner in the area was not impressed with this pagan ritual, and he made some calls to the authorities on his RFDS radio (there was no telephone in the area at that time).

The Rijkers were thus the original owners of Cape Tribulation—that is, in modern times. I've already described Willem, the dress-wearing math genius, at length. He had a brother, Robert, raised in equivalent isolation. Robert sold the property to the Cape Tribulation Commune. He had timbered teak lumber off the property, met an American hippie girl from New Orleans, and had one child with her (a little girl). The hippie girl became his common-law wife. He then went to New Zealand and bought a sixty-four-foot sailboat to sail around the world. During that time, his wife secretly left him, taking their daughter with her and returning to New Orleans, Louisiana. He sailed his boat from Australia to New Orleans, straight into the harbor. He found his little girl, allegedly kidnapped her from her mother, sailed to Florida, and headed back to Australia. What happened to him after that? I only know the details that circulated in North Queensland. Robert Rijker was a powerful man, and he made his own rules. He sued the mother of his child, a police officer, the United States government, and several federal officials for damages connected with the arrest for allegedly kidnapping his daughter.

Aside from enjoying the colorful details about the Rijker family and the ex-convict who owned the property afterward, Cape Trib was very famous. All its owners were Australian environmentalists who would not allow a road to be built to the Cape. When the authorities tried to construct a road, these people lay down on the ground in front of the big D8 Cats (Caterpillar vehicles). Not just adults but young kids too. This was not a stunt but a sincere attempt to stop commercial development of any kind. These commune dwellers planted and cultivated their own orchards and gardens, with the goal of being self-sufficient. They had a "sustainable" farm long before it was fashionable!

After buying the property from the Rijkers, the Cape Tribulation Commune purchased other plots of land all along the coast. Huge parcels were bought and sold; it was a huge land boom encompassing some of the most beautiful rain forest in the world, adjacent to one of the natural wonders of the world: the Great Barrier Reef (as described in Lieutenant Cook's log). This wonder truly defies description in words. The best documentary cannot do it justice, either. You have to be there, see it live, in order to fully appreciate its beauty and grandeur. I agree with Cook, though; it is a labyrinth, a marine maze that is a scientific marvel.

I could talk about the Great Barrier Reef forever, but back to the land boom. I was part of it but not part of the commune. I just fell in love with the magnificent rain forest—with the raw beauty of the landscape and with the simplicity and serenity of the lifestyle.

Seeing Cape Tribulation for the First Time— North Queensland, Australia (1974)

Jack Duncan, the ex-convict turned messiah and leader of the Cape Tribulation Commune, said that if I were interested, he would make arrangements for me to look at the property. I told him I might be interested and that I definitely wanted to see it.

I was far more anxious to buy my ideal property than I let on; I wanted to drop out of the rat race, to find the ultimate fantasy land, the paradise of my dreams.

He probably picked up on my excitement, in spite of my trying to play it cool (not that easy to accomplish when still high from some of the most incredible pot I've ever smoked), and he started telling me about Cape Trib. The way he described it, it sounded too good to be true, a real Garden of Eden—the paradise that most of us seek but never find. Along with a dream lifestyle, the property had sixty-eight fruit- and nut-bearing trees, including pink grapefruit trees, breadfruit trees, lemon trees, lime trees, mango trees, papaya trees, banana trees, macadamia nut trees, avocado trees, and others. All of them bore unbelievably delectable fruit and nuts, to hear him tell it.

The white-sand beach was loaded with coconuts trees, offering yet more fruit, and milk too. An established traditional vegetable and herb garden yielded a bounty to eat as well. There was an artesian spring that produced living water, the purest water you can get for drinking and irrigation. A pristine jungle stream that was loaded with jungle perch flowed through the property to the Coral Sea. Surrounded by some of the most beautiful rain forest in the world, it was full of magical waterfalls, complete with a reef that teemed with lobster and fish. In the mangroves, you could go mud-crabbing with a spear, and those mud crabs were delicious. (Mud crabs hide, and if caught, will instinctively try to grab you with their claws. If they do get a hold of your finger, they will clamp on you … and they hold tight! In fact, one claw is used to hold, the other to cut. You can often hear mud crabs cracking seashells in the mangroves. These crabs can shatter a human finger or toe if given the chance.)

Whether it was the dope I was still high on or the charms of this ex-con/messiah, I can't really say. All I can tell you is the prospect of rain-forest living sounded as delicious as the mud crabs—perhaps even more so. Once again, I remembered how Charlie had called Cape Trib "magical." I wanted to see for myself just how magical it was. Cape Trib was a siren song I couldn't resist. Not that I'd ever been able to resist sensual pleasure, much less tried to.

The time had come at last to completely withdraw from the rat race. Ali and I had been living in Port Douglas ever since the sale of Broman International. Our oceanfront living there was beautiful, but it wasn't enough. Cape Tribulation beckoned. Even if I'd known in advance about the near-fatal disaster in Cyanide Creek, I wouldn't have missed out on my life in Cape Trib. Not for anything.

I was about to dive into a new moon pool.

PART II
Moon Pool in the Rain Forest—Cape Tribulation, North Queensland, Australia

Words cannot adequately express the beauty and meaning derived from living amidst the magnificence and grandeur of the rain forest in Cape Tribulation, North Queensland, Australia. Snapshots I took personally of Cape Trib don't adequately capture the exquisite beauty of the place. You'll have to just take my word for it. I know that's an awful tease, like using words to describe a beautiful woman, when a photo or an oil portrait will take your breath away in an instant. But I am a storyteller, and I hope by now you feel that my story is worth waiting to hear as it unfolds in full.

The contrast between the exquisiteness and serenity of my new home and the rat race I'd left behind is far easier to express and explain in words than the beauty of the landscape of Cape Trib. Embarking on a life of tranquility and deeper meaning is rewarding enough in and of itself, but when it happens on the heels of a frenetic lifestyle filled with tremendous responsibility, the experience is incredible. The contrast between the two ways of life is breathtaking in the same way that great beauty and prophetic revelations are breathtaking. A single instant becomes transcendent and transformational at the same time. Anyone who has ever experienced it is never the same again; I certainly wasn't, and I never will be.

In a moment, you'll step beneath the green tree canopy with me, into the Cape Trib rain forest. The deep turquoise waters of the Coral Sea wash the perfect white-sand beaches, and unique creatures of earth, sea, and sky become friends and neighbors. Yes, I became a hippie. Ali did too. We loved living in nature, being one with it, gently using resources without laying waste to the environment or sacrificing it.

I went from successful entrepreneur to self-proclaimed hippie, seemingly on the turn of a dime. But I never looked back. And I never regretted it. Owning Broman International was a great ride, but, as I said, dropping out of the rat race was an even greater ride. Sure I was sad to say good-bye to the company I'd built and run on a daily basis, but I was relieved too. It was a complex mixture of emotions: sadness and relief. I felt sad about the end of all those great deep-water diving adventures and yet relieved that I would no longer be responsible for my crewmembers who engaged in dangerous work day in and day out. All major life changes involve a mix of emotions that stir us up. Remember, they are moon pools! And that's what moon pools are—seemingly tranquil harbors where we can rest and regroup, readying ourselves for the next big challenge, and yet always aware that the tranquility might not be as calm and smooth as it seems. Life isn't really about the surface; it's about the depths. That's what I learned from deep-water diving and living in secluded cove at Cape Trib.

I will describe my life and work as a deep-water diver later on. For now, follow me beneath that glorious rain-forest canopy, so close to the sea that its gentle roar always purrs in the background. Let's enjoy the surface for a while. We'll get to the depths in due time.

First Trip to Cape Tribulation: The Drive of a Lifetime—North Queensland, Australia (1974)

Jack Duncan made the arrangements for me to look at the property of the Cape Tribulation Commune, just as he said he would. I traveled that twenty-eight miles of rough track for the first time, riding alone in my new custom four-wheel-drive Toyota Land Cruiser. I drove through the rain forest, awed by its magnificence as I crossed the streams. The streams and rough terrain posed no problem for the Land Cruiser. It was the perfect bush vehicle: a special-order flatbed that was similar to the Land Rovers I'd had in Mozambique, Africa, and Port Moresby, Territory of Papua, New Guinea. (Obviously, the perfect bush vehicle was no match for creeks turned to raging rivers by the force of nature in the wet season, but I would have to find that out the hard way—just as we all do with the moon pools in our lives.)

I soon entered no man's land, exiting the main road and taking the ferry north. This was the only cable ferry operating within tropical Australia, and it ran across the Daintree River, which cut Cape Trib off from civilization. Even as I rode the ferry across the Daintree River, known for its saltwater crocodile population, I couldn't help but find everything around me magnificent and breathtaking. (Remember, this was before the trip that would become a fateful, life-threatening moon pool for me.)

The mighty Daintree River flowed out to the Coral Sea and the Great Barrier Reef. At various points along the meandering track, the foliage of the rain-forest canopy thinned out, revealing views of the white-sand beaches and the turquoise-blue Coral Sea below. I'll say it again: breathtaking.

In truth, I think the danger made Cape Trib even more beautiful and tantalizing than it would have been otherwise. I just knew that this was going to be my new home. I can't explain it any better than that. In the midst of all the danger I knew was there, a big moon pool was forming. I let the tranquility draw me in, even though I knew it wouldn't and couldn't last forever.

Cape Trib is probably the only part of the world where the coral reef actually meets the rain forest. There are miles and miles of unspoiled rain forest where the trees tower overhead, forming a large, dense canopy of lush, emerald leaves on jungle branches. The Great Barrier Reef is just offshore. The only sounds you hear are the wildlife rustling in the underbrush, the birdsong in the canopy and the air, and the siren song of the roaring ocean just steps away, not to mention the numerous cascading waterfalls with thunderous roars all their own. All the way through this twenty-eight-mile stretch of some of the most exotic rain forest in the world, everything is unique and matchless in its beauty for all the senses.

Driving is not the only danger of the trip, nor is the ferry ride across the crocodile-infested river. The many waterfalls can be extremely dangerous too, as the extreme rainfall increases their output in the same way that it swells the streams and rivers.

Nature in this rain forest is also dangerous. In fact, its danger is equal to its beauty. Remember, this paradise is loaded with wild boar, crocodiles, and cassowaries, to name but a few of the potentially deadly creatures that call the rain forest home. I've already shared plenty about crocs, and I'll share more stories about boars in a bit. As for the cassowary, it is the most dangerous bird in the world: it could rip a human apart with one swipe of its claw. And let's not forget the deadly plant life, some of which is so poisonous that the sting of the nettles could be lethal. The coastline is a haven for sharks and fish of every kind—yet again, a perfect mixture of danger and beauty, fascination and calm.

During that first drive to Cape Tribulation, all I could think about was how exquisite it was. It made me realize exactly what the word *breathtaking* really meant. The road was sometimes dangerous; it's just a just a dirt track that only four-wheel-drive vehicles could make all year round. There were many steams to cross. Sometimes drivers would wade in to make sure of the depth, as the rains of the day or week could change the water levels, and wading would offer assurance that the streams were indeed fordable. I faced no real dangers on that first drive.

As I drove along this track, I caught glimpses of the Coral Sea through peepholes in the jungle canopy, and in some spots I drove right alongside the white-sand beaches. The fauna and rain forest were exquisite. I found myself fascinated by the cockatoos squabbling over food and flying overhead like they were guiding me to my new home. They were cheeky, happy, and very noisy. The exotic grandeur and deep beauty were intoxicating, almost hypnotic.

At one point, I stopped to walk a stream to check if it was fordable, and a wild boar approached, bearing his tusks threateningly. I backed off and beat a hasty retreat for the Land Cruiser. A while later, while fording another stream, I encountered yet another boar, this one with an entire family in tow: a sow and six or seven little piglets trailing momma. They were very cute, but just like us humans, cuteness and innocence only last so long, and then they grow up and can become quite ferocious, savage, even dangerous. They crossed in front of me. The papa boar was fierce and arrogant, his tusks deadly. I stayed calm, letting them pass. I loved the entire experience; I was already getting used to what I knew would be my new home, so exciting and so dangerous.

I had lived in Mozambique, Africa, for two years, and so I was out in the bush a lot, watching and photographing the wildlife—elephants, kudos, antelope, lions, cape buffalo, giraffes, zebras, hippos, hyenas, baboons, monkeys, and crocodiles, just to name a few of the animals I saw on my safari adventures in Africa. That was magnificent, but this was different, even better: a tropical island paradise that I would own. It would be completely mine.

The very thought filled me with a blend of excitement and deep satisfaction as I drove my ultimate bush vehicle through a stream, feeling the water splashing and splattering the undercarriage and the sides close to the floorboard. I loved that too, especially because my superb, first-class bush vehicle seemed unperturbed. I thought, *I will need to get a snorkel on my exhaust system so I can go even deeper.*

When working throughout Southeast Asia and transferring to the drillship from remote tropical islands, I had thought those were the most beautiful places on earth. Up until the moment of my journey to Cape Tribulation, my favorite place had been Bali, Indonesia; it was exquisite and elegant. Cape Trib was different. Its beauty was raw and untamed. Plus, I was going to own it, possess it utterly, and live in my own personal, private paradise for as long as I wished.

Right at the end of the Cape Trib track there is the most amazing view of the bay and the rain forest meeting the ocean. This is one of the only places in the world where the rain forest reaches right into the ocean. The turquoise water is very tempting, and the property fronts on the Coral Sea. The blue-water cove is fringed by the reef that protects it from the open waters of the Coral Sea, and the grandeur of the Great Barrier Reef is right there. And all of it is surrounded by the enchanting rain forest. I was mesmerized by the beautiful cove, the white-sand beach, and the glorious jungle overhanging it all.

Even seeing the landscape with my own eyes, hearing the sounds with own ears, and smelling the heady fragrance of all the flowers and fruits with my own nose, I could not believe that such magnificence could exist together in one place. I would have my very own jungle, beach, reef and ocean, and lagoon. Was there any paradise that could compare on this green earth? I thought not, and I have traveled the entire world. The farther along the dirt road I traveled, the more certain I was that I'd found my dream home. (And, by the way, I never found a paradise to compare with Cape Trib, and I doubt I ever will.)

I cannot overstate that mere words could never do justice to the beauty of Cape Trib or to the hold it can have on a person. That hold was powerful in my case. Powerful indeed.

But now for the logistics of my trip. Jack Duncan had arranged for his girlfriend to meet me when I arrived. She was to show me all over the property, and then I would make my decision about purchasing it. Rumor had it that this woman was very beautiful, with long, black hair and an exotic look. This commune was known for its beautiful women. Jack's girlfriend was a half-caste (Asian-Australian), and she had the choice to sleep with whomever she wanted because she was the leader's woman. She surely exercised this prerogative frequently! But this was the free-love era and an accepted way of life by anti-establishmentarians at that time.

My instructions were simple: at the right time of the tide, I was to drive halfway down the beach. On my left, there would be a jungle stream that would burst out of the rain forest into the ocean, where I would see a huge coconut tree. The ocean tide dictated when you could drive the beach to get to the entrance of the rough, hand-cut driveway into the property that was hidden from the beach.

I followed the instructions. As I drove up the track and alongside the jungle stream, I came upon a grove of mango trees that lined the rough-cut drive. The trees were loaded with ripe fruit, and I reached out my window and picked a mango. I peeled it, took a bite, and fought to swallow hard as the juice ran down my chin. It was moist and luscious. The delicious taste of the mango brought back memories of the mangosteen, my favorite fruit from Southeast Asia. While living in Port Moresby, Territory of Papua, New Guinea, when working for International Divers, I discovered this delectable fruit during a trip to Bali. It tastes like a combination of a peach and a pineapple and is about the size of a tangerine, with a leathery, maroon rind that surrounds moist, fragrant, snow-white, fleshy fruit. (In fact, I went on and on about how much I loved the mangosteen quite often—so much so that it intrigued my friend Wyatt. He went to Bali, got some seeds, and planted them on his property in North Queensland. Eventually, he had several hundred trees, the largest orchard in the area.)

The mango I was eating now was every bit as good as the ambrosial mangosteens I remembered from my time in Southeast Asia, even though their flavors weren't the same. I couldn't wait to see how heavenly the rest of Cape Trib was going to be.

I didn't have long to wait, soon seeing a sawmill that had been used by the original owners of Cape Trib (the Rijkers I've already introduced you to). They harvested and milled exotic teak wood and red cedar. A small teak cabin was adjacent to the mill, surrounded by banana and papaya trees, ferns, and palms.

Passing the mill and cabin, I saw a football-field-length open clearing, with an orchard loaded with fruit trees and another cabin alongside the jungle stream. This cabin had a metal roof, and the entire area was exquisite. The way of life here was totally self-sufficient. Sixty-eight fruit and nut trees, plus the little private reef out front loaded with lobster and fish, provided all the necessary food. Not to mention the place was filled with hippie women to snuggle and cuddle with, trip on magic mushrooms and smoke joints with—and, best of all, have incredible sex with, all the time. Paradise. In every way.

It was getting close to sundown now, and I followed the rest of my instructions. I was to set up camp at the sawmill cabin. So far I saw no one. I walked down to the beach, and the sunset was overflowing with amazing deep yellows, oranges, pinks, and purples. The stream was powerful and beautiful, bursting out of the rain forest and emptying into the Coral Sea. The ocean cove was overwhelmingly beautiful and serene and yet filled with the quiet excitement of complete isolation.

It was the perfect location. When you finished spearfishing and diving for lobster, or just swimming and snorkeling on the small reef off the beach, you could stop to swim in the pool of the freshwater stream to wash the ocean's salt off your body. So refreshing.

It was getting darker, but still no sign of humans. By the time I got close to the cabin, it was almost full dark. I could see a lantern flickering inside the cabin. There was a bed made up with fresh linen and covered with a batik spread, and that was about all. I was tried from the trip, so I started to lie down.

And then, from out of nowhere, a young, attractive, black-haired girl in a sarong appeared. She held a bowl of fruit against one hip. "Do you want a bath?" she asked me. She was very pretty, sweet, and shy.

I wasn't shocked by the offer. This was how everything was going; this was the hippie era. I loved it.

I said, "Yes, I'd love one. Thank you."

I followed her outside to a little porch. She had heated water in a copper tub, and there was cold running water from a pipe that came from an artesian spring deep in the rain forest. This was living water, soft and sweet and pure, with no chemicals.

She had me strip down naked, and then she gave me a bucket to dip in the copper tub after lathering me up and rubbing me with a versatile loofah.

I poured the hot water over me and then rinsed with cold and hot water. She took off her sarong while bathing me, so she was completely naked. Muscled and strong, with beautiful brown skin from working in the garden, this young Aussie hippie girl was about eighteen years old.

The experience reminded me of my military days in Japan with my jo-san bathing me. (More about my jo-san later, in part IV.) After drying off, I felt so relaxed.

The Aussie hippie girl offered me a joint, and then she lit some incense. "I'll see you tomorrow," she said, and then she left.

I was aroused. She liked me, and I liked her. I found out later that she and the leader's girl had already checked me out as I entered the property. She was told she couldn't sleep with me; the leader's girl had made a claim on me first, but it was agreed that she could be with me later, and that did happen several times. And it was very passionate, as this Aussie hippie girl liked sex sweet.

Just as I was getting ready to doze off that first night in the cabin, a stunningly beautiful Asian-Australian girl came in. She took off her sarong and stood naked in front of me. The lantern she held flickered off her glorious bare skin. She looked at me, signaling quietly and shyly that she wanted to get in bed with me, and I lifted up the batik covering so she could climb in beside me.

As our skin touched, we blended sweetly, making love on and off all night. We were both exhausted, limp but satisfied, floating and blissful. Finally, we went to sleep, clinging to each other.

The jungle noises were alive at dawn. Cockatoos and other birds jabbered excitedly to herald the new day, all of them joining in for a beautiful chorus of rain-forest melodies.

As the sun rose higher, she was standing there, beautiful, long, black hair hanging to her waist in silky shimmer. Her sarong was batik, and she had fresh lemon tea and a papaya sliced in half. It was golden orange in color, with beads of juice inside, and a banana along with an oozing, ripe mango and a pink grapefruit all awaited me for breakfast. Again, all the fruit came from the property's many established trees.

I sat up to drink my tea, and we talked. She was very intelligent.

"I liked our lovemaking," she said directly. "I want to make love again."

She took off her sarong, standing before me naked once again. In the morning light, she was even more strikingly beautiful.

I drew in my breath at the sight of her, putting down my tea and food.

We made love all through the morning.

Afterward, she led me to the beach for a swim. We frolicked naked in the ocean, swimming to the reef about twenty yards out. We swam with schools of tropical fish, and I dived down to pick a lobster from under the coral. (I had picked many lobsters while living in Port Moresby and all throughout Southeast Asia. I had owned a lobster business that I started in Singapore with my agent, Glenn Wood.)

We were very stoned on the way back to the cabin, so we stopped by the freshwater pool from the stream to rinse off. It was heaven on earth. We smoked another joint and took a nap on the beach under a fig tree. She told me to follow her up to the top house (the main cabin), and I did.

This cabin was open, and it had a metal roof, as I described earlier. It was enchanting, perfect for me, handmade of polished teak and red cedar, with a concrete floor. It had a huge, long, low fireplace that was used for cooking. Camp ovens were used to make bread, and a grill was used to cook the fish or wild pig if so desired. No other power sources existed. (There was one worldly convenience, however: an old propane refrigerator.)

The master bedroom belonged to Jack Duncan, and it was the commune leader's privilege to have whomever he wanted to sleep with every night. He had seven women to choose from in the commune, but that amount fluctuated on a nightly basis, with young hippie girls constantly visiting the commune, looking for an alternative lifestyle. They sought to escape the city, to live the hippie lifestyle of free love, pot, and magic mushrooms. There were only two men in the commune: Jack Duncan and his right-hand man, an ex-Australian Special Forces guy named Tom Riley. The two of them had their pick of women.

The rest of the main cabin was one big room with built-in benches that served as beds and divans. They all slept together, men and women; it was an organized commune in the outer room. The stream that ran alongside the open kitchen area was where you cleaned your catch of the day: fish, lobster, prawns, etc.

There was a prawning boat that would often anchor overnight at the far end of the cove during the prawning season. They never came on shore, but we would go out by boat and trade some fruit or fresh bread for some fresh prawns, and they always had fish that they had caught in their nets. We could have our pick. Heaven.

But I'm getting ahead of my story. Back to my first visit to Cape Trib.

The young Aussie girl who had given me my bath the evening before was in the outdoor kitchen, alongside the freshwater stream with the small waterfall. She gave me a sweet, shy smile. She was topless, her young, magnificent breasts full and inviting, set off beautifully by the sarong around her waist. I gave her the lobster I'd picked off the reef. She smiled again, very impressed. I knew I was going to sleep with her soon, as the leader's girl was done with me.

I was intrigued by the Aussie hippie girl; I had been from the moment we met. I let pleasurable thoughts of her fill my mind while I waited for our inevitable time together. And it was worth waiting for. We made love many times, and it was always fresh, exciting, and mutually satisfying. I loved making love to women who loved sex.

In the meantime, I enjoyed all the other sensual delights of Cape Trib.

Water for the cabin came from plastic pipes connected to an artesian spring up in the mountains of the rain forest. Gravity caused the water to flow to the property, where it was used for drinking and irrigation and bathing, providing all the water pressure you wanted.

The gardens had large selection of vegetables, and orchards provided a wide variety of fruit and nuts. The papayas and bananas were the most succulent I'd ever tasted. I had never had breadfruit before, but it was incredible. The fruit grew on a tree, and when cooked, it tasted like potatoes.

If I could design the paradise of my dreams, it would be Cape Trib. I felt that way the moment I saw the place, and I feel that way to this very moment. I always will. Nothing could ever compare to the secluded lagoon, the ocean reef, the white-sand beach, and the rain forest beauty.

Literally feet from the coconut trees that fronted the beach side of the property was the most beautiful, exotic rain forest in the world, complete with the danger that made it even more magnificent—not just the extreme rainfall that caused the streams, rivers, and waterfalls to swell but also the wild boar and cassowaries that roamed the territory, and the saltwater crocodile always lurking and patiently watching.

I cannot overemphasize what a profound effect that first visit to the Cape Tribulation Commune had on me. This was going to be my new home. I had found my dream property, and I'd already decided what answer I was going to give Jack Duncan.

Duncan wanted forty thousand Australian dollars for the property. I had the money, as well as an extreme desire to live there and start a new way of life. I would have the paperwork drawn up by an attorney as soon as I got back to Port Douglas. I could hardly wait to own this beautiful property and live this exciting and exotic lifestyle.

As soon as I got back to Port Douglas, I contacted Jack Duncan. We had the contract drawn up by an attorney, and I bought the property for the agreed-upon forty thousand Australian dollars.

I was working on several other tracts to acquire as well; one very interesting one included Pascoe River. Another thirty miles of beach frontage and a river running through it was being sold as leasehold but could be converted to freehold if you did a certain amount of improvements. It was all promising, and I looked forward to having as many holdings in the gorgeous area as I could afford.

The Cape Trib Commune had a beautiful, lovely house in Cairns that they shared with a wealthy businessman, and he shared in their lifestyle, which included sleeping with their women.

I was at their house in Cairns, and one of the women who were part of the commune was there also. She was one of the sexiest women I had ever been around; she had a newborn baby that she was still nursing. She put her baby in a crib and came to me in bed, and we started making out. So erotic, sensual, and passionate. We made out with long, wet kisses. We were on fire. Her breasts were full of milk, and I loved the feeling. She loved it too, attaching herself to me, grasping and clinging. We held each other tight, and it was so very sexy. We couldn't get enough of each other.

It was the perfect experience to wrap up my purchase of Cape Trib: beautiful, sensual, exotic, and exciting. My new moon pool was starting on just the right note.

Paradise Found: Life at Cape Trib, My Dream Property (1974)

With all the legalities squared away, I was now the proud owner of the property at Cape Tribulation. This isolated, secluded, potentially dangerous, legendary, raw, untamed, exotic, and in all ways phenomenal place that was the perfect setting for me after dropping out of the rat race. Truly my dream home.

I've already talked about the beauty and the dangers, so now I'll describe what it was like to live in Cape Trib 365 days a year. In a word, it was heaven. Granted, the rainfall and deadly wildlife took some getting used to (and I never even talked about the pythons, wide array of other poisonous snakes, or the infamous deadly tick that could kill an animal or human through paralysis), but none of that diminished how much I loved living there. I'll say it again and again: it was an incredible lifestyle— exciting, beautiful, isolated, and as perfect as any place on earth could be.

Ali and I would start our day early in the morning, waking up to the sound of the Coral Sea gently lapping our beach and the birds singing their melodies in the rain forest. Our eyes would open just as the sun's first light burst, casting a glorious array of colors—yellows, oranges, pinks, blues—through the sky. With yellow sunlight bouncing off the turquoise water, dawn gave way to full daylight, making a sheet of glittering diamonds that covered the Coral Sea. This sight was breathtaking to witness, and we never grew tired of it.

Next, it was time to start the fire in our ten-foot-long fireplace. I had my own fire starters (small, chopped-up pieces of coconut husks). I had become skilled at husking coconuts, soaking the husks in the kerosene that we used for our lanterns, chopping them into pieces that we stored in empty coffee cans, and then using tongs to grab a piece of husk out of the can. I would throw the piece of husk onto the pile of wood in the fireplace, throw a lit match on it, and a blaze would start in seconds.

Ali made the dough for our bread, but I helped. We would put it in the freezer of the dented, beat-up, old propane fridge, so we always had a supply of dough. Then, all we had to do was take a ball of frozen dough, oil it up, drop it in a camp oven, and set the camp oven on top of the fire. That's bread baking in paradise! As the first set of coals got the ovens hot, we'd add just enough wood to reach the perfect temperature. The camp ovens would keep it at that perfect temperature throughout the day, and we would leave the bread to bake. It would stay warm and fresh, and it was a delight to take the lid off the camp oven and have the aroma of fresh bread engulf and consume us—especially my world-famous cinnamon bread! We usually baked two loaves at a time (which meant using two camp ovens). Ali's bread was both healthy and delicious. My cinnamon bread was also delicious; how healthy it was I can't really say.

Ali always laughed at me with my peanut butter and what she called my "junk-food bread," but she loved the lobster that I caught on our little reef and the fresh fish that I speared. We cooked these over open fires too, and there is nothing more delicious than fresh-caught seafood.

With the breads baking in the camp ovens, we would throw some wood in the cut-out space at the bottom of an empty forty-four-gallon drum. We had cut the top out also, and we had a copper tub sitting in it. We would fill the copper tub with water, and the heat from the fireplace would keep the water hot all day and night—for washing, for doing the dishes, and for the wonderful baths we took at night.

Our kitchen was awesome, with a metal roof and a concrete floor, and standing right next to the jungle stream and a waterfall. The artesian spring brought us pure, fresh water right there.

With those tasks completed, it was time for breakfast. Ali always had papaya, which she loved for its sweet, musky undertones and soft, butter-like consistency. Christopher Columbus reputedly called it the "fruit of the angels." This exotic fruit was Ali's favorite breakfast, mixed with pink grapefruit and banana. Papaya trees produce fruit year-round.

I preferred mango for breakfast, and I would grab a fresh one right off a tree every morning for breakfast. A mango should be fragrant when held near your nose so you know it's ripe. When ripe, this is such a sweet, luscious, and juicy fruit.

By the time we finished our morning chores and breakfast, the heady tropical sun would already be warm and wonderful. We would decide what we were going to do that day—work in the garden, go for a swim, play with the dogs (more about our two dogs and how we got them in a little bit), and get the boat ready to explore some more of the Great Barrier Reef. Every day was exciting and wonderful, different from any other time in my life … mellow, rich, and relaxed, even though danger always lurked in the rain forest. But that is the price you pay when you live in paradise, and it is well worth it.

The only time we had a more structured schedule was on "Boat Day." This was the day when the cargo/passenger/mail boat from Hayles Company arrived in our cove en route to Cooktown. Boat Day occurred once a week, at which time we received the mail delivered to us and the supplies we had ordered in advance so they would arrive on time. We would take our boat and meet the supply boat in our private little cove, and then we would transfer our supplies and mail from the supply boat to our boat. Sometimes they would have a forty-four-gallon drum of fuel that we had ordered. We would roll it off into the water and then tow it in to the beach with our dive boat.

All through these exciting activities, of course, the majesty of the rain forest and the magnificence of the Great Barrier Reef were mere steps away from us. Can you blame me if I keep on saying it was incredible?

Before I go any further, I need to tell you some more about my longtime girlfriend, Ali. We had lived together in Port Douglas before moving to Cape Trib. Among her many talents, Ali was an excellent record keeper, and she always knew exactly what our supply inventory was, from our living essentials to the pleasure items we enjoyed. For example, we smoked Drum tobacco that we rolled ourselves. It was a great smoke, and I always had a packet on me. Come to think of it, I'm not really sure if that would be an essential or a pleasure item! Regardless, Ali was the one who kept track of everything, and she always made sure I had everything I needed and wanted. She was amazing.

Not only did she take excellent care of me, she taught me things no one else could. Ali would nail me on things when I was wrong. She never judged me, but she'd give me this look that said, "Busted!" That was the end of it; I could never again pretend that I was right on that particular issue. I learned so much from her about life and women. She was the most loyal friend I ever had. To show you just how loyal she was, when we crossed the Daintree River by ferry, she would carry our joints in a baggie in her panties. That's about as loyal as you can get!

In addition to being loyal (or maybe because she was so loyal), Ali never lied. I could trust her with my deepest secrets, my life, my heart, and my soul. This little, sexy, beautiful, gorgeous fox from the American Midwest, with the low, sexy voice and the drop-dead body and the thick, jet-black hair, was a one-of-a-kind woman. A once-in-a-lifetime woman. Spoiler alert: I let her go, but I had to—my addiction wouldn't let me stay with one woman. I was cursed. I loved her enough to let her go, but it hurt. She loved me enough to let me go, and I know it hurt her too. I never found anyone else like her, and that was the greatest loss of my life.

Now that you know how it ended for us, let me share more of our life together. Even the unhappy ending has not dimmed the incredible passion and feeling we shared. It never will. That part of love does last forever.

We would go out to our secluded beach, smoke a joint, enjoy majestic sunsets bursting out of the sky, and make love.

Then, at low tide on the nights when there was a full moon and the tide would be highest, we would set a one-hundred-foot-long net, going straight out from the beach. Sometime around midnight, we would take our dinghy and pull ourselves along the net, picking it up every five feet or so. There would be an amazing assortment of every kind of fish imaginable stuck in the net: hammerhead sharks, reef sharks, plus a variety of tropical reef fish, including mangrove jack, coral trout, barramundi, mackerel, queen fish, and a host of others species. The fish we weren't going to eat we would release from the net, and they would swim off.

That was just one of the many incredible kinds of experiences Ali and I shared. I'll get to more of them later. First, I need to introduce you to the two dogs we both adored: Dee-fer and Midnight.

Dee-Fer and Midnight Join Our Cape Trib Home (1974)

It was pouring and had been for days. We didn't know it yet, but this was going to be one of the wettest wet seasons ever. Aussies call the wet season simply "the wet," with good reason. This wet, in fact, was one for the record books. Safe and snug in our cabin many miles from civilization and totally secluded from our fellow humans, Ali and I cuddled up as the torrents of rain poured down from the night sky. The rain seemed to be an interminable waterfall from the very heavens.

Remember, we lived in complete isolation at Cape Trib. All of sudden, a human voice sounded through the rain-filled night. "Hello!"

Ali and I looked at each other. Was this a warning or alert of some kind? I grabbed my 20-gauge shotgun just in case.

"Hello!" the voice shouted again.

We still didn't know who it was, but in the next instant, there was our friend, a Canadian beachcomber known to everyone simply as Old Bert, standing on the covered porch. He was dripping wet, and so was the black puppy he held.

Ushering Bert inside, Ali brought towels for him and the dog. Ali dried the puppy with a towel. Its coal-black fur was almost the same color as Ali's beautiful hair. The puppy looked up at us with glistening eyes, and Ali smiled at me. I could tell it was instant love, so it seemed like we now had a dog!

Bert settled in. "The mother used to belong to a guy I know. He named her Dee-fer—comes from 'D for dog,'" he told us. "Dee-fer's been at my place for a while now, and she just had some pups. I saved this little guy special for you, Ali," he added, turning toward her with a shy smile.

Ali smiled back, touching his shoulder. "Thanks, Bert," she said in that low, throaty, sexy voice that I loved.

She put the puppy on the bed. The puppy seemed equally thrilled and delighted with Ali.

I wasn't surprised: all the guys loved my girlfriend! Why would dogs be an exception? Grinning, I watched the two of them. Ali seemed overjoyed, and I was absolutely for anything that made her so happy.

By that point, it was just about midnight.

"Time for me to head back to camp," Bert said as he stood up.

"Sure you don't want to stay?" Ali asked, knowing it would be a three-hour walk for him in this storm.

"No, thanks." He took off into the night, the darkness and sheets of rain swallowing him up.

"He'll be fine," I told Ali reassuringly.

Not too many people would willingly make a three-hour walk in any weather—let alone a monsoon—but Old Bert was a rather unusual individual. We both knew that he wanted to get back to his camp so he could drink more of his meth. He seemed his typical higher-than-a-kite self. Now, in Bert's defense, he could walk tripping on meth or acid, in this storm or any other. It wouldn't bother him a bit; he would enjoy seeing the rain forest come alive. The jungle leaves and the eyes of the fauna would glisten; the creeks and waterfalls would burst with energy, beauty, and power, renewed by the rainfall; the frogs, wild boar, crocs, and other wildlife would get their baths, along with fresh food washed up by the rain; the ocean would roll loudly, receiving a massage from the torrents of rain. Most assuredly, Bert would find nature's display quite riveting in his heightened state of awareness.

As usual, Ali seemed to be thinking the same thing I was thinking. "Yeah, I guess Bert being Bert, he'll enjoy the walk." She winked at me, and we both laughed.

We were thrilled with the little black pup, so cute and lovable.

"Let's call him Midnight," we both said at the same time, laughing again. We agreed it was the perfect name for the puppy; his fur was so black, and he arrived on our doorstep at midnight.

We were setting up a little bed for Midnight next to Ali's side of the bed when I saw something on the porch: a beautiful dog with short, shiny, coal-black hair and a white diamond on her chest. This had to be the mother dog, Dee-fer, that Old Bert had told us about. Must have followed him all the way here. She lay down and looked at us and the pup very politely, as if asking if she could come in to see her baby.

"Come here, girl," I said, extending my hand.

She came in, humbly and respectfully, and we put the pup down next to her. She licked him tenderly, carefully examined him, and then went back to the front porch and lay down once again. The dog was clearly exhausted.

We got her some food and water and a blanket to sleep on for the night. I looked at Ali, and she looked at me.

"Mm-hmm," she said.

I gave her a sheepish grin. My love for the momma dog was as instantaneous as Ali's for the puppy. My girlfriend knew me too well. From that moment on, the momma was my dog, and the puppy was Ali's.

Dee-fer and Midnight fit into our life perfectly. Dee-fer was almost a dog genius. She had kept her prior owner in supply of wild pig, in addition to accomplishing a host of other essential tasks. A sheepdog from Victoria, Dee-fer was well trained and, as I said, brilliant. She adapted to the rain forest as well as she'd adapted to her previous habitats.

Given my description of Old Bert, it will come as no surprise that her prior owner was a dope grower. I'd suspected as much when Bert described her as belonging to "some guy I know." Once Dee-fer joined our happy home, I asked Bert more about her origins. It turned out that when her prior owner got busted, Dee-fer took off, heading for the coast and eventually making her way to Cape Trib. Old Bert came across her, recognized her, and took her back to his camp.

Let me back up a little and tell you some more about Old Bert. As I've already shared, Bert was ripped on meth most of the time, and he took LSD too. Actually, he took *anything* that was a drug. He particularly enjoyed mushrooms, but meth was his mainstay. He lived by himself in his camp, but he would be a lookout for the dope growers. In exchange, they gave him money, food, and drugs.

Ali and I knew Bert from the beach. He would come down to the cove on Boat Day sometimes, and we would give him handouts. The handouts were really Ali's idea. Bert couldn't get over how kind she was, and that was how we became friends.

I had all kinds of friends, and I liked Bert. It was fine with me that Ali wanted to help him. That was just the way she was; she treated everyone with kindness. She had this special way about her that people responded to. That was why Old Bert loved her. All my friends loved her too. From Colonel David Hackworth, a decorated military hero, to a beach bum meth-head, everyone—*everyone*—loved her.

But back to Old Bert, that's pretty much the whole story—or what I know of his story anyway. That much meth, mushrooms, and LSD pretty much erases a man's story, memory, and everything else. He had a good heart, though. That was why he let Dee-fer stay with him, why he found homes for her pups. When I told him I was keeping Dee-fer, he was fine with it. He knew we'd take good care of both dogs. Besides, it made Ali happy, and Bert would do anything for her.

In any case, when I found out from Bert what a great hunting dog Dee-fer was, I decided to test her skills myself. I took my Browning 20-gauge shotgun, called Dee-fer, and went out to the porch.

"Dee-fer and I are going into the rain forest for some wild pig," I told Ali.

Wild boar would attack without provocation, and a boar could kill you by brutally goring you to death. I was taking the shotgun more for self-defense than hunting, per se, but I wanted to see Dee-fer in action. I wanted to see myself in action too.

I gave Dee-fer all the common commands that Aussies use, and she knew them all. She responded effortlessly.

As we neared the end of the beach, the trail went into the dense rain forest, beautiful and forbidding during the wet.

I gave Dee-fer a command I had not yet used: "Sue 'em up!" That command was specific for hunting pig.

Reading my mind, Dee-fer took off like a missile into the rain forest.

I was sort of stunned, and I just stood there on a narrow path running on a cliff at the edge of the rain forest. The ocean was right below me, and danger was palpable in the air. Just then, I heard a noise crashing above me. A huge pig burst through the jungle, head high as it leaped through the air just behind me on the path.

I swung and fired off the loaded shotgun, hitting the pig in the rear as it landed. It turned around and started to come at me. I fired the other barrel, hitting it right in the face. It took four or five steps before dropping.

Back at my side, Dee-fer jumped on the pig's back, but it was dead. We bonded at that moment even more so than before. From that day on, Dee-fer was utterly devoted to me and no one else.

The pig was maybe 250 pounds. I dressed it out on the spot. I knew how to, as I'd watched Jack Duncan do it. Stringing up the pig by its hind legs, I bled, gutted, and skinned it quickly. I then carried the pig home on my shoulders after dressing it out.

Dee-fer was so proud and excited, and I was too. I felt like a boy again. There I was, out with my dog, and we'd gotten ourselves a pig—my first wild pig, in fact. I never liked to kill animals, and still don't, but wild boars and crocs I can manage. Imagine how I felt. I was just a guy from the beaches of Southern California. A deep-water diver by training. I'd become a businessman and entrepreneur, and I'd given it all up to become a hippie, a bushman, an adventurer. I loved my life. Living in the rain forest in North Queensland, Australia, and hunting wild pig with my trusty dog was cool. Very cool indeed.

That was the first of many adventures Dee-fer and I had together. We became so close, inseparable in fact. She went everywhere with Ali and me. We loved Dee-fer and Midnight so much. The Australians loved Dee-fer too. Aussies are very proud of their dogs, but many would comment on how special Dee-fer was. Whether out in the bush, in the rain forest, or with us in town, she was a beauty. She would wait outside the pub for us; if we had already done our shopping for supplies, she would wait in the bed of the truck and guard them. What a dog!

Meeting Dee-Fer's Old Owner at the Bloomfield River (1974)

After I had Dee-fer for a while, I had to go up to the Bloomfield River one day. I took my boat, and Dee-fer was with me of course. I pulled into a crude, makeshift, rough-and-ready dock and tied up. Dee-fer and I stepped onto the dock, and there was an Aboriginal outpost station just steps away. We headed for the little store.

About one hundred yards ahead of us, there was a longhaired, hippie-type stoner.

He yelled, "Dee-fer!"

Sure enough, Dee-fer recognized him. He was her former owner, released from jail after that bust on his patch. Dee-fer ran toward him.

I yelled, "Dee-fer! Get behind!"

She stopped halfway between him and me, and he called her. She started to go again, and I yelled out for her to come back to me. It was incredible to watch. Dee-fer stood stock-still. She had to make the choice of who was her master: her old owner or me. She looked at him, then at me, and then she turned around and ran back to me. She sat behind me, tail wagging as she looked up at me. Dee-fer had made her choice, and that was it.

"Okay, man, she's made her choice," the old owner said. He was cool. He still loved Dee-fer, but he saw that she loved me and was loyal to me.

I knew for sure that I was her sole owner now, but I showed him respect.

"Go ahead, see your old friend, girl," I told Dee-fer.

She ran to him, and I could see that they loved each other and had shared so much.

After the greeting, I yelled, "Come on back, Dee-fer!"

He gave her a hug, and she gave him a lick, and then she turned and, like a bullet, ran back behind me. We never saw him again.

Diving the Reef and Other Adventures (1974)

Living in Cape Trib was heaven on earth. Most people never even dream of such an existence, much less have the chance to experience it.

We had our dive boat, aluminum with twin 50-hp Mercury outboards. It was a twenty-eight-footer with plenty of fuel storage, and it could reach the outer reef and the atolls quickly. We would fish by trolling, and Ali loved it as much as I did. She was my bush lady, so sexy.

We would camp on an atoll (a circular oceanic reef system surrounding a lagoon) that was enchanting. This ring-shaped coral reef, way up north on the Great Barrier Reef, was our special place. We would lay on our bedroll ("swag," as Aussies call it), look up at the sky, smoke a joint, and enter another place in our minds, shutting out the world and becoming one with all creation. And then we would make love. She was the best—oh how we could make love. I've described our lovemaking before, but it's hard to put into words. With Ali, it wasn't like it was with other women. With any other woman. The best way I can explain it is to say that Ali and I made love to each other as if we were in another dimension. After making love on the beach one night, she told me that it was magical. It was. Maybe that is the word I've been searching for to describe it: magical. Some women won't trust you enough to let you please them, but Ali did.

The mornings after our nighttime lovemaking on the beach, we would snorkel in the reef, pick a couple of lobsters, spear a few fish, swim back, and then head home. Ali was right with me one time when a huge hammerhead shark started following her. I swam up to her and signaled for her to head for the atoll. It was a dangerous swim back, but we escaped.

Did I mention that Ali was topless most of the time? I loved that, obviously. But on Boat Day, I always tried to get her to wear her top. Usually she did, but when she didn't, the tourists and crew were all in for a treat. Well, it was the hippie era; plus, we lived in isolation, so no one would have noticed if we went around naked—which we sometimes did too.

It was so different from the civilized world in every way. Yet, this amazing lifestyle did have its unpleasant moments, and Ali wasn't always happy about our way of life.

I recall one time when I heard her yelling from a tree, cussing me out. "Jim Broman, you asshole! How did I ever let you talk me into living like this!" Isolation in the rain forest, with no power, with wild boar in the jungle, crocs in the rivers, and sharks in the ocean, was not easy for any woman.

On that particular day, Ali was literally up a tree. A boar had charged out of the rain forest, and she had run into it on the way to the beach. To escape, she had to shinny up a tree. I came running when I heard her yelling, and Dee-fer and I got rid of the boar.

To calm her down, I took Ali fishing on our boat, going along the magnificent, amazing coastline and the clear, turquoise waters of the Great Barrier Reef. She loved fishing on the boat, trolling and hooking the fish. We took our catch back to the cabin and cooked it up, and then I made love to her for hours. She forgot all about that bad old boar. We were so deeply in love. She would get mad at me, but she never stayed angry for long.

That wasn't our only adventure up a tree on the beach because of a boar, by the way. One time Dee-fer and I were playing on the beach. She loved to play with me. I would throw coconut husks in the water, and she would retrieve them. We had our game going, and I was distracted by some fish in the water. I had a hand spear with me, so I figured I would spear a few fish for lunch.

Dee-fer decided to play a joke on me. She knew she wasn't to go after pigs unless I told her to, but she went into the bush, sued up a young boar, and brought him right to me. I didn't have any weapon except for the hand spear, which was useless against this young stud of a boar. Flashing his tusks at me, snorting, and threatening a charge, he was determined to get me.

There was Dee-fer, charging, teasing, and riling up that boar. While she distracted him, I went to the edge of the rain forest to get a rock or something to protect myself. The boar followed me in the next instant. I picked up a rock, but it was pumice stone, which is as light as a piece of balsa wood. I shinnied up a tree, just as Ali had done, so now a boar had me treed.

Dee-fer distracted the boar yet again, jumping on his back and then running away. He chased her, but she was too fast for him. I came down from the tree, and he turned toward me again. It was now just the boar and I on the beach. I did find a big rock; it took two hands to hold it over my head. I stood there challenging him, and he charged. He got almost to my legs, and I smashed him in the head. This stunned him, bringing him to his knees. I ran away from him, stood, and challenged him again, waiting for him to charge. When he did, I smashed him in the head again. We did this for what seemed like hours. Finally, I wore him down and killed him. I was completely out of breath by this time and could barely lift my arms. But I was also excited because the adrenaline was flowing.

Dee-fer just ran up and down the beach like a mad dog. She was crazy happy. If she could talk, I knew she would have kept saying, "We killed the boar! We killed the boar!"

One last boar story before I move on to my next adventure. As I've mentioned, Ali and I were the only permanent residents at Cape Trib once the Rijkers left. Sometimes we wanted a little human contact. I invited my former secretary from Broman International to come up from Melbourne to visit. I picked her up at the airport in Cairns, and we drove back to Cape Trib.

After we crossed the Daintree River by ferry, about halfway home, I asked her, "Do you want to see a wild boar?"

"Yes!" she said excitedly.

I called out to Dee-fer, who was riding in the bed of the truck, "Sue 'em up, girl!"

She jumped out of the truck and took off like a shot into the rain forest. Shortly thereafter, she had sued up a pig. I stopped the truck, got in the bed, and waited for a few seconds. Dee-fer led the boar right below me. I took a rope and lassoed it. The passenger door was open, and the boar went right for my ex-secretary. She let out a bloodcurdling scream, clearly terrified. Now I had the damn thing lassoed, so what was I supposed to do now? He was a mean bastard. I finally got the rope off him, and he split.

My poor ex-secretary. Her heart was beating so fast that I could almost see her blouse move. Needless to say, that was her first, last, and only visit to Cape Trib.

Kangaroo Lady (1974)

We had a good life at Cape Trib, but we had our rough patches too. At one point, Ali went walkabout to visit some American friends in Melbourne. She was seriously thinking about leaving me, and I knew it. I was alone and not very happy. The cabin wasn't the same without Ali.

I decided to visit some friends in Cairns. I asked Johnny Niagara, the aborigine who was the hand on the property sometimes and my friend as well, to look after the place for me. Before leaving, I went down to the beach and out on the reef to pick a few lobsters to bring to my friends in Cairns. They would love that. It just so happened that lobster was my favorite food (barramundi was a close second).

As I was coming out of the water, I saw this stunning Aussie girl on the beach. She headed up my drive, walking a wallaby kangaroo on a leash. She stopped, staring at the cabin and heeling the wallaby.

I walked up the drive to where she stood. "Hello," I said. I was in shock but tried not to give myself away. The truth was, not that many beautiful girls wound up on my beach by accident. I was and am very territorial, just like a cassowary.

"Hello," she said, and then laughed.

She was absolutely exquisite, dressed like a hippie but very cool, classy.

"How did you get here?" I asked her.

"I heard about you in town," she said. "A Yank living on Cape Tribulation. It's such a famous property, and everyone always talks about how beautiful it is up here, so I hitched a ride from some people going to the Bloomfield River."

"Beautiful it is indeed," I said.

I'm sure she picked up on the nuance, but she didn't let on. She went on to tell me that her final destination was Cedar Bay, the big international commune up the coast north of Cape Trib. Her ride dropped her off close to the beach, and she had walked the rest of the way along the isolated beach, ending up next to my driveway. That's Aussie girls for you: they just do what they please, going walkabout whenever the mood strikes them.

"I'll show you around," I offered, inviting her up to the property.

It was strange walking with her and a wallaby on a leash. We entered the property along the stream, and she was awestruck. I picked a ripe mango, peeled it halfway down, and handed it to her.

She took a bite. "Mm … delicious!" she said, flicking her tongue to the corner of her mouth to lick the juice.

When we got to the open clearing with the orchards, gardens, sawmill, and cabins, she gasped. We went up to the main cabin. With the huge, flat, long fireplace, four camp ovens, and huge grills, I thought that we could have some big fish cooking. The fire was so romantic at night. My mind raced at the possibilities. Cape Trib was a property that offered the perfect hippie lifestyle. I could tell she was totally wowed. She made no effort to hide it.

"Want to smoke a joint?" I asked her.

"Yes," she said.

We got high, talking for hours and laughing about everything like you do when you're stoned.

"I was in Kuranda for a while," she told me. "That's when I heard about you."

It seemed I had quite a reputation! What I wanted, though, was to know more about her.

The dope loosened her inhibitions. "I was living with a cattle rancher," she said. "Older and wealthy. But I decided to leave him for Cedar Bay." That meant the hippie movement and lifestyle.

She smoked another joint with me. We got even higher and laughed even more.

"How about a boat ride out on the Great Barrier Reef?" I asked her.

She got really excited, but she was still very cool, real classy. She had a bikini in her swag (Aussie slang for backpack).

I packed some papaya, mangos, and cooked lobster tails in the tucker bag, along with some fresh bread that I'd baked that morning, some honey, and my staple, peanut butter. (I have lived on peanut butter for most of my life.)

We smoked another joint. By that point, I could tell she felt very comfortable with me; plus, she was completely blown away by my lifestyle. It was a glorious one.

I talked her into leaving the wallaby in the sawmill shed with water and food. Johnny Niagara would check on the wallaby and keep an eye on Dee-fer too.

"Don't eat the little fella," I told him with a wink.

It was then I started to think of her as Kangaroo Lady. I didn't share this with her of course. She was mortified by what I said to Johnny. It was the only time I saw her lose her cool. She soon got over it, though. She had smoked too much pot by that point to care about such things for very long.

We took our gear, tucker, and water down to the beach to my boat. We headed out to that atoll I loved. The Great Barrier Reef was its typical gorgeous self. The coral and sea life were incredible, the water so clear we could see straight to the ocean floor. It was a place of unparalleled beauty. She seemed enraptured.

I didn't ignore the beauty of the reef, but I paid equal attention to her. She was young and so very beautiful. I didn't make a move on her; I just enjoyed her beauty from a place of observation, a lookout point. I wanted her to make the first move. She'd never had to do that before; I was sure of that. She was far too beautiful to ever have to initiate things with a man.

We stopped, anchored off, and got ready to go for a swim. She took off her top, looking at me and smiling. I looked back at her, approving of her beautiful, young body. She slipped off her bottoms too. She was extremely sexy.

I pulled the ladder down in the back of the boat so that she could gently slide into the water. I watched her dive down to the bottom. The water was so clear I could see every inch of her perfectly. She came back up, a beautiful shell in her hand and a grin on her face, her white teeth shining.

I stripped, went down the ladder, and dived in naked, hoping I didn't castrate myself. (That's why I love my Speedos.) I went straight to the bottom, grabbed a fresh lobster hiding under some coral, its tail frantically flipping to get away. When she looked at me, she was glowing.

"We have another hour to go before we get to the atoll," I told her when we were both back topside.

I pulled the canvas awning up on the boat so she didn't get sunburned. She had this delicate skin, lightly tanned and flawless. I gave her some sunblock, helping her put some on her back and rear and the backs of her thighs. I was aroused, to say the least.

I slipped my Speedos back on. She put her bottoms back on but remained topless. Aussie girls always went topless, liking the freedom. Plus, it was the hippie era, as I keep reminding you.

We lit up another joint, just a hit or two to keep the buzz going, and then we headed to the atoll on the magnificent, glorious Great Barrier Reef.

I never knew the formal name of this atoll. I usually referred to it as "Coral Reef Island." Its crystal-clear lagoon and white-sand beach were as beautiful as ever. I slowly steered the boat through the opening to the beach, landing the boat on the sand.

We unloaded the tucker, a bedroll (swag), towels, a spread, and a canvas overhang for shelter from the sun. (In Australian historical terms, "swag" is a waterproof bedroll. A "swagman" was a rural worker who carried his bedroll swag, along with his belongings, wrapped in a sack on his back. [This is why swag is also Aussie slang for backpack.] Such swags are typically made with a waterproof outer section. Because these swags were traditionally made of canvas, camping out under the stars around the campfire in a canvas is also called "swag" in Aussie-speak. I had a custom-designed swag that was perfect for me, and it was what I brought with me on that trip to the atoll.)

After setting up, I showed Kangaroo Lady around the atoll, exploring a little, but we were hungry. So we went back to the tucker to enjoy our food. After eating, we smoked another joint. She turned her face toward me, wanting me to kiss her. I didn't right then; I waited, teasing her.

Finally, I did kiss her. She was warm and sweet, and she kissed me back. So sweet and passionate. We made love, and that was sweet and passionate too.

We dozed off, woke up, and ate some bread and mango, washing it down with some of the spring water we'd brought with us.

"Let's go fishing," I said, giving her a mask with a snorkel. I put mine on too.

The reef was loaded with fish: trevally, tuna, schools of barracuda, even some white-tip reef sharks. There were other sharks too: grey reef, silvertip, and hammerhead. We saw many spectacular tropical fish that day.

It was going to be a full-moon night on the Great Barrier Reef. The sunset had the telltale deep yellows, pinks, and range of blues. She loved it. It was glorious.

We spent two days and nights on the atoll, stoned and heady with lovemaking. These were full-moon nights and hours of lovemaking, with wonderful conversation about life, her dreams, and mine too.

As we left the beautiful atoll and lagoon to head back to Cape Trib, we stopped for a swim. I couldn't resist kissing her. She kissed me back, and she kissed so well.

"I have never had lovemaking like this ever, in my whole life," she whispered in my ear. "I want more."

I didn't think I could ever have enough of her, either.

Our trip back to Cape Trib was wonderful. We threw out a line, trolled, and caught a mahimahi. Highly sought because of their beauty, size, food quality, and healthy population, mahimahi was (and still is) popular in many restaurants. I let her pull it in. It was hard to land, but she did it. I helped some, but she was very excited and proud of her catch.

After arriving back at the property, she checked on her wallaby. I checked on Dee-fer, and then I talked to Johnny Niagara.

I cleaned the mahimahi, filleted it, started a fire in the long fireplace, and put the fish on the grill. I threw some veggies in a skillet, browned them, picked some limes and lemons off the trees, and cooked some breadfruit. We had a late lunch that was spectacular. I gave Johnny some vegetables and fruit to take to his family, sent him home, and arranged for him to come back in two days to watch the place while Kangaroo Lady and I went to Port Douglas, Cairns, and then up to Kuranda to visit Rosebud Farm.

While in town, we saw some of the Rosebud Farm girls. There was one cute one, newly over from the States and going with one of the founders of Rosebud. She was a beauty, with that classy, East Coast, blue-blood air about her, sweet looking and a real turn-on.

Kangaroo Lady and I stayed in Cairns, in a house I kept for when I would go to town. We ate dinner in the pub. She kept the wallaby in the house. We had a good time, but then she did go on to Cedar Bay. It was good while it lasted, very special.

I've said that I was cursed with an addiction to women. Too many special ones drifted in and out of my life, Ali most of all. But that's just the way it was. In their own way, women were and always will be the biggest moon pool of all for me.

The Ribbon Reefs (1974)

And now for a brief lesson in oceanography and Australian history, followed by some marlin fishing.

The Ribbon Reefs are covered in colorful corals that attract an overabundance of reef life, big and small. Sandy gullies separate them.

There are several ways to dive this site, which is located at the northernmost tip of Osprey Reef. It can be done as a drift dive, abalone divers' style. This was how we did it off the coast of Southern California. Santa Barbara commercial divers called it "live boating."

When current is present, and a deep dive running down to 130 feet, North Horn Wall is practically a dive site in its own right, with lots of ledges and gorgonian fans and the bigger the blue.

Eagle rays and manta rays often cruise around the vicinity, and it has been known for divers to spot sailfish at this Great Barrier Reef dive site. Diving in Australia at Osprey Reef, you will marvel at the sheer size of the gorgonian fans and catch sight of marine life, such as green loggerhead turtles. Chances of encountering a manta ray or an eagle ray are good, as these are regularly seen in the area, thanks to the reef acting as a huge magnet, drawing in vast amounts of marine life from the surrounding blue.

Also seen at Osprey Reef are some of the "big ones," such as whale sharks, beaked whales, sperm whales, bottlenose dolphins, sailfish, and marlin. Plus, not to be missed is the resident shark population, whose large numbers always ensured that these adrenaline-filled wall dives would be among the highlights of my diving in Australia. Coral Sea, Osprey Reef, regularly boasts visibility of more than one hundred feet. Its home, the Great Barrier Reef, is often referred to as the eighth wonder of the world. The reef stretches over 2,000 kilometers and is home to tens of thousands of species of brilliantly colored fish and coral

Lizard Island is Australia's northernmost island. An absolute tropical paradise and truly a wow place. My very good friend ran some wonderful charters with his fantastic boat, *Big Mama,* along this island. It is located 150 miles north of Cairns and 57 miles northeast of the coast from Cooktown.

In 1770, Lieutenant James Cook first ventured into these uncharted reaches as the last chance for a crew seeking freedom from the beautiful but deadly coral reefs of the Great Barrier Reef. Cook anchored in one of the island's bays and climbed to the top of the hill now known as Cook's Look. There he surveyed a suitable passage away from the island. On Lizard Island, goannas can be found almost everywhere, and they were so common when James Cook first landed that it didn't take him long to name the island after them.

It is paradise! Lizard Island is renowned for its diving. At the world-famous "Cod Hole," one of the many unforgettable dive sites that are close by and a favorite spot that fascinates divers, you'll get to experience the countless and dazzling array of tropical fish and come face to face with a massive yet curious potato cod swimming right up to inspect you with childlike curiosity.

The waters surrounding Lizard Island boast some of the most exciting fishing in the world. Each year, black marlin, some weighing a massive 1,000 pounds or more, are caught here. The outer reef fishing grounds can be reached in fifty minutes. The fish caught in this area of the Great Barrier Reef include mackerel, tuna, trevally, mahimahi, sailfish, and, of course, black marlin at certain times of the year.

I have fished and caught black marlin. On one trip, Wyatt's father and uncle (who was the manager of my Lafayette, Louisiana, operations, as well as an attorney and later a judge) chartered a marlin boat, and we all went marlin fishing. The actor Lee Marvin was in the boat next to us, his crew loading up with supplies, like fifty cases of Aussie beer. I don't really know exactly how many cases, but it was a lot; we had just about as many. Anyway, we were going out far, and they had a mother ship out there if you wanted meals and to sleep there.

We all took turns fishing, and everybody caught a marlin, catch and release. My turn came up again, and I was very hung over from the night before. We had been feeling pretty good, more than pretty good, so we got in the dinghy and started going around Lee Marvin's boat, drunk and singing "Wandering Star" from a movie he had been in. Anyway, I really didn't want to fish because I was so hung over, but I had to take my turn.

My friend was my witness: I hooked a record marlin. When it jumped out of the water, it was a monster. The skipper and the crew went crazy. This could be the record of all time for them and their boat. I fought this monster fish for two hours; they were pouring water all over me to keep me alive. Oh, I got it to the steel leader and close to the boat, but I couldn't land it because it was foul-hooked. The skipper was so disappointed, but what a fight.

We all went shark-looking after that. Snorkeling was great, and we saw a lot of them. That monster marlin was one of a kind, though. I'll never forget it.

Charlie Dean, Brother of the Famous Howard Dean (1974)

As I mentioned earlier, in between selling Broman International and buying the Cape Tribulation property, Ali and I lived in Port Douglas, the sleepy, charming seaside village along the Great Barrier Reef, just north of Cairns.

We rented an oceanfront house, and we enjoyed the beaches and diving in this wonderful place. If you want to get a feel for how magnificent this area is, get some books with my favorite photographer, Peter Ilk. (I don't know him personally; I only know his brilliant work. If I ever do meet him, I would love to tell him how much I admire his brilliant work.)

Living in Port Douglas was a moon pool too. I was still unwinding from selling my company, sad for the loss of something that I had created from nothing and made into a very special enterprise. The experience kind of emptied me, preparing me for my next adventure. This would be moving to Cape Trib, but I hadn't yet found my dream property. In the interim, I just went with the flow of the moon pool I found myself in, knowing that change can be joyous or painful—or even both at once—but that's the deal if you are to live life to the fullest. Whether you go deep or go shallow, you never know what you'll ultimately find when in a moon pool.

While in Port Douglas, I met a great young man named Charlie Dean. As I've mentioned, Charlie was a close friend of my good friend Wyatt. Wyatt introduced me to Charlie. Charlie and I spent some time at my house and on the beach and spearfishing on my boat. Wherever we went, we talked about life; the more I got to know Charlie, the more I liked him. He was a great friend. Charlie always spoke about how much he loved his family, especially his brother, Howard. I have never met Howard Dean, but if he's anything like Charlie, I'm sure I'd like him too.

My story is very different from that of the Dean brothers. And, yes, Charlie's brother is *the* Howard Dean who eventually became the governor of Vermont and the head of the Democratic Party for a time. He also ran for president of the United States.

Charlie spent a year in Australia with a group of friends from the exclusive St. George's School in Newport, Rhode Island. One of those friends was Wyatt, who was the son of a US congressman. (You'll remember Wyatt's battle with the crocodile in part I, and you'll also remember that it was Wyatt who introduced me to Jack Duncan, the leader of the Cape Tribulation Commune.) Charlie and Wyatt had a friend who was the son of a DuPont executive. They'd all dropped out of college after the riots following the Kent State shootings. Coming to Australia, they established an agricultural commune in Far North Queensland called Rosebud Farm. Great guys. I remained friends with Wyatt. One day, Charlie told me he was thinking about buying some property way up north, similar to what Wyatt had at the Bloomfield River. "If I could buy property at Cape Tribulation, I'd never leave Australia, Jim," he said.

I had only heard of the legend of Cape Trib at that point. "It does sound like a wow place," I said.

"You don't even know. It's a magical place. You have to go see it."

I told him I would. Later, when Jack Duncan first tried to sell me on Cape Trib, Charlie's words came back to haunt me. In a way, I guess Charlie was the one responsible for my finding my dream property. If he had bought it instead, things would have been very different. But I get way too sad thinking about that.

Ultimately, Charlie decided not to buy any property in North Queensland. He wanted to go to Laos, do some photography there. It proved a fateful choice. He never came back.

In September 1974, Charlie Dean and Australian companion Neil Sharman disappeared somewhere along the Mekong River. Months later, it was discovered that they had been taken prisoner by communist Pathet Lao soldiers. Held captive in a crude prison camp for three months, who knows what Charlie and Neil had to suffer before the Pathet Lao executed them by rifle fire.

What a waste. Charlie was a magnificent human being and a talented, creative person. He had so much to offer the world, and he would have done great things with his life. I truly mourned his passing and still do. I consider it an honor to have been his friend and to know him for a short time. He sought to fight the establishment, to make the world a better place, and he paid with his life.

Telling you about Charlie Dean was my roundabout way of explaining exactly how and why I fully embraced the hippie lifestyle. He is part of the reason I found my paradise on earth, yes. Even more important, he is the reason I found my purpose. Charlie, Wyatt, and their friends opened my eyes to an alternative lifestyle—not just the sex, drugs, and rock and roll I'd enjoyed in San Francisco (more about that later) but truly living in harmony with nature. These young men turned their back on the private, prestigious schools they had attended and on their wealth as well. I, too, turned my back on the establishment, hoping to make things better. In part, I did that to honor Charlie. If I picked up his torch, maybe his purpose and spirit would live on, even if his life had to be snuffed out so tragically early.

When I dropped out of the rat race, it pissed off a lot of people—business associates, family, friends, and so on. You've read enough to know I don't regret it. I only wish I could have lived the life I found and also had my good friend Charlie Dean in it longer.

The Aborigine, Johnny Niagara (1974)

I've already told you a lot about my various friends in Australia. A colorful cast of characters. You learn a great deal about a man by seeing the kinds of friends he has, I think. That's as true for me as it is for anyone else. So now I'm going to tell you some more about another friend of mine: Johnny Niagara, the aborigine who worked as my hand on the Cape Tribulation property sometimes. (You'll remember Johnny from my interlude with Kangaroo Lady.) He was a good guy, as different as could be from Charlie and Wyatt, but just as good a friend. And his story is as interesting as theirs too, albeit in a very different way.

Johnny Niagara was a descendant of the Kuku Yalanji tribe. He often came to my place to ask me to hunt wild boar for him. (The Yalanji are fishermen, not hunters.) Dee-fer, my 20-gauge shotgun, and I were always ready to sue 'em up, so this was never a problem. We had some great hunts. Later, after Johnny started working for me and I got to know him better, he would come along. We went hunting all the time—just him, Dee-fer, and me.

Prior to white settlement, the Kuku Yalanji aboriginal people lived along the coastline between Mossman and the Bloomfield River. I have walked some of the ancient trails created by the original inhabitants, gone there on horseback too, always with Johnny Niagara. It was a profound experience to follow those paths in the presence of one of the descendants of those who had created them so many years before.

Living mainly along the coast, the Yalanji relied heavily on seafood, and their lifestyle caused little to no damage to the rain forest. Because annual rainfall in that area is eight to nine meters (that's 315 inches per year), they had all the water they needed too. I learned a lot about conservation just by observing them and talking to Johnny. We were "green" and "ecofriendly" at Cape Trib long before that was de rigueur—long before those were even terms people used.

But back to Johnny's story. He also often worked for a big landholder miles away from us. That property was pretty far inland, and Johnny was a native of the coast. He was homesick, so he would come over to the coast to fish. Sometimes, as I said, he would ask me to get a pig for him and his family. I always complied. Ali and I treated him very well, and he appreciated it. I have always respected the native people in the various places where I've lived around the world. I always communicated with them, and they always trusted me (except for the cannibals in Papua). I never tried to change them; I loved who they were and what they were. The different cultures around the world fascinated me and still do. Australia was no exception, especially Johnny Niagara.

At one point, we planned a big trip over some of the most beautiful rain forest ever. I hired Johnny to rent some horses from the landowner he worked for, and also to be my guide on a ride all the way to the Daintree River ferry. That would be twenty-eight miles through the rain forest and along the beaches on horseback. A glorious, magnificent ride, but one with the same many inherent dangers already encountered: snakes, wild boar, cassowaries, stinging trees, and, of course, the ever-present saltwater crocodile. It was an incredible experience to go through the rain forest with a native. I loved it.

Johnny, Dee-fer, and I went into the rain forest often. Usually, it was just the three of us. One time in particular, we took Ali with us. We were in this low area that was very swampy. We arrived at around noon, and the wild boars usually slept at that time. Trees were their favorite napping spots, so you had to be careful as you walked past each tree: if you passed a sleeping boar and woke him up, he would be behind you and could get you from the back and take you down.

There we were in this swampy area, and all of sudden a huge wild boar came out from behind a tree. He charged us head-on, and as he got within thirty feet, I fired. I hit him in the chest, but he kept coming. Johnny was to my left, Ali was on my right, and Dee-fer was going crazy at my feet. In the center of all of them, I fired again, dropping the beast right at Johnny Niagara's feet.

Johnny was trembling and as white as a sheet. In his broken, fuzzy English, he said, "Wow! Close call, Jim."

That boar was huge. It had the most enormous tusks I've ever seen. Dee-fer was in heaven, but I thought Johnny and Ali both might faint.

It was a day in the rain forest none of us would ever forget.

Many Dangers Lurk in Paradise—How to Survive (1974)

There are many dangerous creatures you need to know about in order to survive in tropical paradise. We've talked about many of them already. But there's one ocean denizen that I haven't mentioned: the box jellyfish.

Fortunately, they are not around all year, only seasonally. Nevertheless, the box jellyfish is one of the most lethal animals in the world. Found on the coast alongside the Great Barrier Reef, the box jellyfish possesses extremely powerful venom. This large but almost transparent creature has fifteen ribbonlike tentacles from each of the four corners.

Its stings are terribly painful, causing severe burning and pain in the affected area; the skin feels like it's on fire. Often, the stings are fatal. If stung, immediate medical attention is necessary. The tentacles usually remain in the area stung. Severe stings may cause the victim's breathing to cease or heart to stop, which is why it is so crucial to receive immediate medical care.

A friend of mine, another crazy American, was stung once, and he ended up in the hospital in serious condition. These stings are no joke.

Another deadly menace is the cassowary. I've mentioned this bird, but I haven't yet described any of my run-ins with them. I must remedy that immediately. First, you must understand just how treacherous these birds are.

Known as the most dangerous bird in the world, the cassowary could rip you to shreds with one swipe of its claw. Cassowaries have a reputation for being dangerous to people and domestic animals. Cape Tribulation was known for them, and I personally was stalked and attacked by one. Most other animals will only attack if cornered, but if you accidentally walk into the path of a cassowary, it will track you; it will not let you get away. (That's why I likened myself to the cassowary when I was tracking the Kangaroo Lady.)

After all the adventures I've shared with you about my encounters with big fish, wild boar, and crocs, you might think that a run-in with a bird sounds pretty tame. That's only because you've never seen a cassowary.

Dee-fer and I were deep in the rain forest one time when a female cassowary spotted us. The bird immediately started after me, in attack mode and ready to rip me open with her claws. Dee-fer headed her off, almost doing herself in. She managed to get away, and that saved me. However, the bird continued to follow me until I was out of her territory.

Cassowaries can disembowel a human or dog with one kick, using the long, second-toe claw to cut the gut open. There are many records of humans killed by this bird.

Another danger is one I've mentioned in passing: the stinging tree (gympie-gympie). Found in forests in Australia (Queensland) and Indonesia, this plant is the deadliest and most potent stinging nettle in the world. It's called the stinging tree because merely brushing past the plant accidentally can cause days, weeks, or months of excruciating pain—and even death—for unsuspecting humans and animals. I touched one with my forefinger once just to see how bad it was, and I was sorry I'd done so. It was terribly painful and remained so for a couple of weeks. I'd only brushed it lightly, so I can't even imagine how painful it would be for someone who really got stung. The truth is a severe sting from this plant has been known to kill humans, and it is certainly deadly to pigs, horses, dogs, and most other animals.

Even when not fatal, the sting can cause anaphylactic shock and loss of eyesight. I've heard that the gympie-gympie sting causes the worst kind of pain imaginable; "like being burned with hot acid and electrocuted at the same time," according to one account I read about a man who fell into a stinging tree during military training. Strapped to a hospital bed for three weeks and administered all manner of unsuccessful treatments, he was sent "as mad as a cut snake" by the pain. Another man also told of an officer shooting himself after using a stinging-tree leaf for "toilet purposes." The Queensland Parks and Wildlife Service says this of the stinging tree: "There's nothing to rival it; it's ten times worse than anything else—stinging trees are a real and present danger."

Thanks to the survival techniques we learned and practiced, Ali and I survived the dangers of Cape Tribulation. We thrived there! But we were constantly on the lookout for crocodiles, wild boar, snakes, cassowaries, jellyfish, sharks, and deadly plants. It's a trade-off: if you want to live in the most intensely gorgeous and exotic rain forest in the world, you have to learn to abide by the rules of the bush. If you do, you truly have paradise on earth.

My Friend and Fellow Bushman, Harry Dick (1974)

And now comes a story about another good friend, Harry Dick. Yes, honest to God, that's his real name. Harry was a bushman's bushman. He could walk barefoot through the rain forest. Actually, I never saw him wearing shoes. At least not in the rain forest. He did wear flip-flops in town. I wore the same plastic sandals worn by the Australian Special Forces; you could walk the reefs and swim with them on your feet.

Harry and I became friends. He lived in the rain forest. We respected each other. The aborigines in the area respected both of us. Harry tested me on my bushman skills. He guessed that I was looking for a piece of land to grow a patch on. We never mentioned it, but it was there.

In Cairns, they would talk about Harry Dick and me in tones of reverence. We were both true bushmen. I lived in total isolation, with no power, at the famous Cape Tribulation, where the rain forest met the Great Barrier Reef; he lived up the coast, with his own one-hundred-foot waterfall and reef just off the beach. His property was magnificent. Almost as beautiful as Cape Trib. Almost.

In the pubs in Cairns, they would talk about the legend Harry Dick, the greatest bushman in North Queensland. And with a name like that, he could get into lots of trouble in an American pub!

Maybe that was why we were such great friends. Harry and I loved the bush. Oh, how we loved the bush!

There was another reason why Harry had earned the respect of the aborigines and the people of North Queensland. He was a rarity in this world: he was an honest man, and he kept his word.

I once asked him if he knew of a secluded piece of property that I could buy: a place that was inland and had spring water but that also had views of the Great Barrier Reef. He knew this was the place I wanted for my patch. Again, we never spoke of it, but he knew.

"I know of a property, but it is almost impossible to get to it," Harry said.

I knew he was about to test my bushman skills—again.

Sure enough, Harry gave me an assignment to find this incredible property. He drew a "map" with his finger on the palm of his hand. It was a plateau and a valley that only he knew of. Because it was so hard to find and get to, he'd put a sardine tin under this huge boulder; that way, he could always prove he had been there. He claimed you could see past Cairns and up to Cooktown. He also said that it was almost impossible to get there because the rain forest was so thick and there were so many streams. Plus, at some places, the elevation was such that you had to crawl on your hands and knees.

"One place I have to warn you about," Harry said, jamming his thumb against a spot on the "map." "Leeches. They'll cover your body and face in an instant, suck your blood. When that happens, don't stop, and don't try to pick them off; they will engulf you. Just keep going higher and higher and higher. The increase in elevation will make them drop off."

Turned out, he was right about the leeches and everything else. I even found the sardine tin under the huge boulder, just as he'd described.

I took a friend with me on that trip. We started out as Harry instructed, and it was enchanting going through this beautiful rain forest, passing waterfalls, streams, fauna, tall ferns, and palms, all luscious and green and magical. The terrain started to get steeper, and we had to get on our hands and knees in some spots, just as Harry had warned. We hit the place with the leeches, and they engulfed us. Again, just as Harry had warned.

I looked at my friend; he was covered with them, trying to pick them off. I remembered what Harry had said: "Keep climbing. Get to a higher elevation, and they'll drop off." I called out to my friend, telling him we had to keep climbing. We did, and the leeches did drop off.

Finally, we got to the top. We were blown away by the views, and I found the boulder and the sardine tin under it. I also found a spring and saw the elevation gently increase: a perfect slope to have a plastic water pipe run to a nice area camouflaged to grow my patch on. I already had a name and a picture in my mind for the label!

On the way down, we got disoriented. We reached a place where we could go two different ways; my friend wanted to go one way, and I wanted to go the other way. We argued about the best way to go, but we really were on the verge of total panic. We were lost. I went my way, he followed, and we finally got back.

The next time I went was with Dee-fer. It was still tough, but a little easier. The leeches still attached themselves to me, but I was prepared for it. When I got to the spot, I was even more amazed at how perfect it was for growing marijuana.

The views were more than unbelievable: all the way to Cairns and Cooktown in one direction, and in the other, beautiful rain forest for as far as you could see, and the Great Barrier Reef lying there like a majestic king ruling over a kingdom of coral reefs, atolls with lagoons, and brilliant, white-sand beaches—a whole universe of marine wonder. Islands in the distance along the way were the spots I would camp on as I explored the Great Barrier Reef. This was a different part of it than what we had at Cape Trib. I planned out my camp and what I would need to set it up. Ideas filled my mind.

On the way down this time, though, I had a problem. There was a flash of blue: the treacherous cassowary, royal blue in color, was stalking us. The royal blue was gorgeous, but seeing the most dangerous bird in the world struck fear in my heart that I knew well enough to heed. Dee-fer saw it, but she was quiet. She just nudged me. She was so well trained.

Harry spent a lot of time at my place. We became even closer friends. He actually met his future wife at our place. We had visitors from time to time, hippies that would show up and ask to spend a night or two. If they were good people, we would consent—not often, but on occasion.

A Polish girl was one of our visitors, and Harry happened by while she was there. They met, fell in love, and got together. They had five children together over the years. She was a beautiful, buxom Polish girl, about seventeen; he was in his forties.

I described Harry's property already, but words can't do it justice. A few miles from Cape Trib, it was a very secluded piece of property with a one-hundred-foot waterfall. It was astonishing, by far the most fantastic aspect of the property. It was almost inaccessible by boat because the reef that fronted the property had only one small opening to get through, and that was almost completely hidden. Harry invited me to come up for a visit once; nobody was ever invited to his place. Again he drew a little "map" on his hand of the location of the opening of the reef. I found it. When I arrived on his beach, about fifty yards in, there was the one-hundred-foot waterfall and a beautiful, crystal-clear pool. His open cabin was just beside the pool. It was like a movie set. The power and beauty and majesty of that waterfall were incredible. Nobody knew the bush and North Queensland like my friend Harry Dick, the bushman's bushman who loved the bush.

The Hippie Movement (1974)

North Queensland was getting well-known around Australia and also internationally. By 1975, there were some six thousand young Aussies living on communes.

Marijuana was the drug of choice, supplemented with products from nature's own medicine cabinet: magic mushrooms, gold tops, blue meanies. It wasn't just about a change of lifestyle anymore; it was about altered states of consciousness too.

They headed for Queensland. The Northern Territory was a magnet for the hippies, with its laidback lifestyle, breathtaking natural beauty, and large tracts of uninhabited land. It was a Mecca to the flower children, the ultimate area of choice. They came from all over Australia and all over the world to follow the hippie trail north. A new commune was started at Cedar Bay, a remote cove and rain forest several miles up the coast. (This was the Kangaroo Lady's destination, if you recall.) The word from the grapevine was that there were a couple thousand hippies from all over the world, all nationalities. It was the first and biggest international commune in Australia.

I will never forget my first visit there. Arriving on the shore of Cedar Bay, a coconut-lined beach, I got out of my boat to see this line of naked people just inside the tree line. It was a gorgeous piece of rain forest, absolutely stunning. I stood there taking in the beauty for a moment.

A group of naked men start walking toward me. They were all very friendly. Shouts of "Hey, Jim Broman" sounded. They knew me as the Yank who owned the dazzling Cape Tribulation property, living in isolation and seclusion. They also knew I was a great supporter of Rosebud Farm, the American commune in Kuranda.

We chatted for a bit, and they seemed satisfied that I was one of them, at least in spirit. After accepting me for a visit, we walked to the main camp. The leaders were there, greeting me and inviting me to sit on the jungle floor. They passed a bong around. It was like a group of Indians passing a peace pipe in an old western movie.

I could get used to this lifestyle, I thought.

The party was going to start soon. Hippie girls surrounded us. Some were beautiful, some were bare-breasted, and some were completely naked. Music played—guitars, flutes, bongos. It was a harem of naked and half-naked women from all over the world, stoned and living the free-love lifestyle. Each and every one of them available.

Yes, I could definitely *get used to this lifestyle!*

I didn't stay there, but I did spend the night in a tree house with a sweet hippie girl from Europe. I left a few days later and went back to Cape Tribulation.

* * * * * *

On the morning of August 29, 1976, the hippies at the Cedar Bay International Commune in Far North Queensland were awoken by the sound of a helicopter circling. Some people staggered onto the beach, half-asleep, watching as the chopper dropped off a few policemen. The chopper left, only to return again—and again, and again. All that morning, the chopper kept dropping off police.

The first police group hurried through the camp, stopping for a few moments to chop down the clothesline and tents. They used their machetes for this purpose.

When the Cedar Bay residents challenged the violation of their property, the police said, "We're looking for marijuana plants!"

Shortly after the second group of police arrived, they began searching the huts for marijuana. They started ripping up the food supplies. They threw everything on the floor: bags of rice, packets of tea, packets of soup, cans of vegetables, packets of flour—about a three-month supply of food, all wasted. They bored holes in the water containers. They then started a fire.

When the amazed residents asked the police what they were doing, the reply was, "Looking for marijuana seeds!"

Besides the helicopter, a light aircraft, a customs launch, and the navy patrol boat HMAS *Bayonet* were involved in the raid on Cedar Bay. More than thirty police, as well as Narcotics Bureau and customs agents, took part. The task force assembled to attack Cedar Bay was impressive.

Cedar Bay is a few thousand miles north of Brisbane, but Brisbane's alternative radio station, 4ZZZ, broke the story of the raid through the station's reporter in Cairns. The 4ZZZ report alerted the ABC in Brisbane, which sent another reporter to Cedar Bay. His vivid report on *This Day Tonight* (TDT), showing the burnt houses and the macheted fruit trees and tents, made Cedar Bay a national story.

Early the next morning, they made a raid on my property, mainly because of the group that I'd bought the property from; they even told me they were looking for the previous owner, the ex-convict Jack Duncan. They searched my place. I had a roll-top desk in the cabin, and there was a pound of marijuana in the bottom drawer. I played it cool.

Though heavily armed with banderoles of extra ammo over their bodies, they were very polite. They asked if they could search my place for cannabis.

"Sure, go ahead," I said.

They were thrown off by my confidence, so they weren't that thorough. Long story short, they missed the pound in the bottom drawer of the desk.

It was a real shame what they did to beautiful Cedar Bay. They left my place unspoiled, thankfully. And, thankfully too, they didn't find my stash. It was an unpleasant situation, but I escaped the worst of it. Cedar Bay wasn't so lucky.

Magic Mushrooms, Marijuana, and LSD (1974)

I wouldn't be sharing my full experience at Cape Trib if I didn't describe my experiences with altered states of consciousness. I've already described some of my adventures with marijuana (more about that will occur throughout this book), but I also want to share some of what happened to me with mushrooms and LSD.

Mushrooms first. The "magic" refers to two closely related substances, psilocybin and psilocin, the hallucinogenic components found in most of these types of mushrooms, which are native to many tropical and subtropical areas. Most mushrooms have only trace amounts of psilocin, with higher amounts of psilocybin. The effects of psilocybin can be felt in about thirty minutes and usually last between three and six hours.

The psilocybin in magic mushrooms changes the way you see, smell, hear, taste, and touch. For example, you might think that you can "see" music or "hear" colors. Your body may feel very heavy or very light. Some users feel as though they are having a magical or religious experience.

Physical effects can include increased blood pressure and heartbeat, dizziness, light-headedness, upset stomach, numbness of the tongue and mouth, nausea, anxiety, and shivering.

As is the case with other drugs, magic mushrooms affect each user differently. In addition to the size of the dose, effects are influenced by the setting, as well as the user's expectations, past drug experience, and personality. Sometimes the effects can be overwhelming and frightening. This is known as a "bad trip." If someone is having a bad trip, you can help by telling him or her that everything will be okay.

I never had a bad trip with magic mushrooms or marijuana. LSD (also called acid) is another story. I have taken LSD twice in my life. The first time was with my friend Wyatt, who enlisted me into the hippie movement. We were at a beach in Melbourne. I was hammered, and I went out into the surf. This was good size surf, mind you, and I was really tripping. The hallucinations were intense. I became very confused. I tried to get back to the shore, but the waves and undercurrent held me back. Slowly I inched my way back to where I could catch a wave, but I kept hallucinating, imagining that I would never be able to get back. This forced me back after each wave broke. It was extremely frightening, and I was almost in a full panic.

My friends were watching me from the beach, very nervous because they could see that I couldn't get back in. But they couldn't help me because they were tripping also. At some level, I realized that I had to make an extreme effort; if I didn't, I was going to drown. Finally, I caught a wave that got me close enough to get where I could touch bottom. As I felt the wet sand beneath my feet, I dug my toes in and walked in to shore. That was a close call!

I really cannot overstate what a terrifying experience this was. I was raised on the beach, swam like fish, participated in body surfing and all kinds of water sports, was a champion water-skier, had been on the school swim team, and spent most of my life in the ocean, including my professional life as a deep-water diver. Nevertheless, I almost drowned that day. With all my ocean experience, I almost died that day in Melbourne, Australia, tripping on LSD. I tell you this so you will understand just how powerful—and terrifying—a drug it really is.

But, yes, I did use LSD again. One of my former divers went to Rosebud Farm, and he came to visit Ali and me at a place I kept in Melbourne, bringing some magic mushrooms, at my request, for a party we were going to. He made a soup from the mushrooms. At that point, I had only tried mushrooms once, and they were raw. Fun, good, fantastic.

Ali and I ate the mushroom soup, but nothing happened. We waited and waited; still, nothing happened. The party was underway by this time, and they were passing around some LSD. We took an eighth of a dot. Remembering my experience in the water in Melbourne, I wanted to be careful. Within twenty minutes, the mushrooms finally kicked in, then the acid kicked in, and then we were really in trouble. We maintained, but we wanted to get out of there.

I couldn't function well enough to drive, so I had someone call us a cab to take us back to our place in Melbourne. The cab driver started turning into different animals as we drove along. The hallucinations kept intensifying. By the time we got to the house, the bad trip had begun. We sat together on the floor, holding hands. As each rush came, I would tell her, "Ali, it's going to be okay." We would trip out and have another bad ride, and then I would tell her the same thing all over again. This went on until the next morning. It was a twenty-hour bad trip. We spent it jolted and terrified.

The acid in the ocean in Melbourne was a bad trip; this one was worse. I never used LSD again.

The same things that have made LSD popular also make it creepy. We've all heard the warnings about its many dangers at one time or another. It can "fry" or put holes in your brain, or make you go insane, or cause you to do dangerous things. I testify that it can, and does, do all those things.

LSD was first sold on the street in the early 1960s. It makes sense that it became popular. It's easy to take, colorless, odorless, and tasteless, and ingesting just a tiny amount (less than the weight of two salt grains) is enough for the user to feel the effects. It's also easy to conceal (doses were usually found on tiny squares of absorbent paper). Its being difficult to detect, because of the small amount ingested and the fact that it's quickly metabolized by the body, added to its popularity. Last but not least, LSD is cheap compared to other drugs. That might have added more to its popularity than any other factor.

But the scary truth is LSD disrupts the normal functioning of the brain, making you see images, hear sounds, and feel sensations that seem real but aren't. This can sound fascinating and exciting, but it isn't. It's terrifying. The brain is one of the most important organs in the body, working tirelessly to oversee all of our feelings, actions, and bodily functions. Because of what LSD does to the brain, using it is really a cruel and dangerous trick. Unfortunately, I used it twice before realizing that. I was lucky that I emerged unscathed.

I loved smoking pot, and I enjoyed mushrooms several times. But I did not like LSD. I think it is one of the most dangerous drugs around. No altered-state experience is worth the risk of a bad trip.

Jack Duncan Returns (1974)

As I've described, I bought the Cape Tribulation property from Jack Duncan, an ex-convict. Tom Riley, his second in command in the commune, was said to be former Australian Special Forces. Duncan had bought the property from the original owner, Robert Rijker. Duncan and his henchman both were extremely handsome, dangerous men.

You'll also remember I described that they had a successful patch— Sunshine Marijuana—and they bought large tracts of land with profits from their marijuana business. They were highly successful, and I'll never forget their beautiful printed labels. Rumor had it that they robbed a train going to Cooktown from Cairns, stealing payroll money onboard. I never did find out whether that was true, but they surely did have a lot of money.

Jack Duncan was a genius, and Tom Riley was capable of doing almost anything and doing it well. They were serious about what they did.

I had thought that the transaction of my purchase of Cape Trib would be the end of my association, but that did not prove to be the case. In fact, I had problems with them for quite some time, which was a well-known fact in the area at that time.

They tried to squat on the property after I bought it, despite the fact that they were known to be the most successful marijuana growers in North Queensland and owned many large pieces of property. Let me be clear that I had no problem with them being marijuana growers; that was their business. When I bought the property from Duncan, I knew about their business—everyone in North Queensland knew who they were and what they did. I agreed to let them stay on part of the property for a set time, rent-free, until they could move farther up north to a property they owned. The deal was that they were not to operate the marijuana business on my property, as that would put me in jeopardy with the law.

"When you move, do what you want," I told Duncan.

He and Riley agreed to this.

However, some people don't keep their word, and Jack Duncan was among that number. I paid hard-earned money—forty thousand Australian dollars in cash—for that property, and then I gave them sufficient time to move on to their property up north. As long as they did not grow their patch on my property or operate their business from there, I was very generous. But, unfortunately, Duncan and Riley were assholes who didn't keep their word. I had to go into town to talk to an attorney. Long story short, because I didn't charge them rent, the attorney said I would have a hard time getting them off legally. So I went to them and told them in person that I expected them to honor our agreement.

They did move, but only after a fistfight. So much for the peaceful hippie way of life!

I can't leave a story like this by just telling you that they moved after a fistfight. In fact, to understand what happened, I need to share how I figured out that they were still growing their patch, not on my property, but using a small corner of my property to operate from, which they had agreed not to do. So here's the full version.

I had suspected that Duncan and his people were somehow using a corner of my property to operate their business from, even though they had promised that they would not, per our agreement. I decided to find out once and for all, so one day I followed Tom Riley. Riley was trained to kill, but I secretly trailed him to their patch deep in the dense rain forest miles away. They prided themselves on the fact that *nobody* would ever be able to find it, but I did.

If caught, it could mean death, but I risked it, doing my best to stay hidden. Well, I was caught. Riley saw me, and he pulled a knife. I pulled my puma bushman knife. We stood toe-to-toe in the middle of a creek deep in the rain forest, ready to do battle.

He decided that he would have to check with his leader before he did anything further. Nothing was done without Duncan's okay; he had complete control of the commune. He told me it would have to wait until a later day, and he backed off.

I had found their patch, so it was worth the risk. But I knew that I would be hearing from them soon, and it wouldn't be pleasant. I could take care of myself, but I was concerned for Ali's safety, as well as the welfare of some friends who were visiting us.

Sure enough, the next day, Duncan and Riley came around our place, shooting off handguns (illegal in Australia) in a threatening manner. This was all an attempt to intimidate us, but I wasn't intimidated. Suffice it to say, Duncan and his people turned out to be some very unsavory characters, operating within the hippie movement in a way that was similar to the Charles Manson family in California. I was not going to jeopardize the safety of my girlfriend or my friends. I had made the mistake of letting Duncan stay on my property, and now he was making it clear that he and his group were not going to leave.

My only option was to force his hand, and I did.

All the hippie bullshit just wore off. They had shown their true colors: they were liars and crooks, people who did not keep their word and were capable of causing harm to those I cared about.

That payroll robbery from the train was probably more truth than rumor, but I never did find out for sure. I did know that my friend Colonel David Hackworth (you'll remember him from Cyanide Creek in part I) and the Australian government had good reason to watch Duncan and his people. And they did so.

But back to the story at hand. It was after I had confirmed my suspicions and the handgun display had rattled Ali and our friends that I went to see the attorney in Cairns. Against his advice, I decided to confront Jack Duncan face to face. After all, I was very generous and kind in allowing them to stay for as long as I had. At that point, with all my connections, I could easily have had them busted and put in prison. I didn't want to do that; I just wanted them off my property. In addition to being liars—and I never liked liars—they were extremely stupid to be behaving the way they were, knowing who I was.

Straight to his face, I told Jack Duncan, "I am not a snitch. Just get the fuck off my property, now that you broke our agreement."

Soon afterward, they did move on. I'm certain it was only because I had handled it face to face in the way that I did.

Let me be clear that I loved living in Cape Trib in spite of that trouble. I did not leave because of Duncan or his people or any of their threats. I left because of the Lake Tahoe property issue I described in part I, the reason why I got caught in flooded Cyanide Creek. I was the only person who could remedy that situation, and so I had to return to the States. That happened quite some time after I had removed Duncan and his group.

Their departure following my faceoff with Duncan was not the end of the story, though. Regrettably, I had let them leave some of their belongings stored in the sawmill until they got set up in their new place. This had been out of the goodness of my heart, although they didn't deserve it. I knew that even then, so why I did it I can't really say. My first impulse is always to be kind. Sometimes it gets me kicked in the head—or worse. This was one of those times.

Tom Riley and I finally had it out, not with knives but with fists. He came to get something out of the sawmill, and I finally told him I wanted the rest of their stuff moved off the property within the next week. He went into a rage, and we fought. I was concerned for Ali's safety and for the welfare of the friends still staying with us. I was not sure if he had any knives or guns with him, but I figured the best way to keep those I cared about safe was to fight like hell.

And I did. So did he. He landed some big blows, but I cut up his face with my knuckles, so we were even. I started to pull ahead and knew that I could win if I put my whole self into it. Ali came running outside, yelling for us to stop. I realized then that if I won, he would never be able to save face with his leader, and then they might use force, such as handguns and other weapons. It could easily turn into a Charles Manson type of thing.

I made sure he was marked up enough, and then, when he was close to losing and asked if I wanted to quit, I said that I did. As soon as he asked, I knew it meant that he was tired, realized he was losing, and wanted to quit. I let Riley save face with Duncan. It meant that I had given up, but I was okay with that, knowing I'd only done it for Ali's sake and our friends' sake. As soon as I got her and our friends out of harm's way, all bets were off. Riley now knew I could kick his ass if I wanted to, even though my head looked like a swollen air balloon. His face looked like a lawnmower had run over it, and that was worse.

Later, I heard that their group split up (after I'd gone back to the States). Duncan died of a heart attack in a bathroom in one of the pubs in Cairns. The group sold one of their properties for over a half a million Australian dollars. They moved to Thailand, stayed strung out on heroin, and blew that money in no time. They came back to Australia but eventually disbanded.

I don't know if it's all true, but it is what I heard. What I can say is true is simply this: I wouldn't have missed living in Cape Trib for anything, including that less-than-pleasant experience, but I wouldn't want to repeat involvement with people like that again.

As always, I was ready for another moon pool. Many more moon pools.

I Was Destined to Become a Hippie (1974)

Even with all I've shared about my experiences with the hippie lifestyle and why I loved it, it might still seem weird that a self-made man like me would find that lifestyle appealing. Truth is I was destined to become a hippie. I was born and raised in California, and I experienced firsthand the Summer of Love and a lot of the events in the sixties that really launched the movement. (More about all that in just a bit.)

The lifestyle fit me like a glove. I was born for it.

Ali and I made the *Whole Earth Catalog* our guidebook. Let me explain what that catalog was. The first issue of it surfaced in the fall of 1968. (Original copies of that issue are now next to impossible to find.) In the *Whole Earth Catalog,* you could find just about everything under the sun, from living out in the country, to books on fringe literature, to alternative architecture, to different magazines, to underground publications, to how to survive in the wilderness (tools, camping gear, wood-burning stoves, water pumps, boots, etc.), to how to fix cars and purchase used school buses and trucks, and on and on. I especially liked the fact that the *Whole Earth Catalog* realized that not everyone associated with the hippie counterculture movement was a vegetarian, so they even sold books on how to raise livestock, how to store meat, and so much more. One of the hardest things I ever learned was to milk a cow, but I did it eventually.

This catalog even touched upon communal living, including the real Drop City, which was in Colorado. (Drop City was an artists' community that formed in southern Colorado in 1965. Abandoned by the early 1970s, it became known as the first rural "hippie commune.") The *Whole Earth Catalog* is truly a wonderful resource for those who want to relive the hippie era or learn more about it.

The next must-read publication for hippies was *High Times,* a New York–based monthly. The publication was (and still is) devoted to the legalization of cannabis, which it advocates. It is the largest cannabis-related magazine in the world (at least as far as I know). In 2008, *High Times* launched a digital edition of the magazine, and in early 2010, it began publishing the quarterly *Medical Marijuana News & Reviews.* The magazine was founded in 1974 by Tom Forçade of the Underground Press

Syndicate. *High Times* was originally meant to be a joke, a single-issue lampoon of *Playboy,* substituting dope for sex.

But the magazine found an audience. (In November 2014, it will celebrate its fortieth anniversary.) Like *Playboy,* each issue contains a centerfold photo, but instead of a nude woman, *High Times* typically features a choice grade of cannabis plant. Funny but brilliant. Great magazine.

My friend Wyatt converted me to the hippie lifestyle, but I'd already experienced some of it in San Francisco during the 1960s. (More about that in a bit.) Converts were what hippies wanted most. They were young, so they made it seem possible that this lifestyle could last. *The Hobbit* was the Bible of the movement; hippies saw themselves as the new risk takers, adventurers like Bilbo Baggins.

The article "Hobbit and the Hippie" is an interesting piece that tries to shed light on how a hippie could enjoy *The Hobbit* and also *Lord of the Rings,* by the same author, J. R. R. Tolkien. In these books, there is a lot of struggle and some violence.

True hippies were peaceful people who believed that violence should be avoided at all costs. When asked whether they like these books, many hippies claimed that they love and even worship the *Lord of the Rings* books.

Hippies compared themselves to the hobbits. Hobbits, just like hippies, are peaceful people that live in a part of the world where they have no worries; they call it the shire. I called it Cape Tribulation, North Queensland, Australia.

The hobbit lives a simple life of growing a garden, smoking pipe weed, eating mushrooms, and having a few pints with friends and family.

The hippies respected this lifestyle because they, too, wanted to live a simple life that consisted of sitting with friends, catching a buzz, and using only the bare necessities of living.

But in the book, there are a few instances where the hobbits get caught up in the fight for the hippie movement.

Past generations have impacted the lives of young Americans. In the sixties and seventies, young people went through drastic measures in order to change their lifestyle. Young people at that time refused to follow the teachings of their parents, instead creating an unusual culture of their own.

Often called a counterculture, these changes would alter the values and morals that had been passed on through prior generations. The Vietnam War impacted young people tremendously. They were now drawn to love, peace, happiness, and freedom as a means of escaping from the tragedy they had to face.

This new generation rebelled against society; therefore, the establishment gave them their own name. They came to be known as "hippies," "freaks," or "flower children." They shifted their interests to protests, rock and roll, freedom, peace, and equality. Their unique way of dressing excluded them from the rest of society, reflecting their views of the political and social aspects of the world.

Later in life, I had a girlfriend from Tennessee. She told me she would answer her phone by saying "happiness" instead of "hello." Her mother told her not to answer the phone that way. I don't know about you, but I'd far prefer to be greeted with "happiness" than "hello" anytime.

The hippie era was my time, my destiny. Now I'll take you back to the 1960s when it all began—both the movement and my place in it.

The Summer of Love—San Francisco, California (1967)

The 1960s provided one of the most dominant oppositions to the establishment. Protests at that time truly attacked the status quo. They made the Occupy Movement of the twenty-first century look like mere posturing.

The Summer of Love was a social phenomenon that occurred during the summer of 1967, when as many as a hundred thousand people converged on the Haight-Ashbury neighborhood of San Francisco, California, initiating a major cultural and political shift.

That was the beginning of it all.

In 1966, I was living in a really cool place: San Mateo, California. It was fairly close to where I was born (Richmond, California). I was just breaking in as a hard-hat deep-sea diver on the San Mateo–Hayward Bridge being built across the San Francisco Bay. I joined the pile drivers and bridge builders union in San Francisco: Local 34. This was just after my honorable discharge from the military in 1964. I loved to party. The bars were hopping, always playing soul music. I loved to dance and meet new girls.

Living in San Mateo, I spent a lot of time in San Francisco and all around the Bay Area just as the Haight-Ashbury scene started. The movement was fresh and new then, and it was so exciting to be part of it when it was just getting into full bloom. San Francisco was, is, and always will be a beautiful city, with its harbor and multitude of bridges. The hippie movement thrived there. It was a very cool place. Just across the Golden Gate Bridge was the most unique houseboat community ever: Sausalito.

My tender was very involved in the scene at that time. (The tender is the diver's assistant who takes care of the diver on topside, holds the diving hose, dresses him in, talks to him on the phone while he's underwater, and so on.) He had a Victorian house right in the city, just blocks from Haight-Ashbury. His girlfriend (who later became his wife) could have been a poster girl for the flower children. (When I first saw the album cover for Carole King's *Tapestry,* I immediately thought of that girl.) As a couple, they were hard-core for the "new world movement," as he called it at that time.

Although the hippies also gathered in major cities across the United States, Canada, Australia, and Europe, San Francisco remained the epicenter of the social earthquake, which would come to be known as the Hippie Revolution. Like its sister enclave of Greenwich Village in New York City, San Francisco became even more of a melting pot of politics, music, drugs, creativity, and a total lack of sexual and social inhibition than it already was. As the hippie counterculture movement came farther and farther forward into public awareness, the activities centered therein became a defining moment of the 1960s, causing numerous "ordinary citizens" to begin questioning everything and anything about them and their environment as a result.

Some hippies had no interest in political affairs, preferring to spend their time involved in sex, drugs, and rock and roll music. I was in *that* group of hippies!

Music and Philosophy, Hippie Style (1966–1969)

Music ruled us in the hippie era. Our souls cried out, "Listen to us! We are serious."

Much of the music of that time was based in San Francisco too. The legendary Bill Graham was a well-known music promoter who successfully managed several bands, organized concerts, and made several concert venues famous, most notably the Fillmore. The original Fillmore was in an older part of San Francisco. Graham later moved it to a new location in the city, renaming it the Fillmore West. In both locations, the Fillmore was the heart of the psychedelic music scene in San Francisco. The Fillmore East was his New York venue. In the 1960s, both Fillmores were must-play venues for the most popular artists of the day.

The Fillmore enjoyed a legendary reign at the center of the San Francisco music scene and the counterculture of the sixties. Nearly all the most popular bands of the day made an appearance there, including the Grateful Dead, the Jefferson Airplane, Santana, Quicksilver Messenger Service, Big Brother and the Holding Company, Moby Grape, the Butterfield Blues Band, the Doors, the Jimi Hendrix Experience, Cream, the Who, and many others.

One Fillmore West show in February 1969 was particularly famous. It began with a Tibetan monk playing Tibetan gongs and also featured music by the Grateful Dead. The Fillmore West closed with a concert featuring Santana, Creedence Clearwater Revival, the Grateful Dead, and Quicksilver Messenger Service, as well as a poetry reading. In addition to the fantastic artists featured, the venue also had an amazing atmosphere, which made it a focal point for the youth counterculture. Concerts at the Fillmore often featured light shows, strobe lights, and wild dancing. Also, Fillmore concerts often continued long into the night, much to the dismay of the San Francisco police. The Fillmore East offered equally spectacular light shows and artists; it was a true companion venue for Graham.

As I've said, the hippies were an eclectic group. Many were suspicious of the government, rejected consumerist values, and generally opposed the Vietnam War. Many, like me, just loved the sex, drugs, and rock and roll.

The Woodstock Festival of 1969 was the culmination of the hippie era, an iconic counterculture event. Referred to simply as Woodstock, it was a three-day concert (that rolled into a fourth day) that involved lots of sex, drugs, and rock and roll—plus a lot of mud.

There was a philosophy behind the counterculture. The hippies saw the human body as beautiful and lovable. It wasn't all about sex. Hippies also valued affection. They wanted to hug one another, to be naked without shame. They saw the body as a temple to revere with natural foods, beneficial exercise, herbs, baths, massage, and deep understanding. They wanted intimacy—again, not just in the sexual sense—but in terms of community and humanity. They didn't want to live in neighborhoods where people didn't know one another, or where all they did was consume and compete. To them, there was a lot more to life than just keeping up with the Joneses.

I knew all this about the hippie lifestyle when I first met Wyatt in Australia. I was immediately intrigued, not just because of how much I wanted to drop out of the rat race but also because of how much that lifestyle had resonated with me years before in San Francisco. Wyatt was really a farmer in his heart. Like his family, he was a land person; I was an ocean person, like my family. Wyatt learned from me, and I learned from him. He created an agricultural community based on farming and gathering. Like most hippies, he and his group wanted people to live and work together, and to seek deeper contact with creation individually and together, from cradle to grave. They truly viewed the community as an extended family. They shared everything, even their women.

The commune lifestyle was based on giving and sharing. They (by which I mean hippies, including me) wanted a culture that thrived on those precepts. They hitchhiked, shared their food and drugs, gave away their possessions; it was anti-consumerism. People who could not afford land were invited to live with them. They wanted to open free stores, free clinics, free kitchens—everywhere they went, they wanted living proof that goodness was taking care of them, and, therefore, there was no need to hoard.

Hippies also wanted to live without the constraints of time. They wanted to wake up each day and decide what would be the most fun to do that day—or just find out as the day went along. They wanted to go with the flow, follow their bliss, be here now. This was in complete opposition to society, to their backgrounds. It truly was a counterculture in every way.

They wanted new ways to value each other, by things that had meaning, rather than by wealth, status, looks, achievements, machismo, or any of the things valued by society or the establishment. They didn't want to buy in to the media's messages; instead, they wanted to value one another for being lovable and real.

And the philosophy went even deeper than that. Very deep, in fact. They valued spiritual depth, which they referred to as "heavy." Happiness was something they also valued, and they admired it in one another. They also admired those who offered selfless service or peaceful resolution of conflict. They wanted spiritual roles that actually caused individuals to grow as people, which was far different from attending so-called religious gatherings that were really about social status. They wanted to be guided by their own inner spirits, not by clergy or other authority figures.

In a way, this was a big reason why drugs were involved in the counterculture. Hippies thirsted for spiritual awareness, grace, and sacred transformational experiences. Psychedelic drugs were portals to these experiences, but many hippies were happy to attain those experiences without psychedelics or in addition to them. Many hippies would spend their last cent on a weekend workshop that promised to "change your life forever," with or without drugs involved. That was how so many gurus found followers in those days.

Most of all, I think, the hippies wanted to live in harmony with nature and one another, in body, mind, and spirit, and in connection with the Great Spirit of all creation. This was more important than the establishment's stupid, arbitrary rules, and they sought to eliminate these for themselves and for their children. Some children of hippies became conservative as adults, rebelling against their parents' teachings in much the same way as the hippies had. But other kids raised by hippie parents grew up to be hippies themselves. So in some sense, the counterculture became a new culture that continues to this day. It was successful for a time. And fun. It still is to a certain extent. It did not widely take hold as hoped.

Was it a failure in the end? I don't think so. The consciousness lives on in the ecofriendly mind-set of the twenty-first century, in the increased open-mindedness of more people than ever before, and in the readiness to question authority and the establishment when warranted, with or without protest or activism. The hippies made the world take notice, care more about the earth, and think and feel more deeply. None of that could ever be construed as "failure" in my opinion.

My Adventures in Deep Water: Diving into the Real Moon Pools—Southern California (1964–1967)

I've spent a lot of time describing living in the magnificent rain forest and enjoying the hippie lifestyle, as well as explaining what drew me to both. You know that I worked as a deep-water diver and owned an international deep-water diving company. But I haven't really talked about diving, other than to explain moon pools. The time has come to relate my diving experience. So, without further delay, let's just dive in!

I was the youngest hard-hat deep-sea diver in the California union. This was an elite group. I was trained and raised by the best.

Torrance Parker, a deep-sea-diving legend and the author of *20,000 Jobs under the Sea,* tells the story of the first time he met me. It was in my dad's garage. I had found a can of gasoline, and I drank some of it, which of course made me retch and gag. I got really sick, needless to say; it was quite a display. That was just me, though. I was always doing something that created drama. I didn't even have to try. I'm still that way.

Anyway, it was a real kick to read Parker's description of me as a kid. I idolized him. Deep-water divers are heroes. There should be a day dedicated to them. I hereby proclaim June 2 as Deep-Sea Divers Day and Deep-Water Divers Day.

Most people don't realize how crucial deep-water divers are to the world stage. Let me explain exactly what they do.

Some deep-water divers do construction and maintenance of underwater structures. They begin by inspecting the structures and areas they are assigned to. For example, they may inspect the hulls or propellers of ships to find damaged areas. When they find damaged areas, they repair them. For this work, they use welding equipment, drills, and other tools.

Divers also work on underwater construction of bridges and other structures. To make room for the structure or to level the ground, they may remove rocks or other obstacles. Some items can be removed by cutting them into smaller pieces. However, divers sometimes must blow up rocks. They drill holes in the rock, add explosives, and set up other equipment needed to trigger the explosion. Once the area is clear, divers begin building the structure.

It's dangerous but essential work. You can see why I said deep-water divers deserve their own "heroes' day" and why I proclaimed it. Next June 2, remember to give thanks for deep-water divers. Seriously.

Deep-water divers risk their lives to build bridges and install underwater pipelines. This is how we get safe, clean drinking water into our homes; it's also how vehicles travel safely over water. In addition to building pipelines and bridges and repairing underwater structures, deep-water divers build and maintain marinas, maintain subsea equipment on oil rigs, and explore salvage ships to look for treasure. That last part definitely sounds the most glamorous, but the maintenance work ensures the safety of billions of people worldwide, and that's what makes divers heroes.

Taking a brief trip back to San Francisco, think of the world-famous Golden Gate Bridge. We all recognize its beauty, but not everyone is aware of the engineering behind it. When you think of its construction, you probably picture men perched high up in the air, on iron beams and scaffolds. In truth, much of the bridge's construction occurred underwater. The same is true of most famous large bridges, including the Brooklyn Bridge, which was built way back in 1883.

These divers wore brass or copper helmets (hard hats) and used air lines that provide air from the surface. (Deep-water divers wear hard hats and use air lines to this very day.) They worked shallow and deep. They had to fight extremely strong tidal currents and murky water. Nevertheless, divers built the Golden Gate Bridge foundation and its fender, which helped protect the bridge from stray ships caught in the famous San Francisco fog. As with other underwater construction, these divers used explosives and other tools to blast away rock, smooth the ocean floor, and clear away debris.

I use the Golden Gate Bridge as an example because it's easy to picture what the bridge looks like, and that makes it easier to understand what deep-water divers do—and how dangerous it is. As an experienced hard-hat diver, I can relate to what it must have been like working underwater on the Golden Gate. Some of my own diving experiences were pretty harrowing; others were just incredible. The danger was always there. When you dive for a living, there's always a moon pool. I learned how to survive and thrive there. Keep reading, and you'll see just *how* I did it.

San Onofre—Nuclear Generating Station (1964)

I received my honorable discharge from the military in March 1964. My father, Art Broman, was the diving inspector for Edison Company, so I went to work as a tender (diver's assistant) for him. He was really hard on me. But the work was hard; he didn't have a choice but to be hard on me. He had to crawl underwater to inspect the divers' work: laying of the seventy-two-ton, twenty-four-by-twelve-foot pipe for the big outfalls.

Welcome to the world of commercial deep-water diving. It gave me incredible experience, and it made me a world-class diver.

San Mateo-Hayward Bridge (1964–1967)

The original San Mateo-Hayward Bridge was the longest bridge in the world at that time. It was replaced with a modern span in 1967. The total length of the bridge is seven miles. There's a high-rise section, and the western end of the bridge is composed of multiple steel girder spans.

We were the team of divers responsible for the underwater foundation and the installation (the start of the bridge on the ocean floor; that is, the bottom of the bay). I say the most important part of the bridge is the foundation. We divers always get slighted. The engineers who design the bridges get all the press and recognition. I always resented that and still do. They just draw lines on paper. It's the divers who build the bridges. Wouldn't you agree that the most important part of the bridge is the foundation? After all, if it doesn't hold, the bridge will collapse. It is incredibly difficult to build the foundation underwater, and, without deep-sea divers, such construction would never even be possible. With the powerful, mighty currents of San Francisco Bay, combined with zero visibility on a muddy, sledge bottom, this was an extremely dangerous project. A definite moon pool, literally and figuratively.

Cuss I (1967)

Making helium (one of the chemicals used in deep-water diving) dives on the *Cuss I* with Bob Benton, Ted Benton, Pete Blommers, and Paul Pettingill (ex-master diver in the US Navy) was an incredible experience. Diving with these guys was the greatest compliment another diver could receive; they were truly the elite of the deep-water diving business. Torrance Parker, whom I've already mentioned, was another legend. So were Jack Fonner and Woody Treen.

These were just a few of the great divers I worked with. Working with them and learning from them gave me an edge. Later, as the owner/ operator and head diver of Broman International, I became the leader of this success story.

Yes, I learned from the best. My godfather, Scotty Chisholm, was the owner of Chisholm Divers. Scotty had taught my dad how to dive, and now he was taking me under his wing too. He took me on underwater burning and welding jobs around Oakland Harbor as part of my training.

I learned to crawl upside down with the hard-hat equipment on the Moss Landing job. It was to inspect the seventy-two-ton pipe on the ocean floor. On my first dive, the bottom joint of the first connection was a half-inch gap between the two joints, and I told this to the tender over the phone. The inspector for Pacific Gas & Electric (PG&E) was impressed. This was his first underwater inspection; he had never been around any hard-hat divers before.

I managed to get all the readings, and I said, "Diver coming up."

I did well, and Scotty was proud of me. At sixty-five, he was the oldest hard-hat diver in the union; at twenty-two, I was the youngest. We had an agreement: if I worked as his tender, I would get a chance to get some dives. We were a great team.

Because of my dad, I had made my first hard-hat dive when I was just sixteen years old. The best in the business said I was the best diver tender. I was. The best hard-hat divers in the business had trained me, and I had a tough father who was also a legend in the business. He even had the only hard-hat diving school in the country at one time. I didn't always like his methods, but he and Scotty made me a great diver.

Moss Landing (1968)

Moss Landing was a tough job. Where the pipeline started, it was shallow (twenty feet or so), but it got deeper as the pipeline got longer.

I can tell you this: on my first dive, I was all screwed up. I was at the lip of the pipe, with no visibility, and the surge was brutal, pinning me under the lip of pipe. We had to make long runs in the pipe, checking all the joints for spalled areas outside and inside the pipe. The surf was hard to deal with at first, especially with that big hard-hat equipment. As I said, the start was shallow water; the pipe was twelve feet across, twenty-four feet long, and weighed seventy-two tons. To get inside, you had to hang on the lip of the pipe, fighting the surge that sucked you out. The pipe was smooth inside, so you couldn't hang on to anything; you had to blow up to the top of the pipe, pull your hose, and crawl twenty-four feet until you got to the joint where the two pipes connected.

There was a piece of steel that had areas cut to different thicknesses to check how far apart the connections were between the pipes. When you stuck your gap-reading gauge in the joint, you could hold on until the surge came back in, and then go around the joint, checking the gaps to see if they were tight enough to meet PG&E specs. You usually did three pipes at a time, about one hundred feet back in, but then, later on, you would have to go back and check the pipes to see if there was any settling. This was usually on the final inspections, after all the pipe had been laid. I had to make long runs; we had a diver go through a manhole and pull hose for me. He was a former master navy diver.

After finishing that job, I had a big reputation in the industry; it was a big accomplishment. It was a big deal because the contractors laying the pipe were a large outfit: Pomeroy-Gerwick-Steers. They said that it was The quickest and best inspection diving that they had ever seen.

"Best hard-hat diver" was what I wanted to be called. I was ambitious. I was proud of my accomplishment, but this was just the start. I wanted not only to be the best but to be the best *ever*. This is the kind of diving that very few ever survive. Scotty Chisholm had taught me in how to handle the hard-had equipment, how to weld and burn underwater. I got to dive and practice every day while he trained me.

Now I was inspecting the work of a legend: my dad. It was bizarre. He tried to trick me a few times, but it didn't work; it only made me more determined to do even better. I'll say it again: my dad and Scotty gave me the best training in the world. I became a great diver because of them.

How I Got My First Major Diving Job (1967)

Remember, I learned from the best, growing up with legendary hard-hat divers. All the divers I worked with respected that. They knew my dad. They also knew Scotty Chisholm, who taught first my dad and then me.

A lot of the divers I worked with later on had known me when I was three years old and hanging out in my dad's shop. (No doubt creating some drama without even trying, even then!)

But my growing years were not just about diving. I grew up with two different lifestyles, really. There was the diving side with my dad; if Art Broman the deep-water-diving legend was your father, you couldn't not learn how to dive. And then there was the softer side I learned about through my mother, Colleen. My mother was so beautiful, a real Doris Day type. Don't just take my word for what a knockout she was. Colleen Broman was picked on the beach to be Miss Marine Stadium.

I guess that didn't mean much to my dad. He was a womanizer. (I guess I inherited my curse from him.) And, as I've said, he was a legendary diver. He was wild, smart, charismatic. I was drawn to him and to diving, spending lots of time in his shop with the hard-hat helmets and canvas suits. The suits looked like monsters hanging from the walls. Everything about diving intrigued me: the big copper (sometimes brass) diving helmets (hard hats), the air compressors, the lead weight belts, the ankle weights. I loved it.

When I got older, I built my own room in my dad's shop. I wanted it as a place to take girls to. My dad helped me build it because he wanted a place to sleep in that room. We built a coffin. It had cushions on the top, and the lid had hinges on it so you could keep the bedding inside it. Old Art would sleep inside it, with the lid closed. (He had drilled holes in it for air when the lid was closed.) One night, I had a girl over. We were making out, and the lid started to open. The girl screamed, jumping to her feet. Up came Old Art out of the coffin. She kept screaming hysterically. Finally, we got her calmed down, but what a scene.

That was Old Art. He did crazy things like that all time.

My dad was proud of me, though, in his own way. When Torrance Parker interviewed him for *20,000 Jobs under the Sea* (Parker's history of most of the greatest hard-hat construction diving jobs done up to that time), my dad talked about how I'd inspected his work on the famous outfall at Moss Landing, California. (That was while Scotty Chisholm was training me.) But Old Art also made a point of telling Parker that I was overseas in New Guinea, working with Pomeroy-Gerwick-Steers, one of the premier big construction companies in the world. The superintendent on that job always said I did the best inspection they'd ever had done, and the fastest, which saved them a lot of money because work was at a standstill for less time than usual. I was proud of that accomplishment. I don't know how much of that Parker knew, but he did mention that I was one of the hundred pioneer deep-water oilfield divers.

Even though I had done some of the deepest helium dives, built diving bell systems, and worked on the *Glomar Conception* out of New Guinea as the diving superintendent for International Divers, I wanted more. That was why I founded Broman International, and I'm proud that it was known as the most successful deep-water diving company in the world.

I'm getting ahead of myself again. First, I'll tell you about working for International Divers in Santa Barbara. We'll get to bigger dives—and, eventually, to Broman International—all in good time.

Arriving at International Divers (1967)

When I arrived in Santa Barbara, I went straight to International Divers to apply there. Woody Treen and Pete Blommers owned the place. I went to their shop because I'd heard that they were going to have a contract to go overseas to the Territory of Papua, New Guinea, on a new state-of-the-art drilling vessel, the *Glomar Conception,* which was the talk of the industry. That was the main reason I wanted to work for them. I went into the office and spoke to the business manager. His name was Frank, and he took all the applications from anybody who came in looking for work.

I had other chances with the two other top companies: California Divers and Associated Divers.

Frank said, "We need someone with tending experience."

I said, "Well, I've been a tender, and I will do that for a while, but I want my main job to be a hard hat, a deep-water diver. I just finished Moss Landing."

I had hard-hat experience, so I was very convincing and confident.

When I told him my name, he said, "I've heard about you. Your dad's Art Broman."

I just said, "Yes."

"Hey, they won't hire you here. Why don't you go work for your dad?"

I said, "Well, we don't get along. I'm not going to work for him, and I want to try to interview here."

Both owners were up in Alaska on diving jobs. They wouldn't be back for another two weeks or so.

Undeterred, I told Frank, "I'll just check in when they get back."

But I didn't wait two weeks. Every couple of days, I went to see Frank at International Divers. I'd drop by, talk to him, just shoot the bull.

He ended up liking me and was impressed by my confidence. We became friends, but he still didn't believe that the owners would hire me. "Being Art Broman's son is not giving you any pluses," was the way he put it.

I still kept coming around, checking in. I went around and applied at the other deep-water diving companies too.

John Culbertson, the head of California Divers, had already told me that they would hire me and send me to Australia on a new contract they were getting. But I wanted International Divers.

Pete Blommers finally returned from Alaska, and I went in to get an appointment with him. I pulled up to the shop, and Pete was there.

When I walked in, Frank said, "Yes, Pete's here. I'll tell him you're here."

I heard Frank in Pete's office, saying, "This Jim Broman's here. He's been bugging us about trying to get work. I told him you probably didn't have any room for anybody."

"Yeah, tell him we're all filled up; we don't need anybody right now," Pete said. But I guess he was curious, because then he said, "Wait. Jim Broman. Is that Art's Broman's kid?"

Frank said that I was.

"I heard about him from the Moss Landing job."

As I said, word traveled fast in the industry about how I had nailed that job.

I couldn't hear Frank say anything else.

"Nah. Tell him we're full up," Pete said.

Frank came out said that there really wasn't anything available.

I wasn't sure if he realized that I'd heard their conversation. I took a chance. "I'd really like to talk to him," I said.

So Frank went back in and said, "He really would like to talk to you, Pete."

And Pete couldn't resist. "Okay."

I went in. Pete sized me up, and I sized him up. He was a good-looking man. Forties. Canadian. He had black hair, olive complexion, blue eyes. I'd heard he was married to a real beauty, but he was a big-time womanizer. Another diver who was a womanizer. Big surprise!

"Listen, we just don't have any room for you," Pete said. "Why don't you go work for your dad?"

"You've worked for Art. You know why I don't want to work for him," I replied.

"Well, we just don't have any room; we've got plenty of guys."

I didn't say anything else. I walked out and went directly back into the shop. I knew where the shop was; I even knew where all the equipment was. On my various visits, I'd been back there looking at the equipment and talking to their equipment man (he was a tender, not a diver). I put on a pair of coveralls and went to work on some equipment.

Pete came out of his office and walked into the shop. He said to me, "I thought I just told you we didn't need anybody."

I said, "Well, I'm not charging you for this. I'll just help out in case you do end up needing somebody."

He shook his head and said, "Well, okay."

I heard him tell Frank, "He's cocky, cheeky."

So, I was allowed to work on the equipment, but I wasn't getting paid. But then, guess what happened? Exactly what I thought would happen: they got a call to go out to a rig, the *Salvor.* They needed a diver and a tender, and I was already there, so I got to go. That was my opportunity, and I got paid. So I tended this other diver, and I did an excellent job. Remember, I had a reputation of being the best diver's tender in the business, trained by the best—Art Broman and Scotty Chisholm—so I started working my way in from that moment on.

Not too long after that, they got another call. Again, I went out as the diver's tender. This time, the diver ran out of bottom time, and they needed another dive made.

I was out there on the rig, and, pointing to me, the diver said, "This guy here's a hard-hat diver."

And the tool pusher said, "Man, this kid's too young to be able to handle the hard-hat gear." (They always say things like that.)

They called in to the beach, tried to get another diver, but no divers were available. So, instead, they had a tender sent out, and they suited me up, and I made the dive.

It was 183 feet of water. I'd never been down past one hundred feet. You get something called *nitrogen narcosis,* raptures of the deep. It's a sense of light-headedness, and if you get it bad enough, it causes hallucinations. The equipment was a BOP (blowout preventer). It was close to 30 feet high and 15 feet wide. Very intimidating, especially when on the verge of hallucinating at 183 feet! It was scary.

I went down. I was very narco, and I had never felt that way underwater before. I was ripped, disoriented. I'd never seen a BOP before; it was huge. I was confused, and had to choose between two valves that looked similar. I took off the wrong one. They wanted to change the cement valve, and I took off the wrong one. I was completely disoriented and couldn't finish the job.

When I came up and they put me in the decompression chamber, the tool pusher for the rig was furious that an inexperienced diver had messed up the job like that. And, most important, it shut down the rig, which meant big money.

Yes, I changed the wrong piece of equipment. I messed up. To be honest, I was lucky to surface alive: that nitrogen narcosis had me completely out of it.

Long story short, they had to call Pete Blommers out. They got him out on a workboat. I was in the decompression chamber, knowing I failed on my first chance to be an oilfield hard-hat diver. I was so down it was unbelievable. I'd planned for this moment, and in an instant, it was over. Ruined. That was the end of it: I failed.

Pete got on the rig. They suited him up, he made the dive, fixed the mistake that I'd made, and came back up. When he got out of the chamber, he said to me, "Broman, that could've happened to anybody. At least you made it down there and back up, you know?"

I appreciated his saying that. He respected other divers. But I figured I'd never get another chance again.

The tool pusher said, "Never have that kid come out here again. He can never dive again on this rig."

I didn't take failure easy; I still don't.

As I said, I thought I'd really blown my opportunity. Well, the very next day, they called us again. More dives. That rig always had a lot of problems because it was older.

We went out to the *Salvor,* and I tended. They couldn't get anybody else, so I had to go out.

"What's he doing here?" the tool pusher wanted to know.

"He's just going to tend."

The diver ran out of bottom time again and could not finish the job, so they needed—you guessed it—another diver. They could not get a hold of any other divers, so they took one more chance on me.

I had to take off a hammer union that was connected to the drill string equipment on the bottom. A couple of roughnecks put it on the topside and tightened the freaking thing so much that it might take Hercules to get it off. So I had to take a sledgehammer, go down to the 183 feet, and bang on this thing. I was almost out of bottom time when I finally broke it loose and got it disconnected. I came up, job complete. I was successful, so I redeemed myself.

I was now a deep-water, hard-hat oilfield diver. I had finally made it. That was a big turning point in my life. Was I happy? Oh, yes, very happy.

I was proud too. I had successfully completed that moon pool, and it was a big one.

Pete wound up really liking me. I always had girls I was taking out, bringing them by the shop to make him drool. He was such a womanizer. I had my canary-yellow Citroën convertible, a very cool beach car.

I worked in the shop, and I was a good-looking kid. Plus, I was fun. I was good at my job, an excellent tender. He loved that, and I was also a hell of a diver. I got other chances and opportunities, but that 183-foot dive was the deepest for me at that point.

When we were called out again, it could have been a heavy-duty accident. They had this one guy who was real jealous of me. He wanted to be a hard-hat diver. He was in his forties, but he'd never had the opportunity. He was a tender. In fact, he was assigned to be my tender. He suited me up. Once I was suited up, I made the dive. I jumped into the moon pool, literally. I was very good in that diving equipment, a real swashbuckler. "Cocky and cheeky," just like Pete said.

We good divers didn't climb down the ladder. Scotty Chisholm had trained me in Oakland Harbor, dive after dive. I had to learn how to jump the ten, fifteen, or more if necessary feet down into the water, and then I'd bounce back up and hang on the guide wire. I really was extremely good with the equipment. I'd go down the way Scotty had taught me, all the way down to 183 feet or so, my deepest at that point. I would still get narco, but I started getting used to it. I was gaining experience. I'd change the hose, and, all of a sudden, I wouldn't get any air.

"Hey! Diver not getting any air," I'd say into the phone. "Is everything okay up there?"

The tender, the guy who was jealous of me, would come on. "Yeah, everything is okay," he'd say. A real smart aleck.

You should never have anybody like that tending your hose. There's no room for jealousy on a diving crew. He thought he could get away with it because I was so young. Big mistake for him.

This went on for some time. I started climbing the hose bundle and the guide wire myself. I was not getting any air. That big suit squeezed up against me, and the weight was overwhelming. I kept climbing up, getting to about one hundred feet.

All of a sudden on the phone, they said, "Diver coming up. Diver's out of air."

No kidding. I knew that, and I told them so, but I'd been climbing all that time by myself, climbing up the hose bundle.

They caught up with the slack hose and pulled me out of the water. When they undressed me and took off the helmet, I could barely breathe.

The tender admitted, "I fucked up." But he didn't offer any details. (Later on, we found out that the flex hose had broken off from the compressor to the volume tank that stored the air; all the air had leaked out, but he didn't see it. He didn't go check like he was supposed to. The gauge had stuck.)

I knew it was the tender's fault immediately, even though I didn't know exactly why until later. When they took the hard hat off, I grabbed hold of him. I still had the breastplate and the rest of the gear on. I wanted to kill him. He could have killed me and almost did. I threw him back on deck, jumped on top of him, and ground the breastplate onto his head. He couldn't move with the 250 pounds of weight I had on him (between me and the gear). I kept grinding the brass breastplate into his face and head. I had already broken his nose by that point and started on his teeth, trying to knock them all out. I was unstoppable, on the warpath. It took three men to pull me off him, and they struggled to do it. They had no choice, though; they had to get me into the chamber so I wouldn't get the bends (decompression sickness).

There was another tender on the rig, and he went into the chamber with me. The chamber had two locks. He pressured out the outer lock, went in with me, and undressed me. He was speechless the entire time.

That dive was a very, very close call. For me and for the first tender who was so jealous of me.

There was another close call later on, on that same rig.

I'd made a dive, and we had to change a seal. The ship was moving up and down with a big swell. It was a seal on the wellhead, where the BOP was.

This seal was actually on the inside of the connector, which meant I would have to stick my hand up underneath and inside the connecter. I had them lift the BOP up thirty feet. It was on a drill string, but the swell of the ship kept coming down, and I was right over the wellhead too. I stuck my hand up inside, and a swell came up and down. Caught between the BOP and the wellhead, my arm almost got cut off.

So, yes, that was another close call. I wouldn't have traded diving for anything else, though. It was so cool being a hard-hat diver. I loved it. The fear was always there; you felt the fear, but you did whatever you had to do, and that was that. There were many dives made with no drama at all, strictly routine stuff. The underlying danger was what made it exciting. Even when it was routine, there was still always a rush.

I said I loved it, but it was deeper than that. Diving took more than love; it took faith. I did not have religion, but ever since the fifth grade, I'd prayed about everything I did. I had faith. I knew there was a Higher Power that protected me. I felt close to God. Always have, always will. I am sure he didn't approve of some of my conduct, and probably still doesn't, but he still loves me because he knows I love him. Again, always have, always will.

The Bends—Santa Barbara, California (1967)

I've described the danger of the bends. I almost died of the bends once. It was a helium dive (mix of 90 percent helium, 10 percent oxygen) at 263 feet, in Santa Barbara, California.

Associated Divers had a contract with the company Global Marine, but they ran out of divers with bottom time, so they called us to help. It was really deep water.

This was the *Cuss I,* the first of the fleet. In 1961, Global Marine elected to order not one, but several new self-propelled drillships, each with a package and mast rated for centerline drilling of 20,000-foot wells in water depths to 600 feet. The company christened each with the *Cuss* forename, followed by its respective number (*Cuss II, III, IV,* and so on). But because of problems with the Arabic translation of the word "cuss," in 1964, Global changed the rigs' forenames to *Glomar,* followed by the number.

We went out, and there were three divers already on the rig. I was to go out as a tender because this was very deep water: 263 feet. All the top divers in the industry had been out there diving already. Ted and Bob Benton (known in the industry as the Benton brothers). My boss, Pete Blommers, one of the owners of International Divers. Paul Pettingill, who had been a master diver in the US Navy. He was retired by that point, and he ran all the manifold and helium stuff. They had all finished their dives by the time we got there. No bottom time left.

It was a serious issue that all the divers were out of bottom time, because Global wanted to retrieve a connector that had fallen to the ocean floor. This was worth a lot of money. Really big money.

As I said, I was there to tend one of the divers, not to make a dive. But Bob Benton, one of the top divers in the business, said, "Young Broman can make the dive. He has the hard-hat experience."

I was shocked and pleased to have one of the best in the world recommend me.

Benton had finished his dive, and the people at Global were happy. The major part of the problem was repaired and fixed, but they did need one more dive. They just didn't have a diver. That was why Benton recommended me.

Once again, the oilfield bosses were suspicious because I was so young, but they had nothing to lose: it would take them twenty-four hours to get another diver, if they could find one who would go that deep on helium.

Helium dives in the commercial field were still new. I had never made a helium dive before. Plus, this was going to be my deepest dive to date, at 263 feet. They asked me if I would try the dive even though I had not made a helium dive before, and even though this was such a deep dive.

A first helium dive at that depth was extremely dangerous, but that didn't bother me. I agreed to make the dive, so they briefed me on how to handle the dive, explaining what it was like to dive with helium.

Helium is a gas that is lighter than air. That meant that I would need more weight to get down, so more weight was added to my weight belt. I would go to fifty feet, and then they would switch me from air to helium.

"You start counting, one, two, three, and so on, until your voice changes," they explained. "When you sound like Donald Duck, we'll say, 'Diver, ready for dive; you're on helium.'"

"Got it," I told them. I felt I understood the process, but I had no experience diving with helium, and I had never gone that deep. Combining two firsts like that in the same dive was dangerous. They knew it, and I did. Of course, me being me, I did it anyway.

Because I completely lacked experience diving with helium, I couldn't possibly imagine how many problems it entailed, all of which would be seriously amplified when diving depths were greater than 200 feet.

First, there is the problem of communication. I got that I was going to sound like Donald Duck, but that wasn't all of it. Not even close. Everyone knows what inhaling helium will do to your voice. This happens because of the changes in the speed of sound in the gas medium. But what matters for divers is that this effect is a sensitive function of depth. At 200 feet, the diver's speech is still reasonably understandable, even with helium inhaled. However, as depths increase beyond 200 feet, the situation becomes more serious. To someone trying to get a job done underwater, helium speech is no longer funny. Helium speech in this range is totally lost on an untrained ear, though a listener familiar with the voice and the situation can understand certain statements. Often, a sudden change in the topic of conversation will throw everyone off, and it is necessary for the diver to speak slowly, repeat the statement(s), and try to say things a different way. It can be done, but it is a slow process, and, consequently, it is expensive.

Another significant problem is that helium is about four times as good at conducting heat as nitrogen. When at the chilly depth of 263 feet in the Pacific Ocean, this means that the diver will get very cold. In addition, the decompression time is longer.

In any case, I was not really aware of all this. I knew some of the facts, but I didn't really understand all the implications and potential consequences because I lacked the firsthand experience.

They suited me up, and I jumped into the water. I went down to fifty feet like they'd told me to.

Over the phone, I said, "I'm at fifty feet," and then, again like they'd told me to, I started counting as they changed from air to helium; when my voice changed to something like Donald Duck's, I would say, "Diver going down."

I thought my voice sounded more like Alvin the Chipmunk than Donald Duck, but at the appropriate time, I said into the phone, "Diver going down."

As instructed, I headed for the bottom. Remember, this dive was to 263 feet, my deepest dive to date. It was also the deepest for the day on the rig, as the repair work done earlier had been at 179 feet. I was the only one going all the way to the bottom, the only one diving with helium that day.

I started having a problem getting down because I was not heavy enough. Even though we'd added weight, it was not enough, so I had to open my exhaust valve to the max to dump the gas out of my suit. Doing this caused water to come in through the exhaust, and my suit started to fill up with water. By the time I finished the dive, I had water up to my knees, and I was freezing from exposure.

Eventually, I did get to the bottom. It was a long way down. I had to be very careful not to stir up the cuttings on the bottom, because that would result in no visibility. I had a lot of experience diving with no visibility in some of the big harbors—Oakland, San Francisco, Long Beach—it was so creepy. I remember feeling like a blind man. In the harbors, you never knew what you would touch on the bottom. I really didn't want to experience that at 263 feet.

Anyway, I got to the bottom, searched around the wellhead, and found the connector. I had a cable with me and a shackle to wrap around it to retrieve it, but I had gone over my bottom time by a considerable amount of time by that point. My suit was taking on water up to my knees, I was shivering from exposure, and I was freezing.

Next came the nitrogen narcosis. I've described this already. It's commonly referred to as "rapture of the deep." It typically becomes noticeable at depths of one hundred feet, and it is incapacitating at 300 feet, causing stupor, blindness, unconsciousness, and even death. Nitrogen narcosis is also called "the martini effect," because divers experience an effect comparable to that from one martini on an empty stomach for every fifty feet of depth beyond the initial one hundred feet. Remember, I was at 263 feet, so, yes, I was somewhat narco.

This was such a deep dive, and a first helium dive at that kind of depth made the effects far worse.

There's also a bigger risk of decompression sickness (DCS; a.k.a. the bends) at extreme depths. DCS occurs when a diver with a large amount of inert gas dissolved in the body tissues is decompressed to a pressure where the gas forms bubbles, which may block blood vessels or physically damage surrounding cells. DCS is potentially fatal. Because DCS occurs in divers' bodies following the pressure reduction as they ascend, the best way to prevent DCS is to limit the rate of ascent and to pause at regular intervals in order to allow the pressure of gases in the body to approach equilibrium. This protocol, known as decompression, can last for many hours with dives in excess of 160 feet and when divers spend more than a few minutes at these depths. The longer divers remain at depth, the more inert gas is absorbed into their body tissues, and the time required for decompression increases rapidly. Of course, helium makes all this even harder to deal with.

I was already at risk, but I wanted to get the job done.

I had carried down this big wire with a shackle on it, so if I found the collar I needed to find, I could go ahead and hook on to it. Well, I found it, but I was over my bottom time.

Over the phones, they kept saying, "Diver, come up."

They couldn't really understand me that well because of the helium.

Well, I wouldn't come up. All I wanted was to get this thing done, and I did get it done. I hooked it up, and then I came up. But it was about fifteen or twenty minutes over my bottom time, which is significant.

I came up to my first stop. My suit had filled up with even more water by that point, all the way up to my knees, because exhaust was open on my hard hat. I had to open my exhaust, and it leaked, remember. All because I didn't have enough weight on my weight belt, so I had trouble getting down.

Anyway, I got to my first stop (about sixty feet), and I was supposed to spend about an hour there (standard). And then it would be on to the next stop, and so on. Finally, they brought me to the surface and put me in the chamber for a long decompression. I finally finished my decompression, crawled out of the chamber, and headed for the chow hall. All the other divers were there waiting for me. They didn't take the boat in or fly in by chopper or anything else. That was their way of showing respect. I had finally done it: dived down to 263 feet, made my first helium dive, and got the job done. I was 100 percent successful.

"Good dive, Broman," the other divers said.

These were my idols! Legends of deep-water diving. And I was now one of them, a helium deep-water diver. Finally. It felt great to be one of such an elite group. (Plus, I made big money on that dive. Depth pay, overtime, extra union benefits, the whole nine yards.)

Riding high on my accomplishments, I sat down to have my breakfast. All of a sudden, I started going into convulsions. They had to grab a hold of my tongue so I wouldn't swallow it. It was a severe case of the bends. Right there in the middle of the chow hall floor, I was squirming around. (That's what they told me afterward, and having witnessed the bends in others, I'm sure it's true.)

They took me down in the chamber again, and they had to use a new decompressions table. It was a US Navy oxygen table. Paul Pettingill was the expert on decompression and helium. (You'll remember that he'd been a master diver in the navy before retiring.) I knew Paul; he'd pulled hose for me at Moss Landing as a standby diver.

Anyway, they put me on this new decompression table, and it cured me. I've already described what happens during the bends. Mild cases of the bends result in the telltale warning signs of joint aches, rashes, and itchy skin. Severe cases result in sensory problems, convulsions, paralysis, and even death.

We'd followed the precautions, and I'd spent a lot of time in the chamber after surfacing. Part of the problem was that nitrogen is not the only gas that can cause the bends. Helium causes DCS too, and because helium both enters and leaves the body faster than nitrogen does, it requires different decompression schedules. We had followed the schedule, but it didn't work, maybe because I hadn't ever gone to that depth before and hadn't ever dived with helium before, either.

From the *Salvor* to the bends, those were my adventures while working for International Divers, then the top deep-water diving company in the world.

Now that I was a genuine helium deep-water diver, I was ready to take on the world. Soon, I'd be the top diver for International Divers. Not long after that, I would start my own company, Broman International, known as the premier deep-water diving company in the world. I wasn't just the owner; I was hands-on, in charge of all the daily operations. I also always did all the most dangerous, deepest dives myself.

I'll share a lot more diving adventures in the pages that follow. But now it's time to dive into the next moon pool. It's a big one. Enormous. An extremely dangerous dive in Bass Strait. So let's go back Down Under—to Australia *and* into deep water. Very deep.

PART III

Moon Pools in Deep Water—Bass Strait, Melbourne, Australia; New Guinea; Singapore; Mozambique

After recovering from the bends, I set forth on my first real deep-water diving adventure. International Divers sent me to Port Moresby, Territory of Papua, New Guinea. I excitedly looked forward to my new destination.

When I left Santa Barbara for Port Moresby, I broke up with my then girlfriend, a luscious brunette with mile-long legs. She was a knockout. Every curvy inch of her was as close to perfect as a woman could be. I really hated leaving her, but I wanted a career as a deep-water diver—I wanted to be the best deep-water diver in the world, perhaps in the history of diving. She was a California girl, in love with my very cool, canary-yellow Citroën convertible as much as she was in love with me, and the diving life wasn't the kind of life she wanted. You know me well enough by now to know that I didn't even ask. It was great while it lasted, but then it was back to the sea, my true home and ultimate partner.

Now a fully initiated helium deep-water diver, I was ready for anything. Remember that my first helium dive was also my deepest dive up to that time (263 feet), concluding with a horrifying bout with the bends. It was definitely baptism by fire, diver style! I didn't dwell on it, though. I knew that I could have died, but I didn't die. So I focused on how lucky I was to do what I loved to do: dive. The ever-present danger was part of why I loved it.

I didn't overthink it; diving was what I did, what I loved to do and chose to do. I've already shared that I felt protected and didn't second-guess how or why. But thinking back on it now, I recognize that at some level I always understood that the water was where I belonged—it was my sanctuary, my sacred space. Some people look to the sky—to heaven—when they pray for blessing and protection. I look into deep water. Into the moon pool. That's where we can most clearly see whatever Higher Power we believe in. More people than not find the greatest truths to be revealed in reflections, not thin air. I certainly always have, still do, and always will. All the years I was a diver, I knew this at some level, even if I didn't articulate it precisely. It was that deep knowing that got me safely through the danger and made me a great diver. That deep knowing is a Higher Power moving through each of us, connecting with us and protecting us. I found it while diving. You might have found it in some other way. If you haven't yet, you will. We all do eventually find it.

So my years as a deep-water diver were filled with danger and excitement, but also with faith and awe. I developed a sense of the sacred and a deep love for nature, especially the ocean and marine life. Yes, it was glamorous and thrilling and yet simultaneously humbling. Every aspect resonated with me. Still does.

But this is my story of living adventurously, with philosophy and deeper meaning woven in, so let's move on to explore some of the exotic places where I lived and worked over time.

Port Moresby would be the first of many exotic locations for me. I made deep-water dives in Singapore and other parts of Southeast Asia; in the Bass Strait and off the coast of northern and eastern Australia; in Mozambique, Africa; and all over the world. It didn't take long for me to become the top diver for International Divers. But I wanted more.

You already know that I became an entrepreneur, starting my own company, Broman International. Eventually, it was known as the premier deep-water diving company in the world. I could not have been prouder of my divers or my achievement. I was always right there with my guys, so my achievement was theirs too. I wasn't just the owner; I was hands-on. I ran the daily operations, and I also always did all the deepest, most dangerous dives myself. Founding Broman International was a big moon pool for me; ultimately selling it was a big moon pool too. You'll see why the time came when I needed to move on, trading the moon pools of deep water for the moon pool at Cape Tribulation, my rain-forest/coral-reef paradise. These were all big moon pools, none greater than the others. Each was significant and life changing in its own way, sometimes more so as I reflected back on it later on than when I was in the midst of living through it. But that's what moon pools are: reflections—of wisdom, beauty, love, and life in general.

But I'm getting ahead of the story again. There are a lot more diving adventures in the pages that follow. I promise. Starting with my next big moon pool. As I said at the end of part II, this one was enormous. It happened in the Bass Strait, when I was called to perform an emergency dive prior to my arrival in Port Moresby. That deep-water rescue was a gigantic moon pool all its own, but it was also part of an even larger moon pool: founding (and then ultimately selling) Broman International. My time in Australia was really a full-circle moon pool, from diving to living in paradise and back again. I'll regale you with all the details in good time.

For now, follow me into the waters of Bass Strait, the waterway separating the continent of Australia from the island of Tasmania. It's time for an urgent rescue in very deep water. At once an individual enormous moon pool and a key part of an even larger, all-encompassing, life-changing moon pool. Let's dive in.

Extremely Dangerous Deep-Water Dive— Bass Strait, Australia (1968)

Another American and I arrived at the airport in Sydney, Australia. We were both deep-water divers under contract with International Divers for two years. Our ultimate destination was Port Moresby, Territory of Papua, New Guinea. Although headquartered in Santa Barbara, California, International Divers was an elite, world-renowned company with the best divers around.

My traveling companion and I would be working on the *Glomar Conception,* a sophisticated, brand-new, state-of-the-art drilling vessel owned by Global Marine. (You'll remember from part II that I sought to work for International Divers because I wanted to work on this very ship, and now my dream as a diver was about to come true.) The *Glomar Conception* was a floater, the term for a huge (close to four-hundred-foot) drillship that moves on its own power, up to twelve knots in speed, and drills for oil and gas. The rig was now on its way from Houston, Texas, to Port Moresby, where it would drill for oil and gas in locations all through Southeast Asia for the two years that followed. The deep-water divers contracted for the job would be working in some of the most primitive, dangerous areas in the world. Being one of those divers was a chance of a lifetime, and I could hardly wait for the work to begin.

Upon arriving in Sydney and hearing the Aussie accents, I immediately fell in love with Australia. There is just something about this special country that defies description. Even before you leave the airport, this wonderful feeling fills you. Australia is so vibrant, so alive. I felt an instant connection with this country, and I still do, perhaps even more so now than ever before. Australia does something to you; it gets into your blood, your bones, and your soul. In my case, it has never left. Even though I consider myself an American and live in the United States now, Australia is and always will be my favorite country in the world.

We didn't have too much time to enjoy our arrival in Sydney, in the airport or elsewhere. The pilot had given us an urgent message from International Divers just as we were about to land: Check in with the main office in Sydney before heading to Port Moresby. It's an extreme emergency.

Following the instructions in the message, we contacted the Sydney office as soon as we had collected our baggage. The office gave us further instructions, which we raced to fulfill. It seemed that the *Glomar III* drillship was in serious trouble. We were to fly to Melbourne, and somebody would meet us at the airport and take us to the Bass Strait, Australia's great offshore oil production field.

So it was back on another plane, from Sydney to Melbourne. After spending twenty hours flying from the West Coast of the United States to the shores of Sydney, Australia, we were absolutely exhausted. Having to make an extremely dangerous dive when already that wiped out from traveling was not an optimal situation. The manager of the International Divers office in Sydney must have known we would be exhausted. I didn't know what he was thinking. (During the two years that followed, I would discover that I never understood anything that the manager in Sydney did.) Anyway, our escort met us at the airport, and we drove from Melbourne to Sale, the small town where the oil companies deployed their crews to the Bass Strait.

Although not terribly excited about the detour to Melbourne and Sale prior to the real job in Port Moresby, I had no choice. International Divers had a contract with Esso Australia and BHP on the *Glomar III,* a drillship that was in serious trouble because of treacherous, volatile weather. The crew could not raise the equipment off the wellhead on the ocean floor. This was extremely dangerous. Lives were at stake, and a huge environmental disaster was a real possibility. The drillship was shut down because the divers had no bottom time left to dive, and so they could not repair the equipment on the ocean floor. This was very deep water (257 feet), so this was going to be an extremely deep dive, in addition to an extremely dangerous one because of the severe weather. In fact, the depth made it dangerous in any weather conditions. The prevailing weather conditions at the site made it not just dangerous but extremely hazardous.

I knew about the dangers of the Bass Strait. Making a deep and dangerous dive in extreme cold water in one of the most dangerous bodies of water in the world would put us in harm's way. Many planes, ships, and people have been lost in the Bass Strait over time. Theories abound about this, but most losses can be adequately explained by extreme weather events. In short, the Bass Strait has the reputation of consistently being the roughest stretch of water in the world.

I had signed up for work in the tropics, in warm water and the climate that went with it, plus the excitement of being on the *Glomar Conception.* I wanted to be diving off that brand-new, state-of-the-art drillship in Port Moresby, not risking my life at 257 feet in freezing water, in one of the most dangerous bodies of water in the world.

But, as I've already said, I had no choice in the matter. The danger and discomfort were as much a part of the job as the beauty and excitement, and I had signed on for all of it.

The *Glomar III* was the sister ship of the *Cuss I,* the drillship on which I made my first helium deep-water dive to the depth of 263 feet, off Santa Barbara. (You'll remember this from the end of part II. I got a severe case of the bends during that dive and almost died.) If it hadn't been for my tender and the ship's decompression expert, a master diver retired from the US Navy, I probably wouldn't have made it. If not for those skills and the prayers and support of the other divers on that job—some of the top hard-hat divers in the world—I would not be here to tell this story. But I'm digressing again. You already know about that dive; let's get back to the Bass Strait dive, another story altogether but well worth telling.

The diving equipment being used was the Kirby Morgan Helium Hat; a takeoff on the old Mark V Navy Helmet that was used in the movie *Men of Honor.* Kirby Morgan Company improved on that air hat and the helium hat. Their hard hats were the best, and they were my favorite diving helmets for deep water. As a kid, my first helmet was a Desco, and it was a great helmet. I mention all this just to give you nondivers out there some basic information on diving equipment.

As for the rig, it is interesting to note that the *Glomar III* (and the *Glomar Conception* also) had a similar design to the one used for the Hughes *Glomar Explorer,* which was built secretly under the direction of the CIA. Its mission was to salvage a sunken Soviet submarine that had a nuclear weapon on board when the submarine sank.

A JetRanger helicopter brought us to the drillship. JetRangers were ideal for crew changes from one drillship to another, or to stationary platforms, or to and from towns, remote islands, and so on. Each JetRanger can carry six passengers and can cruise at approximately 214 miles per hour. The fuselage is about thirty-two feet long. From one rotor tip to the other rotor, the blades are about thirty-two feet long also. The JetRanger is just shy of twelve feet high. In short, the JetRanger was a popular helicopter in the oil industry because pilots liked to fly it. And because it was so fast.

From aboard the helicopter, we could see the *Glomar III* bouncing around like a cork in these huge seas. I was not happy about descending from the helicopter onto the drillship's helipad, which, from our airborne vantage point, looked about the size of a postage stamp.

If you have ever seen the movie *Perfect Storm* or been to California and seen the Mavericks waves at their biggest, you'll have an idea of the size of these seas. They were beyond rough. This job was going to be almost undoable.

I use the word almost because we couldn't afford for it to be undoable: a huge disaster was waiting to happen if there was a blowout, with human lives and the environment all at stake.

The violent weather was brutal; it might be impossible to even get to the rig with these severe, sixty-mile-an-hour head winds, along with the forty-foot seas. The Bass Strait was living up to its infamous reputation that day: often treacherous, always powerful, and, therefore, totally unpredictable.

It was hard to land a helicopter on a drillship's helipad in the best weather conditions; in these weather conditions, it was next to impossible. In addition, several months prior, the main rotor had come off a helicopter headed for a rig amidst the high winds produced in the Bass Strait. On that fateful day, some personnel were on the deck waiting for a crew change, and just as the helicopter was about to land, the rotor came off. There were casualties and fatalities that day as the rotor shredded those guys like paper dolls. Reports said it was a hideous sight, gruesome and messy, with body parts flying all over, littering the deck and surrounding water.

The chopper pilots that day were a brave and gutsy lot, and most of them had military training. They were accustomed to dangerous flights, a crew of heroes from around the world.

The pilot flying our helicopter was much the same, but, unfortunately, so was the weather. It was impossible to land the helicopter on the helipad. No one wanted a repeat of the recent catastrophe.

We had one chance: if we got close enough, we could roll out of the chopper from ten feet in the air and then onto the deck. But we would have to do it within a split second.

I was thinking on the way down how dangerous it was to even get close with the winds and seas as they were—it was life threatening on the chopper's descent—but the pilot got us in that ten-foot range for that split second. And we rolled out and landed on the chopper deck, without getting hurt and without the wind blowing us right off the helipad. We were lucky—extremely lucky—and equally relieved. The adrenaline rush overpowered the relief, though, and we moved as quickly as we could to the wheelhouse, with the gale-force winds almost blowing us off the deck. It was absolutely insane. But what a rush. There is nothing like that kind of excitement. Nothing in the world.

The offshore rig personnel were there, waiting for us. This included the oilfield reps, the Global Marine reps, the tool pushers, the driller's roughnecks, and the diving superintendent, among others. These were all industry veterans, but they were very scared, almost petrified with fear, and justifiably so.

As we entered the wheelhouse, their relief was palpable. Their saviors had arrived: two helium deep-water divers from the States, sent to rescue their rig before going to their assignment in Port Moresby.

Yes, their relief was palpable, but it was mixed with disappointment when they saw how young I was. Their supposed savior was just a kid in their eyes. For these seasoned oilfield men, the level of fear they exhibited was a testament to just how dangerous the situation was. Had I been in their shoes, at their age and in comparable circumstances, I would have felt the same way. They had witnessed their own divers making dives with helium at extreme depths, and they knew how dangerous it was. The hazards would multiply exponentially in the prevailing extreme weather conditions.

We were immediately taken to the galley dining hall for a debriefing. Long story short, the rig was in bigger trouble than we'd been told. There was no doubt that was true. The seas tossed the ship, punctuating the words spoken. It was nerve-racking and very terrifying, to say the least, as we bounced off the walls while trying to focus on our instructions. Fear had spread throughout the ship, and the personnel were almost on the verge of panic.

The ship was on an active well, and if the blowout preventer (BOP) got ripped off the wellhead, a blowout would be possible. That could suck the rig underwater. These were seasoned members of the industry from around the world, and they had seen similar situations. They knew what to expect, and that's why they were so scared.

I was lucky that day. In the first place, I didn't have enough experience to understand just how dangerous it was. In the second place, the head diver and supervisor in charge of the diving operation for International Divers was there. He took charge of briefing us, which was a blessing. He was one of the best in the business, and he had been on this operation for several years.

"I made the last dive, but I ran out of bottom time before the weather got so severe," he told us.

Clearly, he understood the gravity of the situation. He looked at me, the "savior," just a kid with only one helium dive to his credit.

I held his gaze. Using the hard-hat diving equipment, I was going to have to make a 257-foot helium dive in perilous conditions. This, my second helium dive, was only six feet less than my first. I forced myself not to think about the depth or the treacherous weather conditions or the bends that had nearly killed me the last time. I had a job to do, and I intended to do it.

You're all they've got, I told myself inwardly. *The only hero available. You're the best available at this time. No, you're the best in the business at any time.* I had to feel that way, or I wouldn't have had the courage to make this dive. As I repeated this encouragement to myself in my head, I started to believe it.

We left the galley, and the other divers warned us about the bronze whalers, powerful and aggressive sharks. These are magnificent animals that like to hang around the equipment on the bottom because of the schools of fish that also hang there. The divers had been having problems with the sharks.

I told myself not to think about the sharks, either.

I focused on the fact that I had the best in the business taking care of me topside. That gave me confidence.

It's important to have confidence in your crew because they literally hold your life in their hands. They run the manifold that delivers your air or helium, they check the depth for decompression, and so on. In short, they are your life support.

I would be making the dive because I was the most qualified. The other diver with me was the standby diver. It's critical to have a standby diver in case the main diver gets into trouble, runs out of bottom time, etc.

As we headed to the ship's moon pool, I felt a mixture of fear and excitement. The best deep-water divers always feel the fear; we just move past it. That was part of what I loved most about diving: pushing through the fear to do what I most wanted to do. Doing that every day gives you an unshakable sense of confidence, and then you know you can get through anything.

The support crews and tenders were ready to suit up the divers (me and the standby) for this deep dive in treacherous seas. It would actually be a mixed-gas dive: 90 percent helium and 10 percent oxygen. My life was in their hands, and their lives were in my hands. Suffice it to say that I felt much more reassured than they did! I was a twenty-three-year-old who looked sixteen. A typical Southern Californian, with blond hair, blue eyes, and a tanned olive complexion. The cleft in my chin was the signature of what my boss, Pete Blommers, always called me: "cocky and cheeky." I'd made my first hard-hat dive at sixteen, and I was trained by the best. I was proud of it. Very proud.

They all kept looking at me, as if to say, "This kid can't do this."

As the youngest hard-hat diver in the union, I was used to this. Plus, I'd been around divers since birth. I didn't know whether any of them knew that my father was Art Broman, the diving legend, but it didn't matter. I knew it. My dad was as tough as nails. As I waited for them to start suiting me up, I mentally prepared myself to enter the moon pool, and I recalled something Old Art once said: "There is only one guy I can't beat, and that's my son."

They were only looking at me and wondering if I could do the dive because they didn't know me. All that mattered was that I knew me, and I knew I could do this dive. I could do any dive. I had already made many deep and dangerous dives off Santa Barbara, California.

I'll describe the ritual of suiting up and the details of this actual dive, but first, I want to describe more of the feelings I experienced while waiting to do that dive in such infamous waters. I had a set internal protocol of mental preparation for every dive, but it was more intense than usual prior to this particular dive. The weather conditions, the Bass Strait's notoriety, and all the prevailing circumstances contributed to the intensity.

Every ocean is different. Until you dive it, you can't feel what it's about, neither its dangers and risks nor its comfort and love. Initially, every sea is aloof and mysterious. You have to dive it to understand it. That's what plumbing the depths is really about. When you dive it, you get to know the ocean's currents, as well as its sea life, and that's how you pick up its vibe. There is always potential danger in deep-water diving, as I've said and will continue to say. But successful divers who survive each dive without getting hurt establish a relationship with the ocean and its depths. This is a very real connection, with deep (no pun intended) meaning and joy.

"Joy?" you might be saying right now. "Is he crazy? How can you find joy in the midst of life-threatening danger?"

Well, in the first place, yes, I am crazy. And, yes, deep-water diving brings the diver indescribable joy, even with the danger. Perhaps because of it. This is what we deep-water divers live for. Did too many deep dives make me crazy, or was I born this way? A little of both, I think. I've shared enough of my life, my philosophy, and my personality by now for you to recognize that I've lived the life I craved, and I craved the life I lived. That's all there is to it.

That's enough philosophizing for now. Back to the action, and there's plenty more to come. Even then, at age twenty-three, I knew this was the life I was born for. I knew I could die making this dive in the Bass Strait, but I also knew nothing on earth was going to stop me. If I died trying, so be it. I wasn't going to live with the regret of having not done what I was meant to do—what people were counting on me to do.

The weather kept deteriorating moment by moment. The wind gusts exceeded sixty miles per hour, pushing the sea into a massive, undulating rollercoaster. This was a runaway ride, with swells as high as sixty feet— and that meant the troughs were equally deep. We would be at the crest of the wave one moment, looking over the tops of the other waves lapping at the sky, our visibility blocked by the dense, gray sheet of falling rain and clouds. The next moment, our gaze would absorb the tremendous sixty-foot drop as the ship nudged over the wave crest and plummeted into the gaping trough of intense blue water below us. With our stomachs in our throats and our hands gripping anything we could hold on to, we did our best to manage as the drillship surfed down the back side of the wave, reaching incredible speeds. If the wave decided not to join us on the ship, crashing topside with tremendous force and a thunderous roar, our awareness would be immediately consumed by the swelling of the next wave, whether an onslaught from behind, or the side, or the front, or all directions. And then the whole rollercoaster ride would start all over again.

The phrase "the living sea" cannot be fully appreciated by anyone who has not lived through an ocean storm. As the perpetual and massive movement of the ocean did its dance around us, I understood what those words meant for the first time. The wind would howl and whip across the decks relentlessly. The storm and the sea were alive and dangerous and threatening. And the most exciting part for me was that I realized that living, as used in the phrase, meant both alive and eternal. The sea and the wind had been dancing together in this way forever. We humans were the newcomers.

I know I keep waxing philosophical in the midst of the action, but that's how it was for me that long-ago day. I kept watching the storm, and these deep thoughts would just pop into my mind, unbidden. Maybe that was my mind's way of preparing me for the danger I was about to plunge into. I was afraid for my life, just as I always was before a deep dive, but this one was different. The weather made everything extraordinary.

The lights were on in the drillship's moon pool, and in between the swells gushing out of it, you could see how clear the water was. I had never experienced anything quite like it in previous dives. The visibility was maybe seventy to one hundred feet. It was so clear and so beautiful, intriguing and hypnotic, and also intimidating. I had encountered this before, the clarity in the moon pool and the pit in my stomach because of the unknown I was about to plunge my body into. That is always frightening on a deep dive. But what made this dive so extraordinary was the dichotomy of the moon pool's tranquility and the battering storm's intense wrath.

The ship continued to roll in the high seas and gale-force wind gusts, and it was all terrifying and unnerving for everyone on board, even the veteran divers and oilfield people.

But then, something amazing happened to me in the midst of the chaos topside. I looked down into the eternally tranquil moon pool, and I felt myself go within, to this special place deep inside me. I felt as calm and quiet as the clear water I was looking into. It was then that I first understood all that the moon pool, literally and figuratively, had to offer: wisdom, beauty, tranquility, perspective. I had this sacred, healing place that I could always access, on the ship and deep within me. That was all I would ever really need, and I could go there whenever I needed or wanted to.

Feeling calm, settled, and uncannily energized, I focused on the task at hand, reviewing the equipment specs in my head. This was part of my pre-suiting-up preparation. I would be wearing a Kirby Morgan helmet, which meant that the air or helium intake would be on my hat rather than a belly valve. (Navy Mark V helmets had the intake on a belly valve, and that could jam up as you crawled along the bottom or banged against the equipment while working.) The air (helium) control on the hard hat was a lifesaver. I'd grown up using a lot of different diving helmets—Siebe Gorman, Desco, and Mark V—but the Kirby Morgan was the best, the elite. Eying the helmet my tender had at the ready, I was grateful I would have its balance, visibility, and air intake during the dive that day in the Bass Strait storm of storms.

The canvas rubberized suit I would wear had been made in Japan by Yokohama. It was like the old navy dresses but not as bulky—more pliable, more comfortable, and better in every way. I always wore rubberized chaffing pants with pockets and rope straps that went over the breastplate and were used as a jock to hold the breastplate down. I'd learned to swim in this huge set of equipment on the Moss Landing job, and also on the *Queen Mary* in Long Beach, California. I thought about my training with Scotty Chisholm in Oakland Harbor, how he'd tested me, how he'd taught me to weld and burn underwater with no visibility. Most of all, he'd taught me to be tough. As a result, I could do anything wearing that equipment. As daunting as this dive would be, I was ready for it.

Rigs like the *Glomar III* were used for exploration. That was why they were called drillships: they would drill for oil, and if they discovered oil or gas, they would pump mud and cement down the well to seal it, and then the divers would cap it. After that, the company would bring in a permanent rig, a stationary platform, and then redrill to open up the well and run pipelines or storage buoys so the tankers could fill up and take the crude to the refineries.

Workboats were used to run huge anchors out from the ship in order to hold the ship while drilling. In these rough seas, all we could do was pray—hard and often—that the anchors would hold. Weather-beaten faces all aboard the ship held eyes that said, "Please let the anchors hold." (Such prayers were equally intense on dives at the bottom of the ocean floor. I made one at 340 feet, on air [not helium], off the coast of New Guinea. More about that later.)

Now, remember, all this was going on in the Bass Strait, one of the world's most infamous waterways. To illustrate its wild strength, Bass Strait is both twice as wide and twice as rough as the English Channel. The shipwrecks on the Tasmanian and Australian coastlines number in the hundreds. Strong currents between the Antarctic-driven southeast portions of the Indian Ocean and the Tasman Sea's Pacific Ocean waters provide a strait of powerful, wild storm waves. Thus, the waters of the Bass Strait are notoriously rough and fierce, with strong, wild currents. This "predictably unpredictable" waterway has been the site of numerous shipwrecks, and many vessels, some quite large, have disappeared there without trace or, at best, left scant evidence of their passing.

The *Glomar III* was launched in 1962. This self-propelled drillship (floater), one of the first in Global Marine's fleet of specialized self-propelled floating rigs, played a major role in the establishment of Australia's Bass Strait natural gas fields. The *Glomar III,* brought in from Houston, Texas, spudded the first Bass Strait well in late 1964.

After several months amid high winds and churning waters, the drill bit reached 1,040 meters (just over 3,000 feet) and hit gas. Further success followed, with the discovery of the Marlin Field, the largest gas field in southeastern Australia. There, indications of oil were also revealed, and confirmed with the next discovery, Kingfish, Australia's biggest oil field, containing more than one billion barrels.

A host of other fields were uncovered in rapid succession. Another discovery: natural gas from its first well, the Barracuda I, also drilled by the *Glomar III,* which withstood the brunt of the strait's legendary hostile waters to find the oil and gas reserves.

Since 1969, the Bass Strait—which lies between the state of Victoria, Australia, to the north and the island state of Tasmania to the south, and between the Indian Ocean to the west and the Tasman Sea to the east—has yielded more than four billion barrels of crude oil and more than seven TCF of natural gas.

All this shows why so much was riding on *Glomar III* and why success during this dive was so critical—to the company, to the men on board, and to the environment.

Failure was not an option. I had to succeed.

The tender, an old Aussie named Bryon, who was the best they had, suited me up. Trained by American divers who'd taught him right, he knew exactly what to do. He laid out some woollies for me to put on. It was cold water, and I didn't object. (Woollies are undergarments worn under the canvas suit to keep you warm and cut down on chafing from the rubberized canvas. Back home, I always wore ski pants and ski sweaters under my suit. I always looked "designer correct," because you never knew when you might run into a gorgeous mermaid [especially if you got narco] or, better yet, some sweet, big-breasted woman watching you from the deck after you made the dive and your suit was off. I looked good in ski pants and always wanted to look my best. You know me by now.) My preference for ski pants and turtlenecks notwithstanding, that day in Bass Strait, I was grateful for the heavy, old navy woollies—and the tender who was wise enough to insist that I wear them—and I waited for him to suit me up.

Here is the ritual of suiting up (getting dressed in):

As I put on my woollies and wrist cuffs, my tender laid out the equipment in front of the bench I would sit on. The chaffing pants, rubberized canvas suit, breastplate, helmet, weight belt, ankle weights, and boots all lay before me. There was also a bucket with the brails, brail nuts, and shims inside it, and another bucket with water and soap.

I sat on the bench, and then I slipped on the canvas suit (diving dress), stood up, pulled the suit up to my waist, bent over, stuck my hands in the water bucket, and soaped my hands and wrists. (This was so the cuffs would slip on easily. This creates a seal as you put your arms through the arms of the suit, and then you can easily slip the cuffs over your hands.)

Neoprene wristbands sealed the cuffs. (I always carried several pairs. I never met anyone who wore them except for my dad and me. I had small wrists.) The cuff of the suit went over the wristbands after soaping up.

Next, the tender pulled the suit up to my shoulders, and I put my hands through the sleeves of the suit, one at a time, and then through the rubber cuffs. (The soap eases the hands through the tight cuff folds.)

Now that both arms were into the suit sleeves, he folded the bib around my neck.

Then he lowered the breastplate, making sure to hold the front of it so it didn't knock my teeth out, pulled the bib through, put the corner hole in the suit through the stud at the shoulder, and then put the holes in all the studs around the suit.

I sat down on the bench, with the bucket filled with the brails, brail nuts, and shims balanced on my lap. He put shims on the front and back corners. Then he put the brails on over the suit and breastplate, and then he put the brass wing nut on finger-tight until all of them were snug. With the brail wrench, he tightened them down, first one corner, then the opposite corner, and then all around.

I moved from the bench to the diver's stool, sat down, and slipped on the chaffing pants. I stood up, and the tender put the straps of the chaffing pants over the breastplate.

I sat down again to put the rubber boots on. The tender put the weights on each of my ankles. I stood up, and the tender put the straps of the weight belt over the breastplate, and then he buckled the belt.

Next came the helmet (hard hat). The tender wrapped the hose over the top so he could screw the helmet on, and then he hooked the hose to the breastplate.

Now that I was suited up (dressed in), I made sure the safety lock was set. Most important, I rechecked the lock and the safety pin on the back of the helmet, so that the hard hat could not be twisted off.

Finally, I tested the phones.

There was nothing left for me to do but go to the side of the moon pool and jump. Only a very few divers would jump in rough seas; most had to climb down a ladder or be sent down in a diver's stage lowered by an air tugger or crane. Art Broman (my dad), Torrance Parker, Pete Blommers, Scotty Chisholm (my godfather and trainer), and Woody Treen were among the few I knew who jumped into rough seas while wearing that full set of gear. Of course, I did too. (Big surprise!)

"Watch out for sharks, mate!" said Bryon in the manner typical of an old Aussie tender.

The critical moment of the jump was now upon me. When stepping close to the moon pool to jump, the diver has at least three coils of hose (sometimes more), depending on how much of a drop to the water there might be. This dive was no exception. I jumped, let go, and when I hit the water, I went down a few feet and bounced up like a buoy. There must be the perfect balance of air in the suit when you do this; if you have too much air, you could flip over and wind up upside down. Obviously, that is not something a diver wants to do.

I had already made hundreds of dives in all kinds of situations prior to Bass Strait, but I had never been upside down, except once, and that was on purpose as part of my training with Scotty Chisholm. I did get right side up by myself during that training. Divers had to learn how to do this, because if someone had to get in the water to help you get upright, it would be a major task. Bottom line: you don't want to get upside down in that gear. I spent hours upon hours in Oakland Harbor practicing in all kind of situations, with Scotty Chisholm teaching me what to do. As a result, I could do anything in that hard-hat gear.

Remember that most of the weight is the helmet and breastplate and weight belt, so if you get upside down, you have all that weight at the bottom, and then you have to turn yourself right side up against the extra weight.

I went down a guide wire (typical for a helium and oxygen dive, and you'll remember my description of this in part II). I went down to fifty feet first. I was on free time, up to that depth of fifty feet, before I had to start counting my bottom time. I started counting, and the manifold operator switched me to the helium and oxygen mix to limit the nitrogen narcosis effect. I used them all, the lighter mask and wet suit and the best is the hard hat, or "heavy gear." When your face is scrunched up in a mask, it's harder to communicate, and talking on helium creates enough problems as it is. You can get more work done in my preferred gear because you are not like a fish fighting the elements while swimming; you are warm and have more leverage using tools. I used to have a standby diver come down in the light gear while I was on the bottom in the heavy gear. As soon as he got close, I would grab him in a headlock and scare the shit out of him, just to prove my point. Of course, I was the boss by that time. It always worked, though.)

By that point, I sounded like that mix of Donald Duck and Alvin the Chipmunk, and then I heard through the phone, "Diver on helium."

Into the phone I said, "Diver going down."

A good diver gets to the bottom like a bullet. And I did. I dumped the air/helium as fast as the suit would let me, until it almost squeezed and crushed me.

It was essential to go down the guide wire as quickly as possible, because the quicker I got to the bottom, the more bottom time I had to get the job done. Every second counted, and I didn't want to run out of bottom time. Aside from not wanting a repeat of the bends under any circumstances, I definitely didn't want that in the Bass Strait in the middle of a gale-force storm and towering, roller-coaster seas.

I was pretty narco by this point, and the squeezing of the suit as I dumped the air/helium felt like a giant's hand wrapped around my body, crushing my ribs. I slowed down just a fraction, keeping that necessary delicate balance while going down the guide wire as fast as I could.

I kept my concentration, and I didn't let fear take over. A dive like this one was scary, almost terrifying, and some divers would have panicked by now. (Divers have died on dives like this.) I was doing what I had to do.

I hit the bottom, stood on top of the baseplate, and entered another world. Fully narco (which is the same as being high), I watched a beautiful mermaid swim by and then realized it was just a huge tuna. I spotted the underwater TV, remembering how my dad had introduced me to the man who invented the underwater TV for the oil field. His name was Joe Granville. I was about twelve at the time.

I forced myself to focus on the task at hand: replacing the broken cable connected to the baseplate. The ship's bouncing up and down in the rough seas had broken the original cable. Other equipment had to be brought up to the surface for repair also, but the only way to accomplish this was by first attaching a new cable. I undid the old cable by taking the shackle off from the eye of the baseplate, and then I hooked the new cable and shackled it into the eye on the baseplate.

The crew and oilfield people were watching me via the underwater TV hooked to the baseplate. They talked to me through the phone. I was now at 257 feet (very deep for those days), and I was pretty narco. I was used to the feeling, though: drunk and giddy. My personal term for it was "hot blood." I was confident but not overly so, as arrogance is a mistake that can kill you when diving that deep. Besides, I could feel "hot blood" even when not on a deep dive. (I still can, by the way.)

Nitrogen narcosis was a given, and there was always a possibility of the bends. Other constant possibilities were dangerous currents and aggressive sharks around the equipment on the bottom, especially in Australia, Africa, and Southeast Asia The current could be so ferocious at times that I could barely hang on to the guide wire once I passed the bottom of the moon pool. The water was cold and rough at that depth. There was also always the risk of equipment failure, including running out of helium or air. But the most frightening of all was the unknown—something could fall off the rig floor, for example, or who knew what else. Surprises of the unpleasant variety that could happen on almost every deep-water dive were limitless. And, quite often, such surprises could be fatal.

As I've said before and will say again, all this was part of deep-water diving. Divers had to live and deal with all these things on every dive. I personally never minded nitrogen narcosis. Of course, that might just be me! (I have never heard anyone else say this, but I believe mermaids were invented by divers getting nitrogen narcosis when a big fish came by and they hallucinated that it was a beautiful woman. I did exactly that when seeing a big tuna in the depths of Bass Strait. But, then again, maybe that had nothing to do with being narco. I didn't need to have a big fish come by; I always hallucinated about beautiful women.)

But back to the dive. Now that I had the new cable connected to the baseplate, the remaining task at hand was to safely bring up the blowout preventer (BOP). Accomplishing this was simple but critical. Again, it was not hard to repair the equipment topside, but the only way to bring it up was if the cable was securely attached to the baseplate. The same cable that I had attached to the baseplate was also attached topside.

How was I able to do all this work underwater? I always carried a 36-inch crescent wrench with a marlin spike welded to it, which made it easier to stick the pointed spike into the hole in the shackle pin and unscrew it. But because my gear was on the drillship headed for Port Moresby (my actual destination), I could only use the tools available to me on the *Glomar III*: a marlin spike all by itself.

I was very narco by that point, thinking about my beautiful brunette back in Santa Barbara, sweet and slim and so passionate … I loved how she clung to me when we made love. That thought got me through the last of my duties, and I had the cable hooked and securely fastened to the baseplate. This meant my work was done and I could come up.

I started to ascend and said into the phone, "Job completed. Diver coming up."

Just then, a bronze whaler shark came from out of nowhere to have a go at me. The beast skimmed my right side, and he was in battle mode, humped mouth open and ready to take me. He missed, but just barely, and then another one came in.

I frantically shouted into the phone, "Two sharks are having a go at me!"

As I mentioned earlier, bronze whalers are magnificent creatures, but they are also terrifying. The old Aussie tender's warning about sharks echoed through my brain as I continued my ascent.

"Diver coming up to 120 feet," I said into the phone. "The sharks are still with me."

The bronze whalers kept circling, but I had to stay at 120 feet for at least twenty minutes because it was my first decompression stop; I risked serious decompression sickness if I didn't stay for at least that long, and I was not about to go through another case of the bends. My visibility was clearer at 120 feet (as opposed to 257), and so was my head, so they knew I wasn't kidding about the sharks.

After the first mandatory stop, I went up to sixty feet to my next one, where I would remain for an hour. They sent down a stage for me to sit in. The sharks were still with me, but there were four of them now. They came close to the stage but didn't attack.

Bronze whaler sharks love being around the equipment, which is a haven for fish on the bottom. These were every bit as aggressive as the other divers had warned me they were. I had thought they were just ribbing me. It reminded me of *Lloyd Bridges* reruns. As kids, we loved watching those shows because our dad sometimes did the stunt work as the hard-hat diver.

Watching exciting reruns was a lot different from the real thing, I can tell you that much. Even while I was in the stage, those sharks were too close for comfort. Way too close.

Finally, they brought me up all the way to the surface. The sea was still frothing out of the moon pool, but they got me on deck. They were a good crew. They took off the helmet, dropped the weight belt, and got me to the decompression chamber. Bryon went into the chamber with me (remember that the chambers have a double lock) to undress me, and then I would stay in the back lock while he closed the door, pressured down, and exited the chamber.

He took the breastplate off first, and then he soaped my wrists to slip off the cuffs. "Good dive, mate," he said to me.

"Thanks. You were right about those sharks; they had a go at me and almost got me!"

In typical Aussie fashion, he said, "We couldn't get anybody else to make the dive. That's why we used you!"

He laughed after he said it, and I laughed too.

Bryon was my first Australian tender, and he became my first Aussie friend, staying with me as tender through many deep-water dives in oceans and countries all over the most exotic parts of the world.

The head diver and diving superintendent was on the phone taking care of me. I could see he was very proud as he talked to the oilfield people. The oil companies had to witness firsthand the awesome work done by deep-water divers in order to adequately respect us. He knew the extreme amount of courage it had taken to accomplish that dive, and even though he'd heard I was a "cheeky, cocky little bastard," he had now seen for himself how good I was. I'd just made one hell of a dive, one that commanded the respect of Global Marine, and he was relieved: I made him and International Divers look good.

Even more important, my dive had made me the man—the best for that day! Hey, I had just saved a bunch of lives and possibly averted a huge environmental disaster! I deserved a little celebrating.

When I requested that the Aussie tender accompany me to New Guinea, the diving superintendent okayed it. That's how my Aussie mate became my special tender and standby diver. Plus, he was a genius at repairing equipment. I found out later that he had built his own scuba regulator out of a tobacco tin that he'd tested in the river of his hometown of Sale. Aussies are gutsy.

He was also the one who introduced me to the power head, and from that day on, I always had one in the diver's stage while in the water taking decompression, because most of the time there were sharks, and in that part of the world, they were the most dangerous sharks.

Everyone was happy about the success of my dive. They could now pull the stack (BOP) off the well, and the ship would ride out the storm. That part of the danger was past.

It was great being "the man" after my successful dive. I loved that feeling of awe and respect, knowing I'd earned it and glorying in it all the more because of that. But that didn't protect me or any other diver from the bends. Even the best diver in the world and in the history of diving is not immune from the bends.

I finished my decompression, and the seas got calm enough for us to get on a workboat after two days.

As we sailed toward shore, the other divers told me, "Good dive, Broman." That's all the reward any diver ever gets, but there is none greater. Respect from your peers and your own self-respect are the greatest reward in any kind of work.

Once ashore, we had a two-hour drive to the airport in Melbourne. After making a deep dive, you can't fly for twenty-four hours, but with the time I'd spent in the decompression chamber, I would be good to go. I actually felt really good.

Bass Strait felt like a once-in-a-lifetime dangerous dive right after it was over, but as time went on, there would be many more. (Including the previously mentioned dive I would make at 340 feet, on air, off the coast of New Guinea, shortly after arriving in Port Moresby. Helium equipment would not be available for this dive, the nitrogen narcosis would be severe, and it would end up being a life-threatening dive. More about this particular dive later.)

At that moment, I was still riding the crest of my glory. Jim Broman was gutsy and cheeky, one hell of a deep-water diver. Maybe the best in the business. That was one hell of a dive I had just made in Bass Strait. I was still buzzing because of the excitement—and the relief that I had survived.

Now it was time to move on to Port Moresby and more adventures.

Adventures in Port Moresby, Territory of Papua, New Guinea (1968)

The Bass Strait dive behind me and successfully completed, I was once again on my way to my original destination: Port Moresby, Territory of Papua, New Guinea. The guy who'd accompanied me as standby diver was still with me, and so was my new tender, Bryon, the old Aussie who'd served me so well during my perils in the deep. I was still in hero mode following my diving achievement, and I would never forget the Bass Strait, but I was already mentally in Port Moresby. After all, as I've said, the tropics were what I signed on for! "If you can't grow a coconut on it, I don't want to be there," as one of my many mottoes puts it. Warm tropical water, beautiful ladies (with a bit of luck), some deep-water adventures—who could ask for more?

As the Qantas jet made its final approach, I looked out the airplane window, feeling excited and confident as I caught sight of the harbor. I couldn't believe I'd finally made it to Port Moresby. The Territory of Papua, New Guinea, was like a gentle caress after the hellish rough seas of the Bass Strait.

At first glimpse, Port Moresby was gorgeous: the green tropical landscape, the beautiful, deep blue of the Indian Ocean and the inlet connecting the harbor to the ocean, the clear water of the harbor—it looked like a picture postcard come to life. The harbor was full of every type of boat imaginable: hundreds of small, colorful catamarans sailing alongside the long, dugout native canoes, big steamers that traveled up the dangerous rivers of one of the most primitive countries in the world, hundreds of small boats, beautiful, majestic sailboats on voyages to other mysterious, exotic countries, ports, and destinations.

Port Moresby was the capital of the Territory of Papua, New Guinea. It was a gem of a town in a cove harbor, and it played a major role in World War II. The MV *MacDhui,* sunk during a Japanese air raid, was still submerged in the harbor. And legends abounded of the Coastwatchers and the brave Aussie soldiers who fought the Japanese alongside the natives. (If you want to learn more about the Coastwatchers, see the old Cary Grant movie, *Father Goose.*)

This little town, in a cove harbor with everything built on the hills with incredible views above the harbor and out toward the beautiful beaches, would be my home base for a while. I loved it, but it took some adjusting. Territory of Papua, New Guinea, was still extremely primitive. Some of the natives were cannibals, and many had never seen white men before. A lot of the natives hung out at the international airport, all of them with bones through their noses, and the women bare breasted. It blew their minds to see a Qantas jet land, and some of them had made a replica of an airplane that they worshipped like a god. Seeing the white man was shocking enough; a jet airliner dropping from the sky was really just too much. It would blow my mind too if I'd just come out of the bush and saw this huge lump of metal falling from the sky, landing, and opening to let humans walk out of it.

As I've said, I was in Asia while in the military (Japan, South Korea, Taiwan), but this was my first time in Southeast Asia, and it was much different from the Far East. It was vastly different from my military postings in Europe (Spain and West Germany) too. The Territory of Papua, New Guinea, was the latest adventure to add to my list, and I fully intended for that list to keep on growing. I had only just started traveling the world, living in different countries, and experiencing different cultures. I loved getting to know the people who were native to the exotic places where I lived, and it thrilled me to know that I would spend two years in Port Moresby, working and traveling all throughout Southeast Asia—by helicopter, by workboat, by small bush plane, and whatever other means necessary to transport us to the islands where we would work or to the *Glomar Conception,* a floater drill ship. Of course, I would also take time to travel to the interior of one of the most primitive countries in the world. (But, remember, I already said that the cannibals of New Guinea were one native group I'd just as soon as not encounter again.)

Needless to say, our landing at the airport was quite colorful, with all the natives gathered about. After going through customs, we had to make our way through a massive mob of people. There were a few whites, but mostly it was all natives with no reason to be there; they just hung out at the airport, mesmerized by the planes.

We got a cab and headed for the hotel. I was so excited to be there. It's difficult to capture in words how thrilling it was for me: my first long-term, offshore deep-water diving assignment, on the heels of my success in the Bass Strait. I was on top of the world.

The cab sped toward the Gateway, a plush new hotel near the airport. All the Phillips oilfield top brass and Global Marine top brass stayed there, so that would be our base until we found permanent housing for our two-year contract.

The crew, such as roughnecks and tool pushers, stayed in Brisbane, Australia, making crew changes from there every two weeks. They went straight to the rig by chopper or flew to an island by small fixed-wing plane and then to the ship by chopper.

Staying at the Gateway suited me just fine. It was a brand-new hotel with the latest amenities. We were treated like royalty. It was absolutely fantastic. The *Glomar Conception* was about two weeks out, coming across the oceans all the way from Houston, Texas, USA, so we had time to look around, check out the local pubs and beaches, and explore Moresby for houses and flats to rent—and, of course, meet the girls in the area. After all, it was essential to see what was happening, as we were going to be there for another two years. Most of the big social events, dances, and parties were at the yacht club.

Before long, I found a flat, and it was on the hill above the yacht club. Perfect. I could meet a sheila (as the Aussies and whites in Southeast Asia call "girls") and then stagger home easily. I was fortunate to have found my little paradise so quickly. It had a breathtaking view of the blue-water cove and harbor, beautiful beaches, and the spectacular boats and ships moving in and out of the harbor. I even had my own houseboy, a genuine New Guinea native with a bone through his nose. The exotic flavor of my new surroundings was palpably delectable. I was even more delighted than I'd imagined I would be. Why not? Women from all over the world were in my midst, working for the government and for private enterprise, and there were also some half-caste girls who caught my eye. They were all beautiful, sweet, sexy, and fun. This was going to be more than just an adventure.

Burns, Philip & Company, Ltd., and Steamships Company were the big suppliers; their ships were about the size of ocean liners. It was a special day when you heard that loud whistle of the first one coming into the harbor. The excitement was breathtaking. Then the second whistle would blast, and you knew it was Boat Day. (Yes, I guess that was my first Boat Day; we'd have one later at our cove in Cape Tribulation.) The town took on a holiday atmosphere.

Moresby was small, but it had two other hotels and popular pubs. The top pub at the Papua Hotel was spectacular for the old Moresby elite. It had a one-hundred-foot-long teak bar with natives in white sarongs pushing big fans hanging from the ceiling, like huge sails airing and cooling the place. It had the best-looking sheilas in town. More my style for the evenings, but I liked the bottom pub for daytime lunches, the views of the South Pacific, and time with some of the wilder girls.

Gazing out of the top pub windows facing the harbor off the veranda was spectacular. The view was so beautiful, and the atmosphere was so exciting. It was fun to see when the magnificent ships came into the harbor. The locals would come in earlier on Boat Day, and the government workers all would have the day off. They would go to their favorite pub and wait for the ships. It was the best way to meet all the locals, especially the single, young Aussie girls, and a sprinkle of foreigners too: French, Scandinavian, Dutch, all European nationals. I was in heaven. I charmed them, and I also slept with them whenever I could—and, thankfully, that was often! I had learned to be an excellent kisser and lover from teens on up (thank you, moms and dads, for those make-out parties you allowed us to participate in … more about that later, in part V). My mission in life was to be the most desirable, most passionate, most considerate lover I could be. I loved women. (Remember, women were, are, and always will be my greatest moon pool.)

As I said, the top pub bar was a masterpiece: all teak wood, highly polished, and about one hundred feet long. It was the locals' favorite. The dining room was elegant, with pure silver placements on the tables. The panoramic view overlooking the harbor of Port Moresby was magnificent. When the two big supply ships would dock and unload after coming from Brisbane with the supplies from Burns, Philip & Company, and Steamships Company, it was like a holiday. Clothes and supplies would come in, and we could have our pick. That was Boat Day, every two weeks. Which meant it was a holiday every two weeks in Moresby.

It was the tropics, which meant it was hot and humid, and I put a wall-mounted air-conditioner in my bedroom. Ceiling fans and the soft, cooling breezes coming off the ocean cooled the rest of the flat. Views of the harbor and beaches were spectacular from my new home above the yacht club. I loved living in the tropics. Remember, if you can't grow a coconut on it, I don't want to be there. I decided that in Port Moresby, and I've never really changed my mind.

I was the only young American around, and I found my spot with the locals in the top pub or bottom pub. They would wear white shoes with knee socks up to their knees, and white shorts with safari jackets or brilliant white shirts. I always rolled up my sleeves (that was my trademark), and sometimes I wore a tie loose around my neck and white long pants, depending on the event of that particular night. Wherever the beautiful women were was where I would be also.

I was not only accepted but treated like a celebrity, being an American from Southern California, and a deep-water diver working on the *Glomar Conception* operation. I also adopted a lot of the local customs, which made me an honorary local of sorts. I wore Speedos at the beach under my shorts, and I swam in them.

And then there were the women. As always, they were the best part. The beautiful accents of the women from around the world who looked me in the eye and said, "Yes, you can be my lover for the night, or forever … it's up to you. I am available."

Oh, yes, Moresby was my town. And this was just the start.

There was the native bar where they would get drunk and have fights and shock the whites. Spears were thrown quite often, and the Aussie bartender would wield a club if necessary to calm things down. We heard from the locals that out in the bush you could get saltwater crocodiles and skin and sell them for big bucks to the skin traders who would come over from the mainland.

What a place this was. A thrilling, wild, once-in-a-lifetime place.

By the time I'd found my flat and made all the discoveries I just described, the *Glomar Conception* was still a couple of weeks out, which gave me time to get my flat furnished and squared away. It was two stories, offering magnificent views of the harbor, the town, the beaches, and farther out to sea.

I'd had time to do some shopping locally too, and I had the long socks and shorts and white shirts and some black ties, just like the locals. I fit right in, but I also stood apart just the right amount. Just enough to charm the ladies and seem special to them. How I loved this place.

Oh, how I loved my life. I had finally made it in the hard-hat diving business. I was working on the most incredible state-of-the-art drilling vessel in the industry. I was making fantastic money. I had plenty of available sheilas. And I enjoyed almost celebrity status. It was heaven on earth.

The *Glomar Conception* Arrives—Port Moresby (1968)

At last, the *Glomar Conception* arrived in the harbor of Port Moresby. We were the first to fly out by a JetRanger helicopter; the divers would be needed to make shallow-water dives to check the ship after the long voyage from Houston, Texas.

It was such a beautiful ship for an oil rig, brand-new and fine. To us in the oil industry, it was magnificent. To me, it was my plaything: I had diving, and I had brand-new workboats, helicopters, etc. It was like a luxury cruise ship to me, and we divers got to pick our accommodations. Very nice rooms. The cooks already had buffet-style snacks laid out for us. It was all first class and so very cool.

We had to get our deep-water diving equipment set up and ready: decompression chamber, air compressors, hard-hat diving helmets, etc. Everything had to be set up for the dives at the first drilling location.

The ship was to stay in the harbor of Port Moresby for two full days while we made some shallow-water dives around the hull, inspecting the bottom of the ship, hooking some buoys with the crane. That was electrifying! There were lots of sea snakes around where we were diving, and they were poisonous. I had never seen sea snakes, let alone poisonous ones that swam in the water with me. Sea snakes occur mainly in the warm tropical waters. To be honest, it was very creepy. Nothing I'd wish to repeat. (It reminded me of my scuba certification dive off Catalina Island in Southern California. We checked out the moray eel population during that dive. They were sinister in their little caves, and they look a lot like sea snakes. Freaky and creepy.)

Nevertheless, sea snakes were part of our routine in Southeast Asia. They are thought to have evolved from a family of Australian land snakes. Though creepy like eels, unlike eels, sea snakes have lungs (instead of gills), and so they need to come to the surface to breathe. The left lung of the sea snake is huge, stretching over much of the entire length of the body, which allows sea snakes to stay underwater for a few hours. They have specialized flattened tails, which act as paddles for swimming, and they have valves over their nostrils, which are closed underwater.

On top of all this, like other creatures living in a very salty environment (such as seabirds and sea turtles) sea snakes have special glands that collect the extra salt from their blood. A sea snake's salt glands are situated beneath its tongue, so that each time the creature flicks its tongue, it ejects salt back into the ocean. Most sea snakes are venomous, as I've already described. Close cousins to the cobra, sea snakes have the same type of venom, only much more potent. This venom contains neurotoxins, which act on the nerve cells of the victim, paralyzing the respiratory system and ultimately causing death. Sometimes the venom also contains myotoxins, which affect the skeletal muscles. Even so-called dead specimens found at the beach should not be touched, because some species are known to feign death when stranded by the tide. Besides, some dead and even decapitated snakes can still administer a reflex bite.

Sea snakes feed mostly on fish, which they swallow whole. This explains why sea snake venom is usually so toxic: it must kill quickly, or else a thrashing fish could escape or use its sharp spines to poke a hole in the snake's stomach.

Suffice it to say, those might have been shallow-water dives, but the sea snakes made them anything but low-risk. Learning to negotiate diving with these treacherous creatures was just another skill to add to my arsenal. I felt in my bones that I would be the best deep-water hard-hat diver the industry had ever seen. I would make it happen. I couldn't wait to dive into my next moon pool: the first drilling location in Southeast Asia.

First Drilling Location—Off the Coast of the Territory of Papua, New Guinea (1968)

It took us a couple of days' sailing time to reach the *Glomar Conception*'s first drilling location. The big, brand-new workboats started setting anchors. These boats were huge; they had to be in order to hold an anchor big enough for a drillship, and also big enough for the massive buoys attached to it to mark the location.

As the crew worked to anchor the ship, a big storm hit. One of the buoy wires got tangled up with the workboat prop. My next moon pool was about to begin. They loaded us into the lifeboats from the rig, with scuba and burning equipment to cut the wire now coiled in the prop.

It was the larger of the two workboats that was affected, the *Biloxi*. These vessels differ from platform supply vessels in that they are fitted with winches for towing and anchor handling, having an open stern to allow the decking of the huge anchors, and having more power to increase the bollard pull. The machinery is specifically designed for these types of anchor-handling operations. They also have arrangements for quick anchor release, which is operable from the bridge or other normally manned locations in direct communication with the bridge. The reference load used in the design and testing of the towing winch is twice the static bollard pull.

Anchor-handling tug supply vessels are mainly built to handle anchors for oil rigs, and, in a few cases, serve as emergency rescue and recovery vessels. They are also used to transport supplies to and from offshore drilling rigs.

The storm that hit us was just the edge of a gigantic storm, the full force of which had yet to come. They wanted to have all the anchors up in order to ride out this enormous storm. They were able to get some of the anchors back up, but one of the anchor's big buoy cables got tangled up in the workboat propeller, as I already described. That was when they loaded us into the lifeboats from the rig, with scuba and burning equipment in order to cut the wire tangled up in the prop. The problem was we couldn't get close enough because the sea kept lifting the lifeboat, with us in it, ten feet above the workboat. Finally, the captain took a huge wave, and that wave dropped the lifeboat with us in it on top of the deck of the workboat. We scrambled out, and the crew tied the lifeboat to the deck of the workboat and then unloaded the burning and diving equipment.

Bryon (the old Aussie who was now my tender) and I made the dive. I went down and started using the burning gear to cut the wire away from the prop. The seas were rough, lifting the workboat ten feet into the air, and there I was, underneath the boat and trying to cut off the wire.

Quite a moon pool! Very unexpected too.

Have you ever almost drowned? I have. Several times, in fact. The first time was when I was body surfing as a kid. I was five years old, next to the pier at Huntington Beach in Southern California. This immense wave came in. My mother had kept warning me all day to stay closer to shore, but I took a risk, riding that huge wave. As I took off on the wave, it engulfed me, covering me completely and holding me underwater. It rolled me into a small ball, and I soon started running out of air. I fought to get to the surface, but the water was too powerful. I couldn't get to the surface. I blacked out, and the wave threw me onto the shore. A lifeguard was there, and he pushed the water out of my lungs, according to my mother, who was nearly hysterical at the time but later relayed to me what had happened. That lifeguard saved my life. Drowning was, is, and always will be one of the most fearsome ways to die, in my opinion.

I almost drowned again that day while trying to cut off the wire tangled in the workboat prop.

They sent Bryon down to help me. He was there with me when I ran out of air; they had not checked the tanks before sending me down. The tanks were only half full of air. I pulled Bryon's hand up to my regulator, and he understood I was out of air. So, both of us worked out of his set of tanks, using buddy-breathing techniques. I slipped, fell off the wire, and started to sink. Bryon came down and pulled me to the surface. The crews pulled me up on the deck of the workboat. Bryon finished what was left of the underwater work.

Thanks, Bryon. If not for you, I wouldn't be here.

The job was done, but we still had to get back in the lifeboat and go all the way back to the drillship through these gigantic, turbulent seas. Miraculously, we made it. We got back on the rig and rode out the rest of the storm.

As soon as the weather calmed down, the anchor went back up, and we made our normal, necessary dives, getting them drilling and setting the baseplate, wellhead casing, and blowout preventer (BOP).

I left a crew out there in case a dive was needed, and I flew by helicopter back to the island that had a dirt airstrip. A fixed-wing aircraft flew us from there back to Port Moresby.

The oil company was delighted, once again. As a result of our dive during the storm, combined with my dive in the Bass Strait, we had acquired a remarkable reputation of being heroic, talented, and skillful. Not only was the job well done, but we were extraordinary, to boot.

For the next two years, I worked as the top deep-water diver on the Global Marine contract for International Divers. I built their trust in us, proving that we could perform any dive, in any situation.

Another moon pool—nearly drowning off the coast of New Guinea—was now completed.

* * * * * *

Back in town, I met some young Aussies who were over from Australia on contract to work and play football (that is, rugby league football for the Territory of Papua). It was the game for Moresby, and I ended up becoming friends with one of the players, Darcy. He was a professional prizefighter also. He was a hero to the locals, yet so humble and nice. In no time, we were best buddies. He was the perfect person to introduce me to the local single scene. Hanging around with the most respected sportsman in the country was great fun, and we had our pick of the women. As a deep-water diver off the *Glomar Conception,* I was something of a celebrity myself. The drillship was the talk of the town, and we had the time of our lives.

Through my friendship with Darcy, I was welcome at the prestigious Rugby Football Club. Once again, being a deep-water diver didn't hurt. I received the royal treatment everywhere I went in Moresby.

Darcy was also the middleweight champion. The heavyweight (whose name I can't remember) fought an Australian named Digger who came over from the mainland for the fight. It lasted only two rounds, and we all were disappointed. Digger hit our local in the stomach so hard that he went down and never got up.

Darcy won his match, though. He was tough, wearing his broken nose like a trophy. He was also tough on the rugby field, and he was an exceptional player. I fascinated him, and he fascinated me. Those rugby players were so much fun to hang out with. A member of the rugby club had to invite you to the club if you were not a member. The club had a great bar, and it was a big part of the local social scene, with all the beautiful women loving to hang out there. The rugby players loved to see me chat up a sheila and then score. Most of the players became my friends instantly, just like Darcy did. For the most part, once a friend, always a friend. That's just how Aussies are; they stay loyal no matter what.

They asked me if I could play American football, and I said that I could.

"Try out for our rugby team, mate!" was the chorused suggestion in response.

So that's what I did. I went to the first tryout, which proved to be my last attempt at rugby. I ran well. I was fast and elusive. But when I got hit and tackled, I was almost knocked out. And then the bloke punched me in the face! When I started to fight him, I received a reprimanded for not showing good sportsmanship. Rugby is a rough game and not my cup of tea. It was fun to watch in Moresby, though. The natives would climb the trees, sit in the branches, and watch the games from there.

It wasn't all about fun and games and parties and women, of course. I was there to work as a deep-water diver, and that is hard, dangerous work in any locale. Still, it was the tropics, and so there was always ample opportunity for fun and games and parties and women during my down time. The town was excited about the arrival of the *Glomar Conception*, which had long been awaited by the international community. A few months prior, Phillips Oil Company had built a four-story office building, which was the closest thing to a skyscraper that Moresby would see for a while.

In fact, the wife of one of the geologists had taken some natives up to the top floor to show them around, but when they rode up in the elevator and the doors opened to reveal a view overlooking the harbor, they thought they had been delivered to the heaven the missionaries had told them about, and then they refused to get back in the elevator to go back down. The police and some missionaries were finally able to coax them down, but it was a quite a scene during the interim.

That was just one instance of the colorful and admittedly humorous events I experienced with the natives. Other experiences were equally colorful, even fascinating, and many of them were extremely enlightening as well. I spent much time with our helicopter pilots, making many trips to the outlying areas, landing in native villages, and exploring and looking for artifacts. It was very exciting and extremely dangerous. Remember, many of these natives were cannibals. Traveling to the interior of one of the most primitive countries in the world was an unforgettable experience; in its own way, it was every bit as incredible as working on the *Glomar Conception,* which truly was a thrill for me.

I bought a brand-new Mini Minor car; it could zip around Moresby. I also had an old Land Rover for croc hunting and boat launching. I was looking for a boat and planning to use the Land Rover to load the boat in and out of the water.

The local boat ramp was at the yacht club. I did get a boat, eventually: the water-ski club's ski boat. They bought a new fiberglass boat, but I loved their wooden inboard that could handle the ocean and was a great ski boat. I did put an offer on a sixty-foot teak sailboat. It was superb. But I preferred the ski boat.

I was also about to meet a great friend, the local diver and water-ski champion, who was also president of the club. His name was Harry Heath. We would travel the islands, camping, diving, and spearfishing. Lobsters abound in that area, so we had a fantastic time.

It was a great life for me. A job I loved, a flat with a spectacular view, a great car, a great boat, great friends, a fun social scene, and my pick of women. Mostly, these were mutually agreed-upon casual relationships. One, regrettably, not so much. I hooked up with a very sexy Finnish girl. We met at the top pub. She was pretty, and she drank a lot (wine and gin and tonic). We started to spend a lot of time together. What a sexy woman she was; she wanted sex all the time. She was sweet and nice. Unfortunately, she became very attached to me, and, before long, she wanted more than I wanted to give in a relationship—more than I was able to give. She didn't take it well, following me everywhere (we'd call it "stalking" today). She would come to my flat, begging me to move in with her. It was a shame.

Truthfully, I was already interested in another girl: a beautiful, young Aussie. Forgetting about the unfortunate circumstances with the Finnish girl, I concentrated on the sheila of my dreams.

She was exquisite, with copper-colored hair that had little golden-blonde streaks from the sun. Her skin was bronze, almost like a half-caste girl, and her teeth were white and perfect. Her eyes were also copper colored, with flecks of gold that would shimmer. She had a long, slender body, with beautifully shaped legs, just like a young thoroughbred colt's. I had already seen her in a bikini, swimming at Ella Beach, a little beach in the cove where the locals went. Aussie girls don't have a problem going topless, but they are tasteful and classy, as I've described about Australian girls. Going topless was just natural for them; they were comfortable with their bodies, not flaunting anything or seeking to shock anyone.

My flat was just up the hill overlooking Ella Beach. This was the best beach to meet the sheilas, another reason why it was such an excellent location for me.

I saw my exquisite Aussie again at the Gateway hotel, on the outdoor veranda with friends. She appeared to be a little shy and very quiet, but she was also very sensuous, with long, graceful movements. I made way into her group, and even though I was talking to everyone else, I could see that she was listening to what I had to say, silently knowing that I was really talking to her. We were already falling in love.

Later she told me I was exotic and interesting and very beautiful; she said she had a weakness for blond-haired, blue-eyed, tanned men. My being American made me even more appealing and exciting to her, it seemed. Hearing this thrilled me. Aussie women are so cool and so sexy; they are courageous women who like excitement, but, at the same time, they can be real homebodies devoted to their families. Always ready for a challenge and trying something new, they are honest (no games) and loyal. Most of all, they are beautiful, physically and sexually. I found the Aussie women who liked me gave themselves completely, holding nothing back. (Remember Kangaroo Lady in part II.) That was what I loved most about them.

I was wealthy by Aussie standards, fun, good-looking, and American. I was also very polite and nice to my exquisite, young sheila. Further along in our relationship, she told me that I was so sweet, that she fell for me that night on the veranda of the Gateway, even though we didn't go out until several weeks after that. (Actually, she reminded me a lot of the girl I'd left behind in Santa Barbara, the luscious brunette with the great legs.)

My Aussie beauty was an exceptional girl. Our skin was so sweet together, and when I kissed her for the first time, she was so passionate that it surprised me. I just followed her lead. It was incredibly passionate and intense. She led me through this incredible, loving, passionate journey. We made out for hours. She stayed the night, and it was quite exceptional.

We had this special affair for some time, but she knew it could never be a lasting relationship. I was honest with her from the beginning. Eventually, it was time for her to go back to Australia, and she returned to Brisbane. Yes, I missed her. If I had been willing to commit to a long-term relationship, she would have stayed.

As I've said before, women have always been my biggest moon pool.

Water-Ski Club—Port Moresby (1968)

While in Moresby, I met the water-ski champions, and I also got to know the president (Harry Heath, who was to become my close friend) and vice president of the water-ski club. They introduced me to the ski jump, trick skiing, and the slalom course. I was a pretty good water-skier, as I'd always had a boat, but this was all new. I had never done any of this before— jumps, tricks, or slalom through a course with buoys. When I wasn't on the drillship, I would practice water-skiing.

I joined the water-ski club, encouraged by Harry Heath. He was the local champion and a legend in the area, and he was also the local diver doing the small shallow-water construction work around the harbor. Given the opportunity, he would have made a fantastic deep-water diver. He did all the harbor diving and explored the islands, spearfishing and wreck diving. He could build or fix anything, and he and his brother, Alan, owned a welding and fabrication shop using native labor.

There were two big water-skiing events: the Territory Championship and the Port Moresby Championship. My favorite event was the jump, second was trick skiing, and the third was slalom. I finally did win the first place in jump at the Port Moresby Championship, and then I won first place in jump and tricks in the Territory Championship. Before I left the Territory of Papua, New Guinea, I won overall in the Territory Championship.

When they introduced me to the water-ski jump, they had me go over it, because it was dry. It is supposed to be wetted down before you go over. Long story short, I hit the jump, the skis stopped on the dry surface, and I flew out of them and up into the air. Having me go over the jump dry was an Aussie joke. I also learned that when you land after the jump, you'd better have wet suit bottoms on; otherwise, you wind up with a saltwater enema. Another Aussie idea of a joke.

My friend Harry had a houseboat made out of steel and set on pontoons. He'd built it at his and his brother's fabricating shop, and we would spend days on it, spearfishing, picking lobster, exploring the local islands, and having all kinds of adventures. It was great.

His wife was obsessed with me. She had this thing about American men. She was one very sexy, blonde, big-breasted woman. A real knockout in a bikini. I was interested, of course, but she was the wife of my good friend. I just couldn't bring myself to do that to him; our friendship was too important to me. They did spilt up eventually, and she took up with another man.

Her obsession with me didn't ever affect my friendship with her ex, thankfully, because he was a great friend, and I really enjoyed the water-ski club. It was so much fun there, and the club was so well organized, run just like most of the clubs in Australia: perfectly.

Later on, I was sent to Brisbane, Australia, to compete in the International Championships, where the top water-skiers from all over the world were to compete. Because I was competing with the world's top skiers, I didn't think we stood a chance. We were bunch of wild men from Port Moresby, Territory of Papua, New Guinea. We didn't stand a chance, but it didn't matter. We had a blast, even when we got eliminated. They used us to check the jump distances through a telescope.

An American, Mike Syderhouse, won the overall, but an Aussie named Colin Birmingham beat him to win the jump (my favorite event). It was a great time, even though we didn't come anywhere close to winning a thing.

Back in Moresby, I was a hero just for participating in the International Championships. Aussies love their sports! My friend Harry was not able to compete, and it would have been close if he had. He was recovering from a very serious injury at the time. One of his native drivers had lost control of a tow truck while he was standing between the truck and the vehicle that they were going to tow. The truck smashed his legs. It was horrible. He never whined or complained; he just dealt with it. It eventually healed, but it took time.

In any case, he was there when I competed locally. On the day of one competition, he was the top judge, sitting right up there at the judges' platform. He was so proud and happy to see me win. I wasn't just his friend; I was also his student, "the Yank," as he liked to call me. We were brothers in spirit.

Over the two years that followed, I did so much water-skiing that I got really buff and healthy. I looked the best I ever have, and that foundation stayed with me for many years.

Now that we've spent this time on my socializing, water-skiing, and other fun adventures, let's get back to the real reason I was in New Guinea in the first place: diving.

Shallow-Water Dive off the Coast Inlet to Fly River—Territory of Papua, New Guinea (1968)

We were on a shallow-water dive off the Fly River that opened into the Arafura Sea, collecting bottom samples. Once again, we were in really rough seas along the New Guinea coast. We were close in to shore, close to the entrance of the Fly River.

This was quite a procedure. They had men dropped off on several islands, encamped with equipment. Some were in the old, abandoned shacks of the World War II Coastwatchers. It was their job to home in and set these locations. I never really got into the radio procedures, but I do know that they had aircraft (choppers), and all kinds of things were going on. Dropping guys into the jungles populated with cannibals was not exactly a fun situation. All this was merely to locate a spot for a well.

We divers played a critical role in the process too, of course. We had to go to the bottom to retrieve samples.

My tender, Bryon, suited me up in the Kirby Morgan Ram Mask, our light-gear wet suit with an umbilical air hose and a bailout bottle. We had one of our air compressors loaded on the boat. We were on our workboat, the *Ocean Springs*. (This was a supply boat and somewhat smaller than the *Biloxi*). I waited for the word to make the dive.

Just then, I saw sharks swimming right next to the boat. I then noticed trash floating around the workboat. The crewmembers were Cayman Islanders, and they often dumped garbage over the side, bringing sharks from everywhere to feed. I was ready to make the dive, and right below me were all these sharks in a feeding frenzy.

The oil company representative said, "Okay, ten minutes."

That meant the airplanes and island crews would have the exact location site pinpointed by then, and I should be ready to make the shallow-water dive and get a bottom sample.

"Bullshit!" I told him. "I am not getting in the water with sharks in a feeding frenzy."

He informed me that they would cancel our contract if I didn't do the dive.

I was not keen on jumping into water of any depth that already held feasting sharks, but I didn't really have a choice. Turning toward Bryon, I said, "Tell those Cayman Islanders to stop dumping trash over the side or I'll break their fucking necks!"

I then had Bryon get the power head out and load it, go to the freezer and get a couple of hunks of meat and put them on a meat hook, get a rope, tie it onto the hook, and hand it all to me. I hung over the side, on one of the fenders, and when a shark came after the meat dangling on the hook, I hit him over the head with the power head, killing him. (We used the 303, a British shell that used black powder.) The rest of the sharks went after the one I'd just killed. While they were distracted by their newest feasting opportunity, I jumped in the water, went to the bottom, filled my container with bottom samples, and quickly surfaced.

Another job successfully completed, even with the very unexpected—and very unnecessary—drama in the midst of it. Quick, creative thinking averted a very messy moon pool. It could have ended in a real bloodbath: mine, that is.

Diving with the Oil VIPs—Territory of Papua, New Guinea (1968)

The oil company's bosses let me know that some VIPs were coming out to the rig from the States, asking if I would take them to a place where they could snorkel and pick some shells from the workboat.

Of course I said that I would take them out to a good spot.

I had Bryon load an air compressor on the workboat, along with light diving equipment and the Kirby Morgan Ram Mask, in case we needed to make a dive.

The VIPs arrived by chopper, landing directly on the rig. Bryon and I loaded them onto the workboat, and we headed for a remote spot called Anchor Cay, which was supposed to have mounds of shells.

The cay was beautiful, but the workboat couldn't get too close because of the shallowness of the water.

Bryon and I snorkeled out to make sure everything was okay before we brought the VIPs into the water.

I took my mask off to rinse it, and I was treading water because it was too deep to touch bottom. After putting the mask on again, I lay back on top of the water. Just as I did so, a shark that must have followed us out had a go at me. Came up underneath me, and before I knew it, I was on its back, the rough skin scraping deep into my chest and stomach. There I was, on the back of this shark, and I pushed my thumb into his eyeball. My trick worked: the shark rolled me off into the water.

In total shock, I looked over at Bryon. He held up two fingers to indicate that two more sharks were there with us in the water, meaning that a total of three sharks had followed us out from the workboat. All three were circling us. I signaled to Bryon to float slowly back to the workboat, and after a few seconds of floating, both of us were swimming as fast as we could to the boat.

We made it.

We climbed up on deck. And you never saw so many masks and snorkels drop as did from the VIPs. They'd watched the whole thing from the workboat, thinking we were goners for sure.

It took a couple of months for the shock of that experience to wear off completely. But, man, were those VIPs grateful we hadn't let them head out to snorkel before we'd checked out the water. That was one scary close call.

Another Big Storm Hits the Coast—Territory of Papua, New Guinea (1968)

Soon after the shallow-water dive amidst the sharks, the rig was on another location. I wasn't there; I'd stayed in town. All of a sudden, a huge storm hit the coast of Territory of Papua, New Guinea, leaving the rig out in big seas. There was huge risk that the blowout preventer (BOP) would get ripped from the wellhead, resulting in the loss of a million-dollar piece of equipment and possibly the rig itself. The entire operation was in jeopardy. This was a situation quite similar to the one in the Bass Strait, where I'd made that dangerous and extremely deep dive while en route to Moresby.

They now needed a diver to get the collect connector to release from the wellhead so that they could pull the huge BOP up on deck. If the connector was not loosened, the well would be lost; the rig could easily be lost too, because of the natural gas coming up from the wellhead. It was an extremely dangerous situation; in fact, it could result in a catastrophe.

My crews needed to get me to the rig. No one else could make the dive. The seas were so rough there was no way to get close to the moon pool. The rig was in jeopardy.

They radioed in to Port Moresby in order to get me out there, and they found me at the top pub, the Papua Hotel. I was not drunk, just chatting up a sheila. When I got to the radio, they told me what the problem was. I said, "No problem, mates. I'll be there." They had already gotten a hold of my favorite chopper pilot, Bill, who had flown in Vietnam mission after mission. He was the only one who could land a chopper on the deck with this kind of storm.

I met him at the hangar with the oil rig bigwigs. I got in the chopper, and we headed out to the rig. The wind was blowing fiercely, with the rain pelting the chopper, and I was worried we wouldn't even make it to the drillship, but we did.

Bill said, "Jim, I am not going to touch down for a few seconds."

I nodded, once again remembering the dive in the Bass Strait where we'd had such a similar situation. I'd survived that landing, so I wasn't overly concerned about this one, even though I would have to jump out and roll onto the deck; otherwise, I was a goner or the chopper would crash.

At the appropriate moment, I jumped out of the chopper, rolled onto the deck, got up, and hauled ass to the wheelhouse.

Tossing violently in these huge, rough seas, the rig was in jeopardy. The BOP was on the verge of ripping from the wellhead. I had to get down there fast to release the collect connector attached to the BOP and the wellhead so that they could pull the BOP up into the moon pool.

As of that moment, they were drilling with a floating mud cap. The method for pressurized mud cap and reverse circulation drilling was extremely dangerous; as I said before, this situation could quickly turn into a catastrophe.

All the drilling personnel and oilfield top brass were in the wheelhouse. They were terrified.

"Can you make the dive?" they asked. They'd already had my crew radio me to get me there because they didn't trust anyone else to make the dive.

I just said, "Yes." I was as confident as ever on the outside, but on the inside I felt the same level of fear that I always did prior to making a dangerous and extremely deep dive.

I began to pray inwardly, just as I did in the Bass Strait—just as I have done on every dive I've ever made, even the ones that were supposed to be "routine" (like shallow-water bottom-sample collecting that turned out to be a shark feeding frenzy). I prayed to a Higher Power; I called him my friend.

Our helium gear had not arrived in Moresby. We had been waiting for it for quite some time (again Sydney office manager putting us divers in harm's way), way before we moved to this location. As a result, I had to make the dive on air. This was my deepest dive to date: 340 feet. It was unheard of to make a dive of that depth without helium, because the air would just trickle in the helmet. And you'd get severe nitrogen narcosis. As it happened, though, I lucked out.

My diving crew took me down to get me dressed in. The waves were coming up out of the moon pool, towers of water rushing and cresting. I knew I would be more narco than I'd ever been, diving to that depth without helium, but there was no choice. (I did see a mermaid swim by! Just kidding ... You know by now that I don't need to be narco to see beautiful women, real, imagined, or somewhere in between.)

Once suited up, I went down right away. I hooked the hose to bypass the one that wouldn't work. They hit the emergency release on the collect connector that was at the bottom of the ocean, and that was that. I had them bring me straight up to the second stop. It was a risk to skip the first stop, because I could get the bends. But I felt it was an even bigger risk to be that deep without helium.

It worked. They put me straight into the decompression chamber as soon as I was all the way up. Then they pulled up the BOP and got off the well.

I survived. So did the ship. Another job completed successfully. Another moon pool finished.

MV *MacDhui*—Port Moresby (1968)

No story about deep-water diving would be complete without telling about at least one shipwreck. The view from my flat included the MV *MacDhui,* a wrecked ship half submerged in twenty feet of water. The bow stuck up out of the harbor. It was a Burns, Philip & Company ship that had provided service between Sydney, Territory of Papua, and the rest of New Guinea. The Australian Navy commandeered the ship during World War II. The Japanese later sank the ship during an air raid on Port Moresby (June 18, 1942). Papua, New Guinea, was a big battle area during the war. The Aussies and the natives fought the Japanese and defeated them.

Papua, New Guinea, was the strategic objective of the Japanese forces during the Battle of the Coral Sea and the overland through the infamous

Kadoka Trail. Although Japanese invasion attempts were unsuccessful, the area was subjected to many air attacks. The Kokoda Trail and Sogeri area have a history of bitter fighting between the Australian and Japanese armies during the early days of the war in the Pacific in World War II. The Kokoda Trail passes through rugged mountainous country and rain forest and jungles of ferns and orchids, filled with birds and clean mountain streams that tumble into steep valleys. All this beauty was scarred by war's brutality and bloodshed.

Enter: the Coastwatchers (the group I mentioned earlier, as featured in the Cary Grant film, *Father Goose*). This gutsy group's accomplishments were many but little known. They were a highly unusual and handpicked group of men who preferred the jungles of the South Pacific to the regimentation of normal society and the military Coastwatchers. Primarily, their mission was to provide adequate surveillance along the huge coastline of Australia itself, as well as for the mandated Territory of Papua, New Guinea.

The Coastwatchers' success at Guadalcanal made their position on Bougainville and other islands riskier. The Japanese realized that the Allies had to have eyes in the mountains. They assembled teams of troops and indigenous natives to hunt for operatives. Eventually, the Japanese pursuit of the Coastwatchers became fierce and effective, unfortunately. Many of the Coastwatchers made it back to Port Moresby via submarine. Others were killed by disloyal natives or Japanese troops. Some survivors returned to guide Allied troops as they hunted for stranded Japanese garrisons.

Now for the story of the MV *MacDhui*. Her captain tried to avoid the bombs by maneuvers in the harbor. Unfortunately, she was hit directly amidships, and she lost rudder control. She hit the reef central in the harbor and rolled on her side. Her captain was killed in the attack, along with ten crewmembers. The rest took to lifeboats in calm water and, although shaken, made it to shore. A total of twenty-seven Mitsubishi G4M1 Bettys led by Navy Lieutenant Renpei Egawa, based at Vunakanau at Rabaul, sank the *MacDhui*. Egawa would later lead the first Japanese air raid on Guadalcanal. The dramatic sinking was captured in a black-and-white movie shot by the infamous Australian cameraman Damien Parer.

To this day, the wreck remains on the reef and has become a common landmark of the town. The main mast was salvaged and became the flag mast for the yacht club.

We even made dives on *MacDhui* where the wreck lay submerged in the harbor of Port Moresby. It was creepy diving inside the cabins amid the bones and other remains. We took some brass portholes as souvenirs.

I had my first encounter with a lion fish (highly poisonous), and the wreck was also a haven for poisonous sea snakes. These treacherous, venomous creatures swam around us gracefully as we surfaced and followed us down as we dove. I've already told you how poisonous they are, in addition to being creepy and sinister. Their ability to breathe air makes them even more dangerous.

I jumped into moon pools that teemed with these sinuous creatures. So much for moon pool "tranquility"! But I never encountered as many at once as when diving the *MacDhui*. After a couple of dives, I decided to let the souls lost there just rest in peace in the harbor.

Meeting My New Love at the International Divers Main Office—Sydney, Australia (1968)

It was close to my birthday when I arrived at the International Divers main office in Sydney, Australia. By that point, I was the head diver and diving superintendent, so I had to give a report on the diving operations from the *Glomar Conception* in Port Moresby, Territory of Papua, New Guinea.

The oil companies were hooked on me. Even though I had a complete crew out there, they always wanted to fly me out to make the dive. I let them do that because it gave me the reputation and clout that I needed in order to have the control I wanted. I didn't just want to be the best; I wanted everyone in the industry to acknowledge that I was the best.

That meeting at the main office started a new chapter in my life. As diving superintendent, I was in charge of the operation, but I did have to send reports back to the main office in Sydney. This was the first time I'd had to go to the office to meet with the Australian manager.

My reports were always simple and positive, no drama. There was always drama, though; I just didn't ever mention any of it. My reports read something like this:

Twenty dives made this month. Water depth: 300 feet. All air dives and deep dives made by Jim Broman. Seventeen dives on deck. Fifteen to thirty routine shallow dives. Checking riser, morale good. Oil company happy with operation. No problems.
    Jim Broman
    Diving Superintendent, Glomar Conception

The drama was in the report, right there in the depth of the dives and the amount of dives. I reported it subtly. But there were no complaints from the oil companies, so my reports were always positive. All of our dives were successful, which was why I always made all the deepest and most dangerous dives myself. Success was the bottom line, all that mattered.

The main office in Sydney was another story. It was always overrun with problems from other operations. There was always an emergency going on somewhere. Drama and stress were a given in the Sydney office, where they constantly had to put out fires (figuratively, that is) because of the oil companies' equipment failures. But the *Glomar Conception*—"Jim Broman's operation," as it was known within the main office—had no stress and no drama, as far as the main office was concerned. Everything ran smoothly and perfectly, with no problems. Never mind that I'd almost died a few times, had fired the whole crew on several occasions, and had my share of equipment failures. I took care of it all, so in their minds, my operation ran perfectly.

They thought I was a genius at the main office in Sydney. They would contact the International Divers headquarters in Santa Barbara, telling them how great my operation was. The owners, Pete Blommers and Woody Treen, would check with Phillips at their headquarters in Bartlesville, Oklahoma, and Phillips had only words of praise for "that young deep-water diver, Jim Broman—so young but so capable."

I was their man, and I loved every minute of it.

That was how I met my new love, Renée. She worked in the main office in Sydney, and she got all the reports firsthand from all the operations.

She knew who I was, how good I was, and that I was still in my twenties. More about all that in a bit.

Back to the reason for my visit to the main office. I had been with International Divers for two years by that point, and they had decided to sell out to Divcon International. I was just finishing my two-year contract on the *Glomar Conception.* Phillips Oil Company was more than pleased with my work. I was Phillips' savior many times, making the deep dives necessary to keep the rig operational. I really didn't like the idea of shifting to Divcon, but, once again, I wouldn't have a choice in the matter.

Anyway, I arrived at the main office of International Divers in Sydney, and the manager and his female assistant (Renée, soon to be my girlfriend) met me there. They had my luggage sent to the Menzies Hotel, which was the best and most popular hotel in Sydney at that time. It was right across the street from the office. Everybody had arranged to meet at the bar at six, the time when Aussies hook up. (This was a carryover from the old six-o'clock closings that the pubs had to abide by.)

I went to the hotel and up to my room, showered, changed, and unpacked. (I had to have my room completely organized so that if I had some female company, I would be ready.) I went down to the bar but didn't see anybody from the office. The bar was packed, though. I squeezed in.

I ordered a drink and started to look around. I didn't know it at the time, but the girl from the office was sitting at a table, watching me. She was checking me out. We had seen each other for only a few minutes on my arrival at the office before I went across the street to the Menzies. I did see her, finally. We exchanged glances, and both of us were pleased. Looking at each other for a bit longer, we were even more pleased. And we wanted more.

If you have ever been to a Sydney hotel bar (pub) at six, you will understand what a mob scene it can be. Especially one like the Menzies, which was the spot in Sydney where the young, cool, beautiful people hung out. It was the place to be seen, named after a famous businessman in Sydney. It was loaded with sheilas, girls who worked in offices in Sydney. And it was like heaven to me—all of them wearing miniskirts, showing off their legs and healthy, sexy bosoms. These were young Australian girls at their best, sexy in the most wholesome, honest way that all beautiful women are sexy. Aussie women were so much fun too, no games at all and so beautiful. From my first visit there, I loved Australian women, and I always will.

The Aussie guys were more into their football and their mates (buddies) and their beer. They were fun, but they weren't as addicted to women as we American men were (and are). If you were an American male at an Aussie pub, you owned it; you were a novelty. The guys didn't seem to mind; they treated Americans warmly, and there was always good camaraderie between Yanks and Aussies. They were so proud of their country and people. They just didn't feel the need to be aggressive. I guess they were spoiled; they were handsome men and fun to be with, and they had all they wanted whenever they wanted it.

While I was playing a little hard to get with the girl from the office, a beauty at the bar started to chat me up, and some others joined in after seeing that I was American. One of them asked me how I got so tan, and I told her I was a deep-water hard-hat diver and a water-skiing champion among other things, working and living in Port Moresby. They couldn't resist me. I was interesting and fun, and I had them.

I gave her a kiss on the mouth, so sweet and sexy, and she reacted in a passionate way. She clung to me, and we started making out. She pushed her body against mine. After a few more drinks, I was really persuaded. We were both very turned on.

Before long, Renée, the girl from the office, crowded in front of the sexy sheila making out with me. Renée got my attention.

Just then, the manager of International Divers came in, and the staff from the Sydney main office came in behind him.

Renée grabbed my arm and whispered in my ear, "You're not getting away from me tonight. You're mine, so leave these little girls alone." She laughed.

I looked down at her. She was so beautiful. I had not really gotten a good look at her until that moment. I was smitten, and she was too. She could not keep her hands off me; they would come down from my shoulders, and she would push her body against me at the bar and snuggle close to me. We were getting very warm there together, and she would laugh and charm me like Aussie women can do.

After a while, everyone was feeling quite happy.

She pulled my head down again, whispering in my ear, "Let's go to your room. I had a bottle of great Australian wine sent up already."

"Okay," I said.

At that same moment, another sweet Aussie girl grabbed me, wanting a hug and a kiss.

Renée pulled me through the crowd, laughing, and we went to the elevators and up to my room. She had arranged everything perfectly: first-class view of the lights of Sydney Harbor, a king-size bed, and a bottle of good Aussie wine. She opened the bottle, poured us both a glass, and then started getting undressed. What a body.

That was it for a fortnight, starting with that weekend. She had it all arranged. I met her sister and parents and friends. We did the harbor ferries to Manly and Bondi, took the buses up to Palm Cove, made a visit to Kings Cross, and stopped at all the beaches down to Circular Quay. And, of course, we had lots of room time at the Menzies.

Palm Beach, the jewel of the Northern Beaches, is the northernmost suburb of Sydney, less than an hour by bus from the Sydney Opera House and Sydney Harbor Bridge. Nestled on a landmark peninsula, it is a unique contrast of lush evergreen bush land and beaches of golden sand, next to the pristine, blue waters of the Pacific Ocean. A unique environment, with breathtaking views, quaint cottages, and palatial homes, ensures that Palm Beach will forever enjoy a lifestyle of relaxed and casual affluence. We rode the buses and stopped at every little beach on the way back to Sydney, leisurely exploring and enjoying ice-cold VB (Victoria draft beer) at beachfront cafés and pubs. We walked the Sydney Harbor Bridge, saw a musical at the Sydney Opera House, had romantic dinners on the harbor boats, took the ferry to Manly and on the water in the harbor, and on and on. Most important, though, we had hours and hours of each other.

What a glorious, beautiful, deep moon pool that was.

Back to Port Moresby (1968)

Sydney was so much fun, and for a city, it was the best—charming and exciting and beautiful. The harbor restaurants and spectacular beaches and surf, the beautiful people, all tan and in great shape. How I loved the

Aussies—especially my new love. We were in love. She was amazing. She ran the main office for International Divers like a skilled surgeon ran an operation. And she loved me.

I went back to Port Moresby, and I continued to run the operation on the *Glomar Conception,* making all the deep dives. I still spent my free time water-skiing, diving on the reefs, and exploring. I was getting close to finishing my contract with International Divers, and I wanted to sail around the world on the sailboat I was buying.

Not long after that, International Divers sold the company to Divcon, as planned. Divcon was the largest company in the business at that time. They sent a rep to Moresby to meet with me and talk to the oil companies, trying to ensure them that they would be on for the next contract. The rumor was that it was going to be in Lourenço Marques, Mozambique, Africa, for two years, a joint venture between Phillips Oil Company (out of Bartlesville, Oklahoma) and Sunray Oil Company (out of Tulsa, Oklahoma). That meant they would split the cost of the rig and all the expenses for the service companies and the total operation.

The Divcon rep, Dean Whitaker, came out to the rig where I was making a deep dive (230 feet) to guide a casing into the baseplate. He arrived by chopper as they were suiting me up. I could see he was impressed, watching as my tender dressed me in at the moon pool. This was no piece-of-cake dive: it was very deep, and the currents were strong as soon as you got past the bottom of the ship. In fact, sometimes the currents were so strong that you couldn't move more than an inch at a time on the guide wire until you got past them.

The Divcon rep knew about me, having already heard about my reputation. I was talked about a lot in the industry. Now, seeing me in action, I could tell he was realizing that I really was that good. This was just another deep dive to me. I could tell that he was in awe. He observed the respect that the oil companies had for me and that the Global Marine personnel had for me. I was cheeky and totally in command.

I always roped off the moon pool area and would only allow one oil company rep and one Global rep to be in that area. They liked to listen to the diver on the phones, but the rule was that they could not talk or get in the way. I got a kick out of taking charge of the whole operation. No other diving operation did that; they were intimidated by the oil companies and the rig owner. I wasn't intimidated by anyone—except once in a while by an incredible, sexy, beautiful woman.

I finished my dive, and after I got out of the decompression chamber, the Divcon rep and I went to the galley to talk.

"I'm going to be around for a couple of days," he said. "Any idea what you're going to do after this contract?"

I told him I wanted to sail around the world. He said that I could have a great future with Divcon, now that they had bought International Divers. Divcon was now the largest diving company in the world, and the previous owners of International Divers were going to join Divcon's operating team.

He went on to say that with my reputation as a deep-water diver with the oil companies, I could pretty much name my own terms if I stayed on. But it was what he said next that blew my mind: Divcon wanted to send me to Duke University, make me the poster boy for the "American diver." Jacques Cousteau was a Frenchman. He never did the dangerous kind of work that we did, but he was a media sensation. We did more scuba on our time off than he did working! Off the reefs and wreck diving on sunken ships, we looked down on Cousteau; he was an amateur to us.

We had Aussie divers on our crews who out-dove that Frenchman a hundredfold. We were the real divers of our time: deep sea, sport, scuba— every type of dive. You name it, we did it. We were superior, the best at that time. We just didn't have a reporter on the payroll or the French government backing us. Cousteau didn't hold a candle to my Aussie divers or to any other good divers. My Aussies and I were the best at that time, hands down. That's all there was to that.

Phillips Oil thought I was their savior, as I've said. Many of the deep dives I made for them saved their equipment and kept the rig operational. When you're running a million-dollar-a-day operation, if the rig shuts down, it is serious. Very serious. We were vital to the success of the drilling operation. Most of the problems were underwater, and we were the link to the success of the drilling operation. Without us, there was no drilling operation. We were necessary.

Remember, I made every dangerous deep-water dive Phillips needed to have done for that contract. They didn't trust any diver but me, even though we had divers on the rig twenty-four hours a day, seven days a week. My divers' shifts were two weeks on the ship and one week off. When I was on-call, if an important deep dive needed to be made, they'd find me by boat or helicopter, or they'd radio me, and, one way or another, they would transport me to the rig to make the dive.

That contract was ending, though. I was leaving Port Moresby, and I planned to sail around the world with an all-female crew. I had been interviewing for two years, anyway!

But I had my mind on the contract for the next assignment of the *Glomar Conception*: Lourenço Marques, Mozambique, Africa. With that contract, I could travel, sail, do whatever I wanted to and on my terms.

When Phillips heard about plans with the sailboat and that I was not staying on the *Glomar Conception*, the oil bigwigs were devastated. Working on a rig was like living with family. They approached me, asking if I was interested in staying on with the dive company that they would hire. At that time, no other diving company had actually been hired. I thanked them but said that I wanted to do the trip around the world. They told me that a VIP from their headquarters in Bartlesville, Oklahoma, was flying in to Moresby to talk to the managers about the new operation in Africa, and they wanted me to talk to him.

So we met to discuss my staying on. Phillips had been loyal to International Divers, but that loyalty disappeared when International Divers sold out to another diving company. The bottom line was this: I was the only one Phillips had confidence in and felt loyalty toward. They had seen me risk my life in extreme situations; there had been quite a few close calls where my life was at risk and I could have opted out of the dive, forcing them to spend millions of dollars to pull the equipment up from the ocean floor. But I didn't. I always made the dives. I always got the job done. I always succeeded, and I never let them down.

We had a good talk, and my confidence deepened. I said to this oil exec, "The only way I will stay on is with my own company." My loyalty had waned as much as Phillips' had. International Divers had sold out to Divcon, and I didn't want to work for Divcon.

"Let me see what I can do." He contacted headquarters in Oklahoma to offer a proposal for me to stay with Phillips on the next contract out of Mozambique, Africa.

I would have to load the equipment in Fremantle, Australia, which meant that time was of the essence; all the equipment had to be sent from the States to Australia before the ship left New Guinea, then on to Fremantle, Australia, and from there to Durban, South Africa, and finally to Mozambique, Africa.

I flew back to Sydney, met with Renée (who was still running the Sydney office, but now it was Divcon). Our affair had continued while I was back in Moresby, and we were deeply in love.

We checked into the Menzies because that was the first place we had spent the night together. We stayed together for few days. She kept me excited; I was always aroused with her. My payoff was that she was always excited with me. We were constantly making out, touching and loving each other. I loved to watch her move around; she was so striking.

The Menzies was across the street from the Divcon (formerly International Divers) office, as I described earlier. We decided to sneak into the office late at night to copy the contract International Divers had with Phillips. So, at one in the morning, we left the hotel, went to the office, and crawled up the stairs on our hands and knees so that no one could see us (you could see the stairs from the street). All the while, both of us were trying not to giggle. We opened the filing cabinet using her key, took the contract, and made copies. Then we got back on our hands and knees and slowly crawled down the stairs.

It was so fun, exhilarating, and arousing as we crawled back out while holding in our laughter. We got up to our room at the Menzies with the contract copies, broke out in hysterical laughter, stripped, and had incredible sex. I stayed two days in Sydney. She was so sexy, and she always felt so pleasingly warm and nice. (Oh, by the way, I already had a copy of the contract. The owners had given it to me when I became diving superintendent.)

Meanwhile, Phillips offered me the contract in Mozambique as an owner. All I had to do was to fly to Bartlesville, Oklahoma, and then to Tulsa to meet with Sunray Oil, Phillips' partners for the Africa contract. I would set up a company, sign the contract, and buy the equipment to be sent to Fremantle Harbor, Perth, Australia. This was the highest compliment a young man like me could get. They were going to put all their trust and faith in me. This was going to be a million-dollar-a-day operation between Phillips Oil Company and Sunray Oil Company, and I was going to be their partner. Me, Jim Broman.

I was the founder of this company, and I called it Broman International. Even though my father had a diving company and was a legend in the industry, this was different. This was my creation. This was done entirely by me. I was always very independent and confident. I started my own company because I felt I could do it better than anyone else. I have had incredible dreams and visions for my life, ever since I was a very small boy. I wanted to travel the world. I wanted adventure. I wanted to prove I was worth something. I was like a lot of young men: I wanted to be a hero; I wanted to feel special. I did not want to feel controlled. I was the all-American boy.

I chose Australia as my main base of operations; later, I would be the major deep-water diving contractor in Southeast Asia and the Bass Strait.

I had complete control. I was still in my twenties. People said I was a boy wonder, a genius, to be in charge of diving operations at that age, but, most important of all, to be the lead diver all over the world at such a young age and for the big oil companies. A huge responsibility, a mammoth one.

They took a chance that this twenty-seven-year-old could handle any situation, no matter how dangerous and deadly. And yet, I always did.

For the two years while I was the lead diver and diving superintendent for International Divers on the *Glomar Conception,* they depended on me. I never let them down; I did some miraculous, dangerous dives. Phillips Oil Company thought I was the best in the business, and they had operations all over the world, so they knew who was the best. That's why they offered and then awarded me the contract for their next operation out of Mozambique, Africa. They even offered me to start operations in the North Sea. I could have been huge, but that's not my style. I was not interested; I like my tropical waters, Southeast Asia gigs, and, of course, my beloved Australia. I wasn't interested in being the biggest, just the best. And I was.

I was like a hit album where the star wrote the songs, played the instruments, sang the lyrics, and kept control of the product. This music was created by one person, played by one person, marketed by one person. I was much the same. I made the deepest and most dangerous dives. I ran the operations. And I got the prettiest women. I was just twenty-seven years old, and I was having the time of my life. It was about to get even better.

* * * * * *

And then I went to Bartlesville, Oklahoma. I met with Phillips and got everything going. Back in my motel room, though, I got terribly ill. I had malaria; I had brought it from New Guinea. I could barely move, I was hallucinating, and I had severe tremors. I was alone. I had to go to another meeting with Phillips to finalize the contract. I didn't even have the strength to call a paralegal service to form the company.

Within a week, I was better. The contracts were signed, and I flew back to Long Beach. Before long, I would be headed for Perth and Fremantle Harbor, where the equipment would be loaded and where my next moon pool was about to begin.

The Launch of Broman International—
Perth, Western Australia (1970)

This next big moon pool in my life started in Perth, Western Australia. I had won the Phillips Oil/Sunray Oil contract for the next *Glomar Conception* job, beating out Divcon (which now also owned the former International Divers). Having won the contract as an owner, I was now the proprietor of Broman International, meaning that my brand-new company's first job would be on the finest self-propelled drillship in the business. I'd already worked off the *Glomar Conception* for two years in Port Moresby, so I had total confidence that I could do the job with the same level of skill that Phillips had come to expect. I knew I could handle running the company, which would be based in Australia, even though this first job would be in Lourenço Marques, Mozambique, Africa.

I heard through the grapevine that Pete Blommers, the owner of International Divers, who had sold to and now worked for Divcon, vowed to get me after I took the contract away from Divcon. Apparently, he flew into a rage upon hearing the news and tore up the Santa Barbara office on

159

Stearns Wharf. He ranted that I didn't have a diving bell system, and none were available, so I wouldn't be able to fulfill the contract and would lose it.

So much for what Pete Blommers thought. I was able to fulfill the contract, and I did fulfill it. Phillips knew I would be able to do it; that was why they awarded me a two-year contract as an owner in the first place.

So began Broman International, and that contract from Phillips Oil and Sunray Oil in their joint venture in Mozambique was a real feather in my cap.

I didn't want to leave for Perth before squaring things with Pete Blommers. So, before I left California, I stopped by his office in Santa Barbara to make peace with him. I had the contract, but I knew he believed I would lose it because I did not have a diving bell system. What he didn't know was that I had bought the last system available in the United States while I was in Houston, Texas. Actually, I made sure that he didn't know that because I wanted him to think he had won. When he found out I had a bell system and would keep the contract, he would flip.

Sure enough, he did. I won't lie and say it wasn't satisfying to see that. But I had a lot of respect for Pete and his partner, Woody Treen. They had the best deep-water diving company in their time, and I learned from them. I would never forget the opportunities they had given me, but it was my turn now. They had sold their company. I wasn't being disloyal to them; I didn't owe Divcon anything. Most of all, Pete and Woody were fantastic deep-water divers who could do any dive. They could do the diving I'd gotten the contract to do. But so could I. And I had proved that to them time and time again while working for them—in the Bass Strait, in Port Moresby, in Santa Barbara, and in every location I'd made dives for International Divers.

We deep-water divers were vital to the success of every drilling operation. Most of the problems that occurred were underwater. We were the link to the success of the drilling, and I personally made every dangerous deep-water dive Phillips needed to have done for that contract in Moresby. They didn't trust any diver but me, even though we had divers on the rig twenty-four hours a day, seven days a week. I was the lead diver and diving superintendent, so I ran the show in Moresby. Even though I had a full crew on the rig at all times, Phillips called or radioed me to make every important dive. They awarded me this new contract in Mozambique because I'd earned it. Even better, they'd offered it to me as an owner. They had faith in me, and they knew I would deliver.

I knew I could and would too. I had flown to Oklahoma, set up my company (Broman International), signed the contract with Phillips and Sunray, bought the equipment I needed, sent it to Fremantle Harbor in Western Australia, gotten the necessary insurance, and now the contract was mine.

I suppose at some level I wanted Pete Blommers, who had resisted hiring me to begin with, to acknowledge that I had earned the contract. After all, I'd proved myself to Phillips while doing a great job for Pete, my former boss.

He didn't ever really acknowledge it, at least not in so many words.

"Thanks for giving me my big break in deep-water diving," I said to him as I walked out of his office.

He didn't say anything, but I knew he was thinking the same thing he thought when he met me for the first time: cocky, cheeky bastard!

I was okay with that. That was me. It was why I was the best, why my company became the best. And I was damn proud of it—still am, always will be.

I left California and headed for Australia, my new home base—and my next moon pool.

* * * * * *

I was in Perth, waiting for the *Glomar Conception* to arrive in the beautiful Fremantle Harbor. What a place! Yachts, pleasure boats, and all kinds of amenities abounded. The harbor was right next to Perth, with the Swan River running through it (giving me a new Aussie beer to try, Swan Lager). Perth was and still is one of the nicest cities in Australia.

Fremantle was magnificent, with something to offer people of all ages and at any time of the year. It will always hold unforgettable memories.

The harbor had picturesque old buildings, cultural diversity, and what longtime residents still call the "Fremantle feeling." You get that feeling when you cross the bridge over the Swan River into Fremantle. It's very different from Perth (the capital of Western Australia) and the northern suburbs.

A working port, Fremantle was host to a big fishing fleet as well as container ships and the occasional large cruise vessel. It maintained a vibrant commercial life and was a very cool tourist destination. One of my favorite places to swing by on an afternoon was the south side of the port. There was always something going on the dockside or a ship coming in or heading out. It was also a great spot for sunsets. In just a few square miles, it would be hard to find a bigger variety of sights, sounds, and experiences. And they could be covered easily on foot. I liked to have my midmorning coffee, or a locally brewed beer in the afternoon, on South Terrace, sometimes called Cappuccino Strip for its outdoor-café atmosphere. The venerable Fremantle Markets, also on South Terrace, was the perfect venue for an afternoon stroll.

This year-round working harbor also offered the opportunity of seeing fresh seafood unloaded from the fishing boats prior to export or local dispatch. The many waterfront restaurants in Fishing Boat Harbor thus offered true fresh-caught items on their menus. These establishments also had spectacular views of the Indian Ocean, all the way out to Rottnest Island and beyond. It was an atmosphere similar to San Francisco's Fisherman's Wharf but better, with cuisine catering to all tastes and featuring heavy Italian influences. Of course, the incomparable taste of fresh-caught fish and lobster was the trademark of these restaurants, and I've never tasted better. (Except for the fish and lobster I caught off my reef in Cape Trib!)

I would check in where the oilfield people hung out, keeping in touch and getting updates as to when the *Glomar Conception* would be arriving from New Guinea. It would be a while yet, so I had ample time to explore Fremantle and Perth. Plus, Phillips Oil had given me an advance until the contract started. I was flat broke after buying all my new equipment. It was nice indeed to have a little money in my pocket.

I enjoyed the area, relaxed and recharged, and waited for the rig to arrive. There would be nothing but work once it did. In the meantime, though, there was plenty of fun to be had. And I did.

Jill, My New Zealand Dream Girl— Fremantle, Western Australia (1970)

The second day I was in town, I walked into a restaurant to have lunch. The waitress and I made eye contact, and I knew we had an incredible connection. It was like we had been waiting for each other.

She looked like an angel. Blonde hair and blue eyes, she was sweet and classy looking, and beautifully built too.

I sat down and turned on my most humble, lost American act. We almost started making out right there, the attraction was so powerful. I could barely hold back, and it didn't seem like she could, either.

Before I even ordered any food, I said, "What's your name, and will you go out with me?"

She looked straight at me, the gaze of her piercing blue eyes intense, and she said, "You're an American, aren't you?"

I said that I was.

"We don't usually get Americans in here."

Again, I asked her name and if she would go out with me.

She laughed. "I'm Jill. Meet me here after work."

She said she would go home first to get ready to go out, and then she would meet me at the restaurant.

We laughed and just felt comfortable—and lustful—together.

Jill was a Kiwi (a New Zealander). We went out that night and spent the night together. She had never done that before on a first date.

As we lay together, she looked into my eyes and said, "You're a rogue, Jim Broman. You're going to have a rough life because of your womanizing."

She was right. Her words proved truer than I could have imagined at the time. But while I was in Fremantle and Perth, we were inseparable. She slept with me every night for three weeks. We couldn't keep our hands off each other.

Twenty-one nights of bliss while I waited for the *Glomar Conception* to arrive.

Hull Cleaning of the *Glomar Conception*—
Fremantle, Western Australia (1970)

The *Glomar Conception* arrived in Fremantle at last. The crew had to clean the hull to get the rig ready to make the voyage to Durban, South Africa, for dry-docking after two years in tropical seas off Port Moresby, Territory of Papua, New Guinea. After dry-docking in Durban, the rig was headed for Mozambique, on the Indian Ocean side of Africa. This was where the Phillips Oil/Sunray Oil joint venture would operate from: Lourenço Marques, the capital of Mozambique. (At that time, the Portuguese still ran the country; after independence, the capital would be renamed Maputo.)

The ship needed a complete work over, especially the bottom, where the barnacles were thick and hindered the speed of the ship from twelve knots to about half or less. That meant the voyage to Africa would take twice as long, and in the oil industry, if you're not drilling, you're not making money. If you own a boat, you've probably encountered barnacles adhering to the hull of your ship. It's quite a problem. While many choose to leave the creatures where they are, barnacles actually create considerable drag on your boat, slowing you down and costing you in fuel and time. Phillips was not happy and applied pressure on me to clean the barnacles off the rig before sailing. Problem was they were only stopping in Fremantle for twenty-four hours. And they wanted me to clean two years of growth off the bottom of a four-hundred-foot ship!

In twenty-four hours, I thought. *Give me a break.* But then I decided it would be fun to try. Another challenge.

Barnacles are tough little varmints. But I wasn't going to be defeated too easily, either. I remembered that Global Marine had come up with a hull-cleaning brush several years earlier. In fact, I had used these brushes on the *Queen Mary* in Long Beach. I was one of the first to use them, I believe. The brushes worked, but they were slower than what would be ideal for hull cleaning. Picture using a floor-waxing brush run by air hose; they had stiff bristles, but the secret weapon was the barnacle buster mounted on the brush. This was a piece of steel mounted on a piece of rubber, and the whole contraption stuck out a half inch over the bristles. The idea was that the rubber would give when it hit the barnacle; the rubber would give way, and that would remove the barnacles from the base and the ship.

Global Marine had sent over some of these brushes to coincide with arrival of the *Glomar Conception* in Fremantle. At least I had the tools to get started.

Barnacle removal usually takes place when the ship is out of the water and in dry dock, but in this case the ship had a long trip from Australia to Africa. She was scheduled to go to dry dock in Durban, South Africa—and she still would—but, in the meantime, the bottom was so loaded with barnacles that it would take twice as long to even get to the dry-dock destination. The oil companies were eager to cut the time in half, if not even more so. I wasn't thrilled about having to do it all in twenty-four hours, but I agreed it was worth it to try, given how much we would save in fuel consumption and, especially, time.

I had ten divers lined up: three to get the Broman International equipment loaded on the ship and seven to start the hull cleaning. I did get the job done, and when they saw the hull in dry dock in Durban, there was only a strip up by the bow that we'd left intentionally with barnacles intact: it showed the thickness of the growth we had cleaned off the ship, all in twenty-four hours' time. But I didn't get it done with seven divers; it took twenty-two. I had already made arrangements to fly them in from Sydney and Melbourne. When Phillips and Global Marine saw the results, they were thrilled. And shocked.

After that, my reputation grew. Phillips and Global Marine were completely amazed that I had pulled it off. Word of my accomplishments went rapid-fire through the offshore oil industry. "That Jim Broman can get any undersea job done that we ask him to do—in deep water, shallow water, and anywhere in between." This was big, to clean a ship of that size (close to four hundred feet) that had been in the tropics (Southeast Asia) for two years, with barnacles so thick under the hull that the growth reduced the speed from twelve knots to four to five knots. I basked in the glory. I'd earned it, and I didn't care if it seemed arrogant. Once again, other diving companies that had bad-mouthed me had crap on their faces, and all it proved was that they could have never pulled off that job. But I could, and I did.

After an uneventful dry dock in Durban, South Africa, the *Glomar Conception* headed for its next drilling destination: Lourenço Marques, Mozambique, Africa.

Deep-Water Diving off the Coast of Mozambique, Africa (1970)

My next moon pool had begun, and it was a big one. Very big. The drilling project off the coast of Mozambique was my first contract as an owner. I would still make all the deepest and most dangerous dives, just as I'd done in Port Moresby as head diver/diving superintendent, but now, as the owner of Broman International, I would have all the managerial responsibilities to handle as well. I knew I was up for it, and I was ready. As with every other moon pool in my life, literal and figurative, I just jumped in and went deep.

This was it, what I'd waited for and worked for ever since making my first dive. Nothing mattered but getting this job right for Phillips Oil and Sunray Oil, because it would establish my new company as the best in the business. I already had the reputation of being the best deep-water diver in the business, Phillips' savior throughout my stint in Port Moresby. Now I wanted to be known as the owner of the best deep-water diving company in the industry. I could do it, and I would do it.

Lourenço Marques, Mozambique, Africa, was home now—for two years, at any rate, as that was the length of the contract. Broman International was responsible for all aspects of the deep-diving operation in Mozambique, just as International Divers had been in New Guinea. We set up all of the subsea equipment on the ocean floor. First, we set the baseplate, then we guided the drill string, with a thirty-six-inch bit on the end of it to help guide the string into the baseplate to start the hole for the wellhead. Next, we guided the casing into the hole, after pumping concrete that would go out the bottom through a nonreturn valve of the casing and up the sides to give it strength; that would become the wellhead. After that, we guided the blowout preventer (BOP) into place, changing the seal that got crimped (as usual) when stabbing the BOP on the wellhead. We would also be responsible for maintaining all the underwater equipment that we had set up on the sea bottom. The most maintenance and repairs required were to the BOP on the wellhead located in the collect connecter. However, we were responsible for all the maintenance and repairs of all the underwater equipment. Global Marine and the oil companies watched us work via the underwater TV equipment. All this was standard operation, just as I've described previously about the deep-water dives I made in California, the Bass Strait, and Port Moresby. The only difference for me now was that I owned the company performing the dives. I was the boss—for better and for worse.

I was known to make the deepest and most dangerous dives. My dives were legendary with my divers, with Phillips Oil and Sunray Oil, and with Global Marine. If it sounds like bragging, so be it; that's the way it was. It was how I'd gotten this job, and it was how I held my power and kept control. Doing the deepest and the most dangerous dives was my job, and it was also my greatest talent. Even more than that, it was who I was.

This Mozambique operation was a major undertaking, and Phillips and Sunray would not take a chance with anybody else. I had an established track record that they appreciated and respected. I had made some incredible dives during my two years as diving superintendent and lead deep-water diver on the *Glomar Conception* while in Port Moresby. I had risked my own safety—my very life—on more than one occasion. They trusted me, not just because I was the best but also because I was loyal to the job. I did what needed to be done. I put the safety and success of the operation and the rig ahead of my own safety and well-being. That meant a lot to them. They invested in me because I had more than proved my value to them.

All that said, the danger and risk that I took on were tremendous. A lot of people thought that what I did and the way I did it was crazy. Maybe they're right. Certainly, it was not easy! It was scary, dangerous, and risky, but it was also exciting, thrilling, and incredible. The things that I experienced while diving and because of diving I would never have experienced doing anything else. I loved every part of it—the danger and the excitement and the beauty and the wonder—but in the way that you develop a love of what you do well. It's your passion and your calling and your sacred task. By which I mean that it becomes so much a part of you that it is like breathing, natural and inexplicable all at once, just as everything sacred must be.

So, yes, I had a lot more responsibility as the owner than I'd ever had before, but I thrived on it. Handling the operation of all the underwater work was nothing new to me; I'd been responsible for all that throughout my two years in Port Moresby. On a drillship like the *Glomar Conception,* that was at least a million-dollar-a-day operation. Now, however, as the owner, I was also responsible for my divers' safety, securing new contracts, qualifying with Lloyds of London for insurance, processing the payroll, obtaining all the work permits and visas for the crews, and doing all the paperwork necessary to keep an international company operating in the foreign countries where we worked. But I loved every bit of being the owner. I had total control, and I could still enjoy the action and rush of deep-water diving. All throughout the time I owned Broman International, I continued to do all the deepest and most dangerous dives myself. My reputation was the reason why I had the company in the first place. Besides, there was nothing I loved to do more than make deep-water dives. (Well, except love beautiful women, but it would be way too complicated to do that for a living!)

Life and Times in Lourenço Marques, Mozambique, Africa (1970)

Before I further describe our drilling operations and diving while in Mozambique, let me give you a bit of background on the place. When I lived and worked there, Mozambique was still under Portuguese control, so the capital still had its Portuguese name: Lourenço Marques. After independence, it would become Maputo, as mentioned previously. Regardless of which name it went by, it was the largest city in the country, and both city and country were fascinating indeed.

Arab traders who made their way down the East African coast mingled with African peoples, creating a hybrid culture and language called Swahili. This culture still predominates in several East African countries and exerts a strong influence in northern Mozambique. The name Mozambique is thought to come from the Swahili Musa al Biq, the name of an ancient

Arab sheikh who lived on the northern Ilha de Mozambique. Maputo (Lourenço Marques during Portuguese rule) is also known as the "City of Acacias," in reference to the acacia trees found along its avenues. In addition to the stunning yellow-and-white blooms, the acacia produces a dry seedpod as its fruit. Each pod is a few inches long and contains five to six brownish-black seeds. The combination of its feathery leaves, beautiful flowers, and dry seedpods creates a dramatic appearance during the trees' peak growing years. The city is beautiful beyond its acacias, though, and has long been known as the "Pearl of the Indian Ocean." Famous for the inscription "This is Portugal" on the walkway of its municipal building, as a port city on the Indian Ocean, its economy centered on the harbor, and this was where the *Glomar Conception* drilling operation was based as well.

To give you a better sense of the geography, Mozambique is on the southeastern coast of Africa (Indian Ocean), bordering Tanzania, Malawi, and Zambia to the north, Zimbabwe to the west, South Africa and Swaziland to the south, and the Mozambique Channel to the east. The capital, Lourenço Marques (today called Maputo), is in the south, near the coast.

The terrain ranges from rain forests and swamps to mountains, grasslands, sand dunes, and beaches. The Zambezi River flows west to east and cuts the country into northern and southern regions that diverge, to some extent, in terms of culture and history as well as climate. Mozambique's 1,553 miles of Indian Ocean coastline is mainly made up of empty, palm-fringed, strikingly beautiful sandy beaches.

Navigable Lake Malawi (also known as Lake Nyasa [Lago Niassa in Mozambique]) borders Mozambique and Tanzania. The lake has an incredible 11,400 square miles of surface area, about one-third of which is situated within Mozambique's territory. Its deepest waters, which reach a maximum depth of 2,316 feet, are found in the part of the lake situated within Mozambique.

Mozambique is rich in rivers, with twenty-five of them throughout the country (including the mighty Zambezi). Many of these rivers flow out from the western highlands to the Indian Ocean, or to the Mozambique Channel in the east. Water flow tends to fluctuate, owing to the rainy and dry seasons.

Now that you understand the geography, you won't be surprised that I did my fair share of exploring while in Mozambique. I had done my homework prior to arriving in Africa, loading my boat on the *Glomar Conception* in New Guinea. I offloaded it when the rig arrived in Lourenço Marques. I also bought a new Land Rover (I'd had one in Port Moresby). This four-wheel-drive all-terrain vehicle was the product of continuous advancement and refinement throughout the 1950s and 1960s, with improved stability and a tighter turning circle. At that time, Land Rover took the lead in the developing market for four-wheel-drive vehicles. As a tough, reliable vehicle, countless organizations came to depend on Land Rover vehicles to transport people and equipment into the most challenging situations ... and then safely out again. I added my name to that list. Also a skilled explorer, I have traveled to many remote world locations. The Land Rover name is accepted as standard jargon for a four-wheel-drive vehicle throughout much of Africa.

As I took my boat along the coast through the wilderness, I was consistently amazed by the magnificence of the landscape. Northern Mozambique was the world's last true wilderness at that time. The Querimba Archipelago is a group of islands near the river that forms Mozambique's border with Tanzania. With pristine white beaches, feathery palms, soft sand dunes, and inland lakes all surrounded by the crystal clear waters of the Indian Ocean, northern Mozambique offers a vast selection of delights for anyone who wants to dive deep into the risky and rewarding journey through this part of the world. And you know me; I always dive deep!

In addition to the stunning scenery offered, that part of the country also boasts the mammoth Niassa Reserve, which is twice the size of Kruger Park in South Africa and is home to an extensive selection of wildlife, including elephants, sable antelopes, lions, leopards, spotted hyenas, and the elusive African wild dog. To the north of Pemba, inquisitive elephants stroll right up to the beach. To spot the infamous African fish eagle while boating along the tapered waterways of the traditional African mangroves is an incredible experience—one I will never forget. In short, northern Mozambique offers the opportunity to discover a remote and beautiful paradise that is one of the last undiscovered jewels of Africa.

I had been up the Zambezi with native guides to look at the hippopotami from a small boat; it was thrilling when we got to the spot. A huge hippo came up right alongside the boat. It could have swamped us easily. It was frightening and thrilling at the same time, just like diving. The creatures surrounded us, so close we could touch them. They were no more than an arm's length away, and there must have been twenty of them. They were magnificent, and they seemed so gentle—that is, until they opened their mouths. Those huge mouths were among the scariest things I've ever seen. Mozambique has a great diversity of wildlife besides hippos; zebras, water buffalo, elephants, giraffes, lions, and crocodiles all abound.

The mighty Zambezi, the longest and most important river in the area (total length of 1,650 miles), was another fabulous place to explore. It flows southeast, across the heart of Mozambique and into the Indian Ocean. This river has always been the principal means of transport between inland Central Africa and the coast. Its waters make the soil in the land surrounding it some of the most fertile land in the country. From the Maravia Highlands downstream, the valley is low-lying and has a very gentle slope, with an elevation of less than 500 feet. Much of the area around the mouth of the Zambezi, and south to the lower reaches of the Pongo River is the country's wetlands, providing excellent conditions for many marine species, most notably prawns. (For my favorite Mozambique seafood dish: jumbo prawns with *piri piri* seasoning.)

In the 1960s, Mozambique was swept up in the Pan-African movement toward independence. However, Mozambique would not gain independence from Portugal until 1975. While I was there, it was still under colonial rule (that's why the capital was still Lourenço Marques, not yet Maputo). All the main cities are located on the coast, and they are all beautiful. Lourenço Marques (Maputo) itself is magnificent and every inch the European capital. Its design was based on a European model, in fact, with wide streets, public gardens, and paved sidewalks inlaid with mosaic tiles. The city has two parts: the older residential area on a cliff overlooking the harbor, and the newer industrial area below, where the factories, port facilities, and most office buildings are located. In the 1950s, the Portuguese architect Amancio d'Alpoim Guedes designed many of the city's office and apartment buildings, which combine shapes and symbols from traditional African art with a modern feeling.

So you can see what a fantastic time I had exploring the city and country that would be my home base for the two years that followed. Of course, I didn't have too much time to do this exploring. I had left Durban ahead of the rig to get things set up for the operation and my crews (accommodations, permits, visas, etc.—all the paperwork and logistics that I was now responsible for as owner).

"Grande Dame of Africa"—Hotel Polana, Mozambique (1970)

The Hotel Polana ranks as one of the most famous historic hotels of the world. Designed in 1922 in the Palace Style by one of the most prominent architects in the world (at that time), the hotel's guest list reads like a "who's who" of world politics in the years leading up to and during World War II. Standing in the center of the capital city, the hotel and its environs are indeed a millionaire's playground. The elegance and grace of this unique hotel caused it to be considered not only one of the most prestigious places to stay in southern Africa but also one of the most atmospheric and character-rich hotels in the world. During the war, it was a seat of espionage and counterespionage. As part of the Portuguese empire, the hotel made the ideal neutral meeting place for spies and secret agents from both the Allied and Axis forces. Here, both sides were free of the constraints operating elsewhere on the continent. Indeed, the hotel was renowned as a place where spies from South Africa, England, America, Germany, and Italy were so relaxed as to be able to "exchange courteous greetings" when meeting in the corridors and bars of the hotel that came to be known as the "Grand Dame of Africa."

When I was there, the hotel was still every bit as stunning as it had been during its heyday. At the inlet of the Indian Ocean, its views were magnificent, and it boasted all the amenities of that time (1970): huge pools, restaurants, nightclub, and so on. The Hotel Polana was our base of operations while we looked for permanent accommodations.

Beautiful native women (some Zulu) would come over from South Africa. This was similar to living in Southern California, with the border so close to Mexico, down the Baja coast. Then, too, the Mozambique coast reminded me of Baja.

I had no issue with the Portuguese governing Mozambique at the time, but the real grandeur and beauty of the country was in the native land and peoples. They possessed unique grace and beauty, and they commanded respect. Their talents and abilities were amazing: they all could speak several languages and carry water in huge containers on their heads while also carrying children strapped to their backs. It was almost always the women who did this, each one walking regally with the water container on her magnificent head and her child strapped to her back. I could not get over how beautiful and talented these bare-breasted black women were.

My First Native Girlfriend—Mozambique, Africa (1970)

The African women intrigued me, with their blend of composure and raw passion. It wasn't long before I dived into that moon pool. I'm sure that's no surprise.

I slept with a maid at a house where a friend took me to meet a different woman. I was sitting and waiting when this sexy native woman walked by me to make up the bedroom. She was beautiful and erotic, sensually suggestive, with a breathtaking body. I followed her into the room and gently clasped her hand. She smiled, held my hand, and gave a soft laugh. She had the most beautiful white teeth I have ever seen. As I took off her blouse, she gave another soft laugh. She was stunning and affectionate, so very loving. She then dropped her native sarong, and we started off with sweet, little kisses. She was so beautiful. Her name was Lwandle (meaning "Ocean.") She was Zulu. We were with each other many times over the two years that followed. But that first time was incredible.

* * * * * *

After staying at the Hotel Polana, it was hard for me to move into a house at first, but I found a sophisticated, graceful, well-designed one, and, as always, it had a beautiful view. It also had large maid quarters, and it was essential to have servants in the countries where we did offshore drilling.

They weren't servants in the sense that we know in the States; they became part of your family.

All the wives of the oil company personnel had found maids, so I put the word out. The maid that I hired had worked for one of the heads of an oil company (Shell, I believe), but he had recently died of hepatitis, and so she was looking for another job. She was a big woman but classy, about forty, and she spoke six languages. I met with her, and we hit it off immediately. Her name was Cecelia. She had these amazing, wise eyes, and when she looked you in the eye, you knew she understood everything about you—what made you tick and maybe even your secrets too. She could laugh with her eyes and love with her eyes. I adored her. Fabulous cook too. She knew every cuisine, from English, to French, to Portuguese, to South African. I ate out a lot, but she always cooked my favorite meals when I wanted to eat in.

My favorite restaurant was outdoors, with a tin roof over it and a concrete floor. (Actually, it was a lot like my later home in Cape Trib.) The waiters dressed in brilliant white aprons. It was noisy, alive, and exciting, with lots of different nationalities and languages filling the atmosphere. The specialty of the house was Piri Piri Chicken Piri Piri Prawns—these are spicy dishes with roots in both Africa and Portugal. The dish was created in Angola and Mozambique when Portuguese settlers blended with the natives. *Piri piri* is Swahili for the incendiary red peppers of Africa, primarily those of Angola and Mozambique, which the Portuguese colonized. Because of the seafaring nature of the Portuguese, it didn't take long for these bite-size pods of fire to make their way to Lisbon aboard spice ships returning from the East. This restaurant crafted the dish as a true feast; the prawns were almost as big as lobster tails (and the chicken was good too).

Cecelia liked for me to eat her cooking, and I indulged her some of the time. When I did eat in, she always made my favorites. She did my laundry perfectly and took care of me like I was her friend, not her employer. We had a mutual respect for each other—two people from very different backgrounds but with the same kind of heart.

Her family members stayed with her a lot. The maid's quarters were actually a small house separate from the main house. She knew I liked women, so she always had some pretty girls staying with her.

My divers lived with native women in the villages. They loved the native women too. How could you not? Beautiful ebony skin, perfect bodies, and passionate lovers. Some of them were more than six feet tall. They were absolutely exquisite. Magnificent. And fun too! Native Africans love to laugh and play; they are so much fun to be with. (In fact, after finishing our two-year contract, my divers received a bonus: airline tickets for round-the-world trips, plus cash. They each chose to come back to Africa and stay with their native women.)

One night, we were out with some of the oilfield brass. They wanted to get hooked up with some girls. They had an interpreter to handle the communications. For political reasons, I was being "one of the boys," so I stayed and partied with them.

And then something incredible happened. A very young, beautiful, sweet native girl came in. She was shy, almost timid, but also proud and stunning. She was not a Zulu.

I was the youngest man there. Fortunately, the other beasts were already hooked up and ready to leave with their girls for the evening. I walked over to this beautiful, young girl. I smiled, and she smiled back, the sweetest smile, with brilliant white teeth. She wore the typical native dress.

In the kind of broken English the natives spoke, I asked if she would sleep with me, and she said yes. She took charge, got us a cab, and took me to a village.

Later, I found out that this was her own thatch hut, her home; ordinarily, she would never bring a man here. This was a special privilege, and I was truly honored. We liked each other at first sight. It was almost like a date.

She led me inside the hut, with its thatched roof, and brought me straight to her bed. There was a beautiful batik spread across it, clean and soft.

Immediately, she undressed and signaled for me to do the same, which I did. She slipped into the bed beneath the batik, and I got in next to her. Her body was flawless: slender, with beautiful, large, long breasts. She clutched me hard, deeply turned on. A wild, young woman ready to make love. We were on fire with our mutual passion. She clung to me the whole time.

I stayed until noon the following day, making love on and off all morning. I saw her several times a week after that first night together.

Early one morning, I asked her, "Do you like our lovemaking?"

She giggled. "I like too much," she said sweetly.

I knew she wanted me to be her man. I could have lived with this girl. She was so sweet, with the smells of Africa on her. I would take her out in my Land Rover, looking for game to photograph in the bush. And we would camp. And make love.

I didn't live with her, though. I always went back to my house.

I was asked once if I would want go out with a game warden to kill an elephant because it had turned rogue and was attacking villages. It broke my heart to watch them shoot this magnificent animal, even though it was rogue and a man-killer. It had already destroyed several villages. The natives used every part of the animal: the flesh for food, the hide for shields, the tusks for weapons. I was asked many times to hunt, but I never would. I just could never kill beautiful animals for sport. To protect myself, yes; I never hesitated killing wild boar or crocs, as I've described. But the magnificent beasts in Africa were a different story. I couldn't kill them, but I didn't blame the villagers who did. That rogue elephant was destroying the people and villages; they had no choice. That's the way of wild Africa.

I spent a lot of time in the bush and a lot of time in my boat along the coast. It was dangerous because civil wars were going on. I had to go through many checkpoints. I took my boat to these beautiful, inland freshwater lakes right on the ocean sand. Sand dunes, lakes, rivers, beaches, and the Indian Ocean all in one place. Mozambique was incredible and unforgettable in every way.

New Office in Johannesburg, South Africa; Black-Tie Gala at Hotel Polana in Mozambique (1970)

It might sound like I spent the majority of my time in Africa exploring the landscape and meeting beautiful native women. Of course, I did spend a fair amount of time doing both, but I also worked all the time. Deep-water diving was as challenging and time-consuming as ever, and now I had all the work associated with owning a company, managing employees, and running a business day by day. Having my company based in Australia created logistical problems, so I opened an office in Johannesburg, South Africa, through a friend I'd met in Port Moresby. He had formerly worked for Global Marine but resigned on good terms. Afterward, he set up an agency for companies like mine, service providers that needed representation in Africa.

My agent, Monroe Asworth, was very good at his job. He had lived and worked in Africa before, and he knew the ropes. I would travel to Johannesburg from Lourenço Marques by train. It was incredible! The carriages were very old and dilapidated. It was really just a rickety old train, but it took me through some of the most magnificent country imaginable. I loved traveling through the wilds from Mozambique to South Africa, seeing herds of Cape buffalo, wildebeests, giraffes, and zebras all running alongside the train at different times. It was so serene to watch those magnificent creatures. Sometimes my trips to Johannesburg had less serene views. I once saw a lioness take down a kudu, which was fascinating but grisly. There were many predators in that area, not just lions and other big cats but also African wild dogs, hyenas, and pythons. And, of course, hippopotami, as I've mentioned.

In fact, hippos are one of the most feared animals in southern Africa. It is claimed that they kill more people each year than any other African animal. (You'll remember my voyage up the Zambezi with the natives when some twenty hippos surrounded our small boat. I found them quite fearsome, I assure you.)

I didn't need to spend too much time in Johannesburg, just what was necessary to handle some logistics and administrative details. I still spent most of my time in Lourenço Marques, running the operation, managing my divers, and making the dives that only I could do. I still frequented the Hotel Polana for socialization, especially hobnobbing with the oil bigwigs as needed for political reasons. And, of course, I still had fun with my sweet native girlfriend.

But I had also met some Americans who were not associated with the oil field; they were on an exchange program to teach golf and basketball to the Portuguese. Their father was the instructor for the top Portuguese women's amateur golfer in Africa and internationally. Apparently, she was famous outside the United States. He also taught basketball for the

Portuguese college, and his family was in Mozambique with him: wife, son, and daughter. His son, Mark, and I hit it off and became great partiers together. He was very good-looking, blond like I was but a few years younger. At six feet two, twenty-two years old, handsome, and fun, the women could not resist him. Our both being American was also a plus in those days, so, yes, we were confident that we could get any women we wanted—and we did.

Mark started dating the daughter of the head of the French consulate. Mark was as much a womanizer as I was. (Most American men were in that era.) Anyway, I was trying to date Mark's sister, Laurie. She was cute and nice, but she was loyal to her boyfriend back home in the States. We went out a couple of times, but she would never sleep with me; she was true to her boyfriend. I tried, but she held her ground, so I let it go. We double-dated with Mark and his new French girlfriend. After Laurie went back to her place, I would hook up with my native girlfriend.

One night, there was a big event at the Hotel Polana, a black-tie gala with international dignitaries, wealthy Portuguese, South Africans, Dutch, French, and every other nationality with money and/or power. The oil bigwigs were in attendance, of course, and so I had to attend as well. I invited Mark, his French girlfriend, and Laurie to accompany me.

We arrived at the hotel, and as I passed one of the several bars on the main floor, I saw a bunch of the guys from the rig. They were drinking, and some of my divers were with them.

Old Bryon had passed up Divcon's offer to remain with them, and he worked for me now. He was at the bar, drunk. He spotted me, heading toward me just as I was getting into the elevator to go up to the ballroom. Mark and his French girlfriend had already gone up, because she was a guest in her own right, through her father. Laurie, my date, was with me. Just as the elevator doors started to close, Byron slipped in. He was so drunk, he stank. He could hardly stand up, and there we were dressed to the nines.

Well, on the way up, Bryon took out his false teeth and stuck them, all wet and slimy, in Laurie's hair. He looked like a monster with his toothless mouth wide open. (He was an ugly little bastard on his best day, even sober and with his teeth in place.)

Needless to say, Laurie flipped. She tried to get the slimy teeth out of her beautiful, thick hair, but they were stuck. She started to scream and then sob, and the whole situation deteriorated rapidly.

I grabbed Bryon just as the elevator doors opened to the ballroom, putting him in a headlock. The maître d' stood waiting to escort us to our table; he was rather shocked to discover the ruckus going on inside the elevator: a hysterical girl and two guys wrestling. Finally, we got Bryon's teeth out of Laurie's hair, and she made a beeline for the ladies' room. I slammed Bryon into the elevator and immediately sent it back down. When we got to the bottom, he escaped and ran to the bar, going straight to this big derrick guy for protection. I knew this guy really well, and we got along. I briefly related what had happened.

"Don't worry, Jim," he said. "I'll take care of Bryon. You go ahead and enjoy the party."

This guy was a giant and one of the toughest on the rig, so I felt confident he could deal with little Bryon.

Bryon was wiry and wily. I found out just how wily a minute later. He always rolled his own cigarettes when he smoked. He rolled himself one at the bar, lit it, and started to smoke. I was ready to go back up to the ballroom, but before I could do so, that Bryon pulled the big derrick guy's shirt around the neck and dropped his lit cigarette down the guy's shirt. The guy started screaming while he tried to put out the cigarette.

Bryon took off like a shot, running away to his thatch-roof hut in the village where he lived with his Zulu girlfriend.

That was the most memorable part of an otherwise dull and stuffy evening. Bryon was the best tender I ever had, but he was more than a little crazy when he got drunk. Thankfully, he never took his teeth out and stuck them in any of my other dates' hair.

Trip to Italy (1971)

I was close to losing my company; we were finishing our contract in Mozambique, Africa. This was a big moon pool for me. I felt like I'd only just started Broman International, and now, two short years later, it was about to fall apart.

Agip Oil Company, based out of Milan, Italy, was to take the *Glomar Conception* to Singapore, with Phillips Oil Company as a partner, for one well, which was only three months' worth of work. It was a fairly deep project, as far as water depth was concerned, but Agip Oil owned its own diving company. They felt they had no need of my services; they wanted to use their own diving company on the rig.

That created a huge problem for me. Missing out on the three months was not that big of a deal in itself. The problem was that Phillips was willing to sign a two-year contract with Broman International, to operate out of Darwin, Northern Territory, Australia, but there was a catch: I had to get the Agip contract and have my equipment on board, as they were going to the Darwin contract straight from Singapore, which meant that they would have to leave the Agip diving company on the rig. They would then get the two-year contract for Darwin, and I would be out.

I arranged for an appointment with the powers-that-be of Agip Oil Company. I flew to Italy a couple of weeks before the meeting, landed in Rome, hired a taxicab for a week, and saw all the sights (the Vatican, the Colosseum, etc.). The cab driver had served in the war with Americans, and we became friends. We shared a lot of laughs, ate lunch together every day, and enjoyed each other's company. I met his family, but, as always, I was looking for beautiful women. He was the perfect connection for me, but I needed to be in Milan in ten days.

I arrived in Milan two days before my appointment. I had telexed Phillips to ask them to lobby for me to get the contract, even though Agip owned its own diving company. As always, I scoped out the area, talking to Agip employees just to get a feel for the place. Finally, the time came for my appointment; when I walked in, I could tell the executive had already made up his mind that he was not going to let an American company get this contract before his company.

As always, when in a situation totally outside my control, I prayed. I prayed to get that contract as hard as I usually prayed to survive the most dangerous dives.

I sat down, and the executive addressed me in Italian-inflected English. "Mr. Broman, do you really think you have a chance of getting this contract? You are well aware that we have a very sophisticated and well-equipped diving company. Phillips Oil Company speaks so highly of you; you have been on the *Glomar Conception* in Port Moresby, New Guinea, and in Mozambique, Africa. You are well known for your deep-water capabilities, but, again, we feel we have the same." He went on to express some regret about the decision he had to make.

We talked for a while, and then it was my turn to plead my case. I did, and he listened to me.

Later, I found out he was very impressed with me; I was so young to have the responsibility of a million-dollar-a-day operation. He understood that the divers were responsible if the rig should shut down. He was also very curious as to why Phillips would go out on a limb for a diving company. He knew that Phillips had applied pressure on Sunray in their joint venture, specifically requesting that Jim Broman and Broman International be their diving company. My reputation had preceded me. Some of the dives I had made for Phillips were legendary, such as the dive I'd done at 340 feet, without helium gear, in Port Moresby. It was known that I did whatever was necessary to save the rig and see to it that the operation succeeded.

Remember, the deal I had with Phillips now was that I had to get the Agip contract and have my equipment on board, because they were going straight out of Singapore to the Darwin contract. While they were operating out of Southeast Asia, there would be no opportunity to load my equipment onto the *Glomar Conception*. I would not get the two-year contract with Phillips if I did not secure the three-month contract with Agip; it was as simple as that.

I talked to Phillips; they badly wanted me on the Darwin contract—and they wanted me in Southeast Asia (Singapore) too—but, again, I needed to have my equipment on the rig. They couldn't get the Agip contract for me; it was up to me to get it.

As I have explained before, the *Glomar Conception* was the state-of-the-art drilling vessel in the industry. If I did not get the contract with Phillips (which necessitated getting the contract with Agip too), I probably would have been out of business. It was a do-or-die situation.

I knew the Agip exec knew my story from Phillips, but just as he was getting ready to end our meeting, I brought out another point.

"What will it cost you to mobilize your equipment? What's it going to cost you to charge your bell system with helium and to have your equipment sent from Italy to Singapore?"

He admitted that he had not thought about that.

I had a ballpark figure on what it would cost them not to keep my equipment on the rig, and I told him the number. Furthermore, I said my personnel would not require any crew changes. I had calculated how much I would save him by not having to charge the bell system with helium, pay for flights for employees, and so on. I finished by saying, "I'll cut my contract price by 30 percent."

Now he was upset because I handed him the paperwork and the bid in writing, which meant he would have to show his superiors the offer. It was not going to be easy anymore. Phillips had some say in this; as a partner, they bore half the cost.

Before I left his office, I still tried to get him on my side as much as possible, explaining that if I did not get this contract, it could put me out of business, and then I would never have the opportunity to work for the Italians who I was looking forward to working with. It would have been a big disappointment.

He looked me straight in the eye, and I could tell that he liked me as a person. We were making a good connection, businesswise and personally.

"All right. Get back with me in two days," he said.

I said that I would.

The next day, I went back to his office.

"I said two days," he reminded me.

"Yes, I know, but my life is on hold right now, and I could not stand to worry about not getting this contract."

"What makes you think you even have a chance?"

I replied, "I think my proposal speaks for itself."

We both laughed.

"Come back tomorrow," he said.

I came back the next day, and the day after, and the day after that.

Finally, five days after our initial meeting, I walked into his office.

He looked at me and smiled. "You have a contract," he said. "Sign it, and get out of here."

Once again, we both laughed.

I could tell he had gone to bat for me. Boy, did I celebrate! I stayed in Italy another whole week.

I had more fun with the Italians than I thought I could ever have. The managers and powers-that-be at Agip became very good friends of mine, and we would have a lot of great adventures together.

But, best of all, I had saved Broman International. I was ready for my next moon pool: deep-water diving off the coast of Singapore.

Adventures in Singapore—Southeast Asia (1971)

I flew from Italy to Singapore, talked to Phillips, thanked them for their support, signed my two-year contract, got my crews lined up, and everything was a go. The crews would stay on the rig for the entire job, just as I'd promised Agip they would. We had some tough dives, but we made good on all of them.

My crews loved working with the Italians, and so did I. Talk about partying—the Italians knew how! And did we ever party, with beautiful, exotic Asian women from Singapore, Kuala Lumpur, and all over Southeast Asia.

It wasn't all fun and games, though. I learned a lot about business too. It was in Singapore that some guys at another service company taught me how to get an exclusive contract with the Indonesian government. It took political power; we had to deal with the military and the government officials. These guys I got to know worked for a well-known service company headquartered in Houston, Texas. I got to be good friends with some of them, and they set me up to get contracts for all the deep-water diving on all offshore oil rigs in Indonesia. That meant platform work also.

I was invited to meet with the people involved, and the meeting was to be at the Ming Court Hotel in Singapore, in one of the penthouse suites. The salesman for the service company that set it up included me. When I arrived, my friends greeted me at the door to the penthouse, and I walked into the room.

There were already a few Indonesian generals and high-ranking dignitaries there. And many beauties (Asian women and some Europeans too) filled the room as well. Against the wall there were complete sets of golf clubs, all the best quality, lined up for the taking. These were just some of the gifts given away at these sales meeting.

I had my brochures and letters of recommendation, all the things you normally use to sell contracts and get the work. In Southeast Asia and other similar types of foreign countries, however, that wasn't the way it was done. That day was quite an education indeed.

Everything I learned about how to get contracts in foreign countries I credit to my Texas friends.

* * * * * *

Doing business in Southeast Asia was an ongoing education. I had lived and worked in this part of the world a few years prior while in New Guinea, but it was very different as the owner of the company. The learning process was a challenge, and it was exciting in a way that was different from diving. Diving was my great passion, but I really enjoyed being an entrepreneur, especially in the early years of ownership.

Fortunately for me, I had no learning curve with deep-water diving. That work is pretty much the same in every location. The surfaces of places are where the greatest differences lie; depths are always pretty much the same. When we arrived in Singapore straight from Mozambique, Agip (the Italian oil company) was to take the rig with Phillips for one well, which, as I've mentioned, was only three months' work. It was a fairly deep project as far as water depth went: minimum 250 feet, and possibly as deep as 300 feet or more.

Singapore was very exotic. I had rooms at the Shangri-La, a gorgeous hotel, even though it was not quite complete (the top stories weren't finished, so it was open). My Italian friends and I had many wild times together at the Shangri-La.

The next good friend I made in Singapore was Glenn Wood of Straits Transportation. He was big at the prestigious American Club and very politically connected in Singapore. In addition to becoming my very good friend, Glenn was my agent for Broman International in Southeast Asia. He set me up with an Indian from Bombay, and we formed a partnership called Sigmal: he would supply me with all the cottage goods out of India (shirts, pants, jewelry, pens, pipes). It was incredible! Glenn would eventually become my agent for several other businesses. He was great to deal with.

The oil companies sort of ignored Glenn at first, but I didn't. I could tell right away that he was "the man" in Singapore. I was right, and that was one of the best connections I ever made. He did a lot of favors for me, had a lot of political influence and important contacts, and I valued him. I opened offices in Singapore through my business contacts with Glenn, and he acted as my agent.

One of the first things Glenn introduced me to was Change Alley, a cluster of shops in the financial district of Raffles Place in the downtown area of Singapore. It was managed by the Change Alley Merchants Association. I frequented this area in the days when visitors and seafarers arrived at the waterfront and made their way to Raffles Place through the alley.

Prior to the 1970s, Change Alley was not a famous tourist spot, just a recognized meeting place for European buyers and Asian brokers. There were only a few stalls then, so it was easy to walk through from Collier Quay to Raffles Place (unlike decades later when tourists had to push and shove their way through a narrow, congested space in between the stalls). Named after the Change Alley of London, where stockbrokers always congregated, the Singapore version became renowned in its own right.

But even in 1971, bargain-hunting servicemen and tourists knew about Change Alley. Visitors and seafarers arriving at the waterfront would make their way from the seafront at Collier Quay to the commercial center, Raffles Place, through this alley. The mixture of cramped and dingy shops and stalls offered everything from clothes, batik cloth, bags, briefcases, watches, toys, tape recorders, radios, jewelry, fishing accessories, handicrafts, and all kinds of souvenirs. The goods could be bargained for, and part of the attraction of Change Alley was the opportunity to practice this interactive exchange. The shopkeepers conducted business in various languages, including "broken" forms of English, French, German, Italian, and Russian. The moneychangers, many of them Indian Muslims, ran their businesses within their own little retail shops. There were also many illegal moneychangers stationed at both entrances of the alley, touting their currencies at "bargainable exchange rates."

Change Alley was famous for hackers (not the computer kind of the twenty-first century), a place where no European white entrepreneurs would go to do business. I was the sole exception. I put up six thousand dollars, and Glenn gathered the goods together and sent them to Australia. They sat in the customs warehouse, awaiting my return to Darwin. Glenn and I also set up a lobster-fishing business. We had Filipino divers who would pick the lobsters, and we bought a snap freezer boat that we put the lobsters into, sending them by airfreight to Houston, Texas.

After two incidents, I decided to abandon the lobster-fishing business, sell the snap freezer boat, get my supervisor back to Darwin, and let the Filipino divers go. The first incident involved some Indonesian pirates who chased us, boarded our boat, and took all our payroll, cash, and food. The second incident involved the Indonesian navy, which boarded our boat on the high seas, threatened to confiscate and impound the boat and take it to Jakarta, all because they said our paperwork was not in order. Glenn Wood had been tracking us, and he used all his political weight, contacting the powers that be, who in turn contacted the Indonesian navy, and they let us go.

So that's the long version of how I opened (and closed) Sigmal Company: a lobster-fishing business and an Indian clothes franchise for all of Southeast Asia and Australia. I had an office in Change Alley, Singapore. I had all the cottage goods out of Bombay and an Indian partner to whom I gave three thousand dollars for my half of the inventory.

All thanks to the savvy business acumen of my good friend and agent, Glenn Wood.

As you can see, I packed a lot of adventure into my three months in Singapore. That contract's time flew by. Before I knew it, it was time to head for Darwin, Northern Territory, Australia, and my next big moon pool.

Broman International Operations Base—Darwin, Northern Territory, Australia (1972)

This was one hell of a moon pool I had just dived into, one of the biggest changes that I have ever experienced in my entire life. I had been raised to be an entrepreneur; the vehicle for my entrepreneurship was deep-sea diving. When I started Broman International, I had already been a successful deep-water diver for several years. I had now owned and run the company for a little over two years, having successfully completed my contract with Phillips Oil in Mozambique, Africa. I had then successfully managed to get Agip Oil to sign me on for three months in Singapore (even though they owned their own diving company) and successfully completed that contract too. (Actually, that three-month stint was a joint venture between Phillips and Agip, but my next two-year contract with Phillips had been contingent upon getting the contract with Agip.)

So now that the Singapore operation was over, I was about to start a new two-year contract with Phillips in Darwin, Northern Territory, Australia. I left Singapore, bound for our base of operations in Darwin. All these operations (Mozambique, Singapore, Australia) were on the *Glomar Conception,* the state-of-the-art drillship that had become home to me. I'd worked off that rig since 1968 in Port Moresby, and I loved it. I was so excited about the prospect of living and working in Australia. The time I'd spent there already had been glorious and unforgettable—Sydney, Perth, Fremantle—I couldn't wait to see what Darwin was like.

My excitement could not have been more well-deserved! Darwin was made for me. Its population at that time was approximately thirty thousand, but the people were spread out in the outback and along the beaches. And what beaches! The tides were twenty feet, sometimes even higher. The whole place had a Wild West atmosphere—crocodile hunters, water buffalo hunters, treasure hunters. In addition, there were hippies traveling the world (you'll remember from my descriptions in part II that hippies loved Australia and still do). Best of all were the beautiful, suntanned sheilas who came up from Sydney and Melbourne, looking for adventure and excitement. These Aussie girls were sexy and fun, and they could drink beer as well as any of the blokes could.

This was a great time for me; I was able to enjoy some of the success of Broman International, even though I still had to deal with the responsibility of owning a deep-water diving company. Not that I didn't always have a good time, whether I was working for someone else or running my own show. But it was nice to have fun and enjoy myself while simultaneously knowing that my company was doing so well. I'll describe more of Broman International's operations in Darwin later. For now, back to Darwin itself.

Though it is the capital of the Northern Territory, Darwin is not a city, per se, even by Australian standards. It's too laid back, too small, too friendly. All that was exactly what made it perfect for me. I had so much fun living and working there.

Darwin was the first place I lived in Australia. I'd visited other places and enjoyed my all-too-brief stays there, but my true introduction to Oz (as Aussies call their homeland) was Darwin and the Northern Territory. Did I say how much I loved it there? Yes, of course I did. I just can't emphasize it enough. Australia is my favorite place in the world and always will be.

Darwin is situated on a peninsula, giving it a cool and fun, tropical lifestyle. That worked for me—remember, if you can't grow a coconut on it, I don't want to be there! But, as I learned while living in New Guinea, living in the tropics means not just warm, pleasant weather in the so-called winter but also extreme heat, humidity, and torrential rain in the summer. Because Australia is in the southern hemisphere, the seasons are flipped from what we're used to north of the equator. Their summer is our winter, and vice versa. This meant that the rainy season (summer) in Australia was from November to March. As I've mentioned, these months of monsoonal rains are called simply "the wet" in Oz. (You'll recall several memorable "wets" from parts I and II, including my nearly drowning in the flooded Cyanide Creek that destroyed my Land Cruiser.) There's no escaping the rain during the wet; water and wind are everywhere.

Nevertheless, Darwin's attractions abound. The enclosed marina with a lock immediately intrigued me. You might ask, as I did, why do they have a marina with a lock in Darwin? The answer is very simple: the tidal range is over twenty feet. For a deep-sea diver, the water alone was a source of excitement. You can't even imagine.

Images of Darwin and the time I spent there come to mind again and again. The inimitable outback, with its dry and wild landscape, east of Darwin. Anthills twenty feet high. A pack of dingoes working over road kill with a glorious sunset in the background. The complete melody sung by a bird deep in the bush, rousing you from a sound sleep to wonder if it knew more about music than human composers. All my memories of Darwin are equally indelible.

Most everybody (men, women, and children) participated in sports; that was the Aussie way. They had no TV in Darwin in the early seventies. Instead, they went to drive-in movies, which were always family affairs.

They brought their "barbies" (barbecues) and lounge chairs, visited with one another, and it was just wonderful.

I lived in a suburb of Darwin called Nightcliff, right on the beach. Nothing fancy, but very nice and perfect for me. It was on the edge of the outback, and I had an incredible view of the ocean with its twenty-foot-plus tides and the scenery up and down the coast.

I bought a Yamaha 250 dirt bike, and I would ride along the coast and in the interior bush, looking for crocs and water buffalo and wild boar. I also owned a Mini Moke (made by Morris, the same company that made the Mini Minor version of the Mini Cooper). It was the same kind of car as the one I had in Port Moresby.

I loved exploring Darwin and its environs. Usually, I couldn't stand cities (still can't). If you are like me and prefer to have a simple beer in a simple pub where you can easily strike up a regular conversation with down-to-earth people, even though you've never met them before, then you'll like Darwin as much as I do. It's a gateway to the Australian outback, as well as to Southeast Asia and the South Pacific, from its position in the Northern Territory on the Timor Sea.

The city proper occupies a low bluff overlooking Darwin Harbor, flanked by Frances Bay to the east and Cullen Bay to the west. The remainder of the city is flat and low-lying, and coastal areas are home to extensive beaches and excellent fishing. Darwin has always been prone to cyclone activity during the wet season, during which time monsoonal downpours and spectacular lightning shows are daily occurrences. During the dry season, sunshine, blue skies, and gentle sea breezes abound. Paradise! The harbor is charming and picturesque, and the city is very easy to get around, which is part of what makes it such a fun place. Everything in Darwin is only twenty minutes away from everything else.

The city's miles of wide, unpolluted beaches include the Casuarina Beach and well-know Mindil Beach (home of the Mindil Beach markets). Darwin City Council has designated an area of Casuarina Beach as a free beach, which has long offered a designated nudist beach area. Swimming in the sea during the months of October to May should always be avoided, though, because of the presence of deadly box jellyfish, known locally as "stingers." (You'll remember my description of them in part II.)

Saltwater crocodiles, very common in all waterways surrounding Darwin, have even occasionally been found swimming in Darwin Harbor and on local beaches. They are notorious man-eaters, as I've mentioned previously. Despite the dangerous natural predators, fishing has always been a primary recreation of Darwin locals, as well as tourists. Visitors from around the world flock to Darwin, aiming to catch the prized barramundi, an iconic fish for the region. (This is the same fish that saved the life of my friend Wyatt [in part I] when the croc he was face to face with picked the barramundi instead of him!)

Truly, Darwin was, is, and always will be unique—charming city, picturesque harbor, magnificent beaches, and gloriously untamed surrounding wild (outback). Plus, its demography is as fascinating as its geography. Nearly a quarter of Darwin's residents are of aboriginal or Torres Strait Islander descent. Another big percentage of the population has immigrated from South and East Asia. A total of seventy-five nationalities are represented in the city of Darwin. Any way I describe it, you can see that it was a fascinating and fabulous place to live and work.

Now that you understand why Darwin was an ideal place for me personally, let me explain why it was also ideal for Broman International in terms of business. Darwin's proximity to Southeast Asia makes it an important Australian gateway to countries like Indonesia and East Timor. Darwin is closer to the capitals of five other countries than it is to Canberra, the capital of Australia. It is 1,949 miles from Canberra, but it is just 408 miles from Dili (East Timor), 1,130 miles from Port Moresby (Papua, New Guinea), 1,678 miles from Jakarta (Indonesia), 1,620 miles from Bandar Seri Begawan (Brunei), and 1,396 miles from Melekeok (Palau). Even Malaysia and Singapore are only slightly farther away (2,082 miles). Manila (Philippines) is just 1,992 miles away, and Honiara (Solomon Islands) is just 1,987 miles away. Closest of all is probably Ambon, Indonesia, which is only 547 miles from Darwin.

In addition to its close proximity to so much of Southeast Asia and the South Pacific, Darwin was a key port within Australia itself. Though quite a distance from Canberra and other major cities, Darwin was by no means isolated, even though the Northern Territory was vastly different from the South. The Stuart Highway, starting in Darwin and ending at Port Augusta in South Australia, offered ready access between cities.

All this was essential to the continued success of Broman International. Our reputation was already world-renowned by this time. People like Red Adair and his second in command, Cotton—both industry legends—considered us a first-class deep-water diving company. The guys who put out the oilfield fires on land and offshore held us in the highest regard. This included Global Marine, Pomeroy-Gerwick-Steers, Phillips Oil Company, Agip Oil Company, Sunray Oil Company, Union Oil Company, Gulf Oil Company, Esso, and BP, to name just a few.

I was in the most secure position I had ever been in with my company: big money, big contracts, no worries, well-disciplined and well-trained crews—the best in the business, handpicked and trained by me. Broman International earned a top rating from Lloyds of London; we never had an injury or death, and that was a big accomplishment in our line of work. In fact, it was remarkable. The truth was, though, I was bored. I needed challenges in order to thrive; I couldn't be happy without facing and overcoming the hurdles that stood in my way. That was why I loved and excelled at diving in the first place.

It would be time for a new moon pool soon, but I enjoyed just relishing my success for a while longer.

Life in Darwin (1972)

In case you're wondering why I haven't yet described meeting a beautiful woman in Darwin, I'm getting to that too. It didn't actually take me very long in real time; I just wanted to describe the landscape, climate, culture, etc., before I got into my romantic adventures.

My office in Darwin was in a wood duplex building, with Hertz next door. I had been flirting with the Hertz rent-a-car girl, trying to date this little beauty. I was waiting for a call from her to see if we were going to go out. She was such a cute Aussie girl—blonde, blue-eyed, very classy.

A guy walked into my office just then. (My friend Wyatt, whom I've described many times already.) He and I laughed and talked for a bit, and we just clicked.

Pulling a joint out of his pocket, he asked, "Have you ever smoked pot?"

"Yeah, once. I was about sixteen," I said.

"Want to try it again?"

I smiled, and so he lit it up, and we smoked it together.

I was ready for my friendship with him—more than ready—but it was not the right moment at that time. The seed had been planted, and, as I said, I was bored. I owned a successful international diving company, but I wanted to smoke pot, chase women, and play. And I also wanted to change the world. In short, I wanted to be a hippie. That joint reminded me of the time I had spent in San Francisco. So did the things he talked about. I could tell that he was sincere about his beliefs, and he could see that I was a potential "convert," that I was ready to leave the establishment. What he really didn't know was that I have never been in the establishment. Not really. Given my prior experiences with the hippie counterculture, I was probably more what could be called a revert than a convert.

We talked for a while longer, and then he left. I knew it wouldn't be long before we met again.

A short time later, the rent-a-car girl called me, and I was ripped. I could barely get out of the chair. I went out to my Mini Moke (it's like a golf cart, but it goes eighty miles per hour), started it up, and headed off to meet her. I was so ripped that I could hardly drive. I pulled over in the bush and passed out until about one or two in the morning. The next day, I apologized to her, and we made new arrangements.

I got in touch with Wyatt and told him what had happened. We laughed and laughed. From that day on, I was a pot smoker.

Pot taught me some good things and some bad things. The good things were: I learned to look at nature in different way; I learned to relax and not always be so intense; I learned to see the beauty in things, because pot slowed the world down so I could enjoy it; I learned to be a better lover (I was always a good lover, but pot slowed me down some, which made me even better); I learned to have fun being crazy and childlike; I learned to widen my circle of friends (I liked having friends who weren't business associates); and I learned how much I loved to laugh. The bad things were. Hmm … can't remember and don't much care.

I was becoming a hobbit like Bilbo Baggins; I just didn't know it yet.

The Darwin Oilers (1972)

The Darwin Oilers was a hardball baseball team that I started. As I've said, things were almost too good for me at that time. I was bored, and I needed some excitement. Some Americans who were traveling the world sought me out to put up the money for this team. Our first game was soon scheduled, playing opposite the Aussie team in last place.

That was the start of one of the biggest changes in my life. There were two local hardball leagues, with five to six teams in each league, and they were thrilled that an American team was going to field a team against the Aussies. This was right up their alley. Aussies are very competitive but have incomparable sportsmanship. They loved the game and everybody in the league.

The day before the game arrived, and the Americans who were to play for me were nowhere to be seen. My attempts to reach them by phone were to no avail. The rumor was that they had gone to Singapore. This forced me to look for a team on the same day that the game was to take place. I had no choice, so I did it. I got a hold of all the oil companies and service company managers, asking them to help me scrounge up a team. I had the equipment and the uniforms but no players.

Long story short, I was able to get together a group ranging in age from fourteen to sixty. That was the starting lineup of the Darwin Oilers' first game. Of course, all the Australians showed up to watch the Americans (or "Yanks," as they always called us, and still do) play the all-American game. The game had been advertised on local radio and in the newspapers, and there was a good turnout.

The Darwin Oilers were ready to play, that was for sure. The caliber of the players was another story. We were a motley crew assembled at a moment's notice. We had no pitcher, so I pitched. That was brutally embarrassing. I had not played baseball in years, and the rest of the team was in pretty much the same shape. (Actually, the best equipped to play among us was probably the fourteen-year-old kid!) I could not quite remember how to come off the mound and not balk the batter. I balked the first five batters.

The Aussies knew all the rules and were sticklers for following them. This game was like a comedy routine to them. They couldn't get over how Americans were botching our own national pastime. After nine embarrassing innings, the score was 17 to 1. I had knocked in a run that our guy had gotten on base by a walk. Of course, the town was jubilant—their team had beat the Americans at hardball baseball. It was on radio and in the newspapers, and I really did not enjoy the embarrassment. Truth to tell, I was pissed about those phonies who'd promised to play and then never showed up.

Soon afterward, some new prospects arrived to interview for the team. My prayers were answered when a tall (six-feet-two), lanky, twenty-two-year-old American came to our practice to see if he could try out for the team. He had hair down to his shoulders that he'd pulled back in a ponytail, had a full beard, and he wore an earring, hiking boots, and shorts. The guy was a hippie! And he wanted to play for the most redneck team you could imagine: the Darwin Oilers.

I asked him, "What do you do? What position do you play?"

He said, "Well, I can play outfield and infield, and I can pitch."

We could certainly use a pitcher! And I told him so.

I had a new catcher, a Cajun from Louisiana who had played semipro ball. He worked for Global Marine.

I said to the hippie, "Okay! Show us what you can do." I pointed to the catcher, gave the hippie a baseball, and stepped back.

That hippie threw a really great fastball, and the catcher threw it back. He threw a curveball, and then he threw a knuckle ball—it was beautiful, the best knuckle ball I have ever seen. I knew we had our pitcher.

If I could add just a few more good players, I knew we would have a chance to redeem ourselves and beat the Aussies. We practiced all week. We were to play against one of the mediocre teams, better than the last-place team but not great.

Based on our last performance, the local radio and newspapers all advertised that the Darwin Oilers were going to get whipped all over the field. All the Aussies should come to watch their team beat the Yanks at their own game. The Aussies never did it in a mean-spirited way, mind you. It was all in good fun. It was irritating because there was too much truth to it.

I was still livid about the guys who had promised to play in that first game but who never showed. I really did not know what to do about the upcoming game. I told the team we would practice every day, and I banked everything on our new pitcher and catcher, hoping they'd be as good on game day as they were during practice.

Game day finally arrived. We took our infield practice, and we looked pretty good. I invited the girl from Hertz to come and cheer for us. She did; she was so cute and classy, sexy and really built. I was looking forward to the after game, but I owed it to my team to focus on the game at hand. We had a lot riding on this game, and I did not want to be the butt of Aussie jokes indefinitely.

As captain, coach, and founder of the team, I made all the decisions. I also played second base, which never would have happened in the States because lefties never play second base. It had always been my dream to play second base, and who could argue with the captain/coach/founder? (Yup, it's all about being in control. Diving. Baseball. Everything. By the way, I realize I never mentioned being left-handed before now, but I am. It doesn't matter much in diving, but in baseball it's a pretty big deal, as anyone who's ever played will surely agree.)

I asked the league officials if we could warm up to music. My preference was Creedence Clearwater Revival's "Proud Mary." They still always played "Take Me Out to the Ballgame" to start the game. I loved that song, but this was just for our warm-up and to get the crowd going. The league officials okayed my request, so we warmed up to "Proud Mary."

I was so determined to win, I hit like I never thought I could. I never struck out, and I was the best hitter on the team. Ended up with a 578 average for the season, the best in our league. And won the batting championship.

Our hippie pitcher was incredible. And now I'll tell you who it was: Wyatt. (I wanted to keep it a bit of a surprise.) He was amazing. The Aussies could not hit his fastball or his knuckle ball. We won that game with no problem. It was almost a shutout because of him.

But I was the hitter. You need runs, after all, no matter how great your pitcher is.

That was the start of the Darwin Oilers' undefeated season. After our one loss, we went on to glory. My pitcher (Wyatt) and I became friends—lifelong, in fact, as I've already described.

My life as a baseball team captain, coach, and founder was just beginning.

The Aussies Show Up to Watch the Yanks Lose ... Um, Win ... in Darwin (1972)

When I was a kid, I had wanted to be a professional baseball player; it was my dream. I used to carry my glove on my belt! So owning the team was a dream come true in one way. But the truth was that I had a twofold reason for staring the team in Darwin: childhood dream come true and good business decision. At that time, I still had the deep-water diving contract on the *Glomar Conception* (with Phillips Oil). Several other oil companies were operating in the area (Australia and Southeast Asia), all on different ships. I was always advertising and wanting to take over contracts. I quickly saw that owning a baseball team was a great business tool. The locals loved it, the oil companies loved it, and I loved it. It was win-win-win; that's one more win than the standard expression.

I knew I couldn't lose. Everyone loved the game. All we had to do was play, and we did. We packed them in. I soon had other oil companies involved. They would telex their main offices in the States and give them the rundown on the game. Before long, we were famous: the Darwin Oilers. (In case, you're wondering, yes, I came up with the name for the team.)

Needless to say, once I won the batting championship that year in our league and the Darwin Oilers were undefeated for the rest of the year, the Aussies stopped laughing at us. The radio stations and newspapers stopped advertising for Aussies to come watch the Yanks lose.

Soon afterward, the Aussies started a night baseball league, and they split us Americans up into different teams. I played for a team called the Nightcliff. They were the champions in the other league. Our first game was a big deal in Darwin: night baseball with the Americans playing on Aussie teams. The Oilers' catcher was interviewed by the radio station and newspaper, and his night team was playing against mine, so they asked him if he thought I would get a hit off his new protégé Aussie pitcher. He predicted that I would not get a hit, even though I had already won the batting championship! He had worked with this pitcher, so that was big news in Darwin.

Well, the stands were packed for that game. The locals enjoyed watching baseball, especially when the Americans played. They had a brand-new ball field set up.

I was batting third. I came up to the plate, with cheers and applause all around. The Aussies were so cool; I loved them. They wanted to see what I could do against this pitcher, but they welcomed me first.

The first pitch was faster than any other pitcher had pitched in the league before. The second pitch was fast but a little high. The third pitch came right down the middle, a scorching fastball. I took a nice, easy swing. That crack of wood on leather resounded through the ballpark. I hit it high and long out of the park, straight over the centerfield fence, and by a quite a lot too. I had never hit a ball that far before, but he was fast, and I just made a good swing. Every kid wishes and dreams of being a hero, of hitting a ball like that. It was incredible. That was my last baseball game, and what a way to go! I trotted the bases (I was really pretty slow, to be honest). I couldn't get enough of the cheers and applause.

As I've hinted, another moon pool had already formed. I was about to make some of the biggest changes in my life, but I didn't know it yet. Within two years' time, I would sell Broman International, drop out of the rat race, and move to my dream home—the paradise cove at Cape Tribulation. We've already dived through the moon pool that resulted. Now let's get ready for the one that caused it. I'll relate everything that preceded my selling my company (and all the reasons why I felt I had no choice), but first I want to share some more of my adventures in Darwin.

Glenda, My Black-Haired Beauty (1972)

Glenda was a black-haired beauty from Melbourne. She was twenty-one when I met her, hired by one of my new friends, the manager for Gulf Oil out of Darwin.

Sixty days prior to becoming the office manager of Gulf Oil, my friend had been the janitor at the Darwin Hotel. Believe it or not, that's the way it was in those days; college graduates went hitchhiking around the world, doing odd jobs, with money in the bank from their parents or a trust fund. He had a degree in accounting. And a good line of bullshit. But he was fun. Sammy Roach was his name.

One day, he called me up and said this sheila he had hired was coming in from Melbourne. Would I pick her up? Before I answered, I asked what she looked like. (Of course!)

"She's very pretty," he assured me. "A sexy Italian girl."

Needless to say, I agreed to pick her up.

He made a bet with me that I couldn't win her over and start an affair with her.

I went to the airport to pick her up as planned. And I was quite happy to see that she was all he had said she was—and more. Glenda was beautiful, a black-haired Italian Aussie girl dressed to the nines. She had the nicest body and a great personality. I liked her immediately.

I checked her into the Darwin Hotel, and all of a sudden she got very homesick. I took her to my favorite restaurant and pub, and we sat and talked until closing.

I could tell she was truly feeling the loneliness that fills the homesick—that scary, empty feeling. I always get homesick for the last place that I was, wherever it was. Time takes care of it, but I still empathized with what she was going through.

She wanted me to stay the night with her, not for sex but just to ease her loneliness. So I did. Things got intense pretty quickly. We clung to each other, and I knew she wanted me. She was so passionate. Sweet Glenda. I loved the way she smelled, a beautiful, musky woman.

We started to have sex every night from that night on. (Yes, I won the bet with my friend, and I collected. But getting Glenda was even better.)

It was always sweet and passionate with her. One night, we parked on the beach next to a beautiful tree. We got out of the car, sat on the beach, and looked out at the ocean. It was beautiful in the way a Darwin night could be, with a full moon and a warm, tropical breeze. We started making out in the car, and then we took off our clothes, and I laid her on the fender. We started to make love; we were so into each other, just floating.

I looked down, and beneath the tree about a foot away from us was an aborigine. He was so close he could reach out and touch us if he wanted to. His wiry, white hair stood out against his dark skin, and his eyes were illuminated by the moonlight. He just stared at us, watching us make love, a big, white, toothy grin filling his face. He was as quiet as the night itself.

Glenda followed my gaze, and she saw him too. She was on the verge of panic and about to scream, but I gently put my hand over her mouth. Ever so quietly, I opened the car door and slid her into the front seat, giving her the shush sign. I winked at the old black man, got in the car, and drove off slowly. Once we were back on the road, Glenda and I both burst out laughing.

We stopped on the beach farther on, and I brought my swag out of the boot (that's what Aussies call the trunk), laid it out, and led her out of the car. She was still naked. Oh, how I loved the tropics! Warm and romantic all the time.

I was having my fun, but I kept thinking about my conversation with Wyatt more and more. I could feel a new moon pool forming, but I couldn't see into its clear depths yet. The waves were there, beckoning me, but it was still murky. It would be clear before too long. Deep within me, I was ready to dive in—I just wasn't yet sure exactly what it was that I was diving into. Time would tell. I let the waters gather, and I waited for the moment to jump. That moment came in a singular burst of intuitive knowing. I had felt it on every dive, hundreds of times already. I would know it when it arrived again.

Broman International, Biggest Deep-Water Diving Company in Australia and Southeast Asia (1973)

The year 1973 was the greatest in the history of Broman International. I was now the largest deep-water diving contractor in that part of the world, with offices in Singapore; Johannesburg, South Africa; Perth, Australia; and Darwin, Australia. I also had offices in Long Beach, California, and Lafayette, Louisiana.

The *Glomar Conception* moved to Sale, Victoria, the big oil field near the Bass Strait (the site of my extreme dive en route to Port Moresby). I retained the contract, even though it was to work for Esso and BHP, not Phillips Oil. (You'll remember from the start of this section that Bass Strait was and still is some of the roughest water in the world.)

I was also awarded all the other platform work and diving in the Bass Strait.

If you'll recall from part II, Divcon bought International Divers, so they had all those contracts. They had just bought all new equipment and put their old equipment up for sale in a warehouse in Sydney, with instructions not to sell it to me.

Well, I hired an agent and attorney to make an offer on the equipment without disclosing my name, which was entirely legal. They accepted my offer, and I bought the equipment, went to Esso BHP, and bid the diving work. My bid was accepted, I got the work, and I put them out of the Bass Strait. It was brilliant.

In addition, I had a new contract in Cabinda, Africa, for Gulf Oil, and I had a contract on the *Navigator,* another floater (oil rig). The company was poised to expand past diving to become an oil rig provider for the entire offshore field internationally.

I moved from Darwin to Sale in order to be closer to the Bass Strait. The property was 250 acres, with the oldest house in Sale, Victoria, beautiful and full of antiques. The house had many huge rooms, seven fireplaces, and a horse barn. A river ran in back of the house, and there was the most beautiful rose garden I have ever seen, even to this day. I will never forget seeing that house and grounds for the first time, especially the rose garden. I drove up to the house and got out of the car, and my dog, Dinkum, followed me. (He was a Queensland blue heeler, the ultimate cattle dog. I'd gotten him as a pup from a cattle station in Darwin. These dogs grab the cow or steer by the heel, just above the hoof, bite the tendon to stop the animal from moving, and then twist until the animal falls to the ground. The dogs stand guard until the drovers come to tie up the cattle and brand them. Australian cattle dogs are sometimes generically referred to as "heelers," and Aussie herdsmen are called "jackaroos.")

It was while I was living in Sale and running my operation off the Bass Strait that my friendship with Wyatt deepened. I started hanging around with him and his friends in Melbourne (you'll remember my description of Charlie Dean in part II) and also at their commune, Rosebud Farm, in Kuranda, North Queensland. We had lots of adventures in Melbourne. I once almost drowned in the waves off Melbourne because of a bad acid trip (you'll remember my experiences with LSD from part II also). But the psychedelic mushrooms we sampled in Melbourne were a much better experience.

I briefly mentioned this episode with mushrooms in part II. Now I'll tell you the longer version. The band Chicago was putting on a concert in Melbourne. I got tickets and sent someone to Wyatt's in North Queensland to bring back some mushrooms. (Rosebud Farm's psychedelic mushrooms were legendary.)

We were hanging out inside my hippie van, waiting for the show to start. We took the mushrooms, smoked a joint to take the edge off, and waited for the effects to kick in. I really didn't feel anything, and I told that to my friend Hank, the guy who'd picked up the mushrooms.

"Give it some time, man," he said, laughing in his typical laid-back way.

We got out of the van and went inside the concert venue, which was about the size of a high-school auditorium. Our seats were fantastic: about twelve rows back from the stage. We were right in the middle of the action, and the place was packed, mostly loaded with Aussie girls who loved watching American musicians play.

Anyway, there we were, looking around at the sheilas and the other people attending the concert, all of us waiting for the band to come out. It was very cool.

Just as the band came onstage, I had the most incredible, exciting sensations I have ever experienced. The guys in the band became so vivid— bright colors, sharp outlines, dimensions that were beyond what I had ever seen, almost like an old Technicolor movie with goofy 3-D special effects. The sound was phenomenal, with the horns and guitars and vocals more incredible than anything I had ever heard. Don't get me wrong, Chicago is a great band, very political (which I enjoyed), and they were brilliant at that concert. But what I was experiencing was not the band's considerable talent. The mushrooms had kicked in.

I started going crazy, tripping all over, but not in bad way. I was in another dimension, partying with this giant, boogying in another world.

Mark's voice came from what felt like very far away. "Calm down, Jim."

It sounded garbled; I could barely make out the words, much less understand them. Then we both just started laughing. What an amazing experience! Mushrooms were the greatest thing ever.

At some point, one of the Chicago band members asked the Australian audience, "Do you guys party?"

Up to that point, the Aussies were just sitting in their seats. But after that, they started partying big time. Aussies love their fun!

After the concert, we left and headed back to my van. The windows were iced over. We got inside, lit up a joint, and I started the engine, driving through Melbourne with the windows frosted over.

We laughed all the way. It was a major trip, to say the least—and in more ways than one.

The most memorable concert I went to, aside from Chicago, was the Rolling Stones show at the Kuyong Tennis Courts. They were superb; I took my whole company to see that concert. What an event.

But it was the mushrooms and the pot that deeply affected me, more so than the music. Don't get me wrong, I loved the music. But the drugs were opening my eyes, heightening my awareness, making me realize that there was more to life than money and success. More to life than diving. That was a big realization; I had always lived to dive (and to love women, but with my heightened awareness, love was even better than before).

Mushrooms, even though I tried them only twice in my life, were made for me just like Australia was. I wanted more than what I had—I craved it—and as that yearning became ever more apparent to me, it became harder and harder not to answer it. My next moon pool was ready for me. The water was clearing. It was just a question of my discerning that perfect moment when I would say my prayer, steel myself, and jump into the deep.

The *Navigator*—Bass Strait, Australia (1973)

I got a bit sidetracked telling you all about my house in Sale, the concerts, and the magic mushrooms. There was a lot more to the story of my winning the *Navigator* contract, so let's get back to that.

The first item of business was that I needed a new diving bell system. Of course, there were none available, so I decided to build one. I had to meet with some Englishmen who ran Vidor Engineering, a big manufacturing firm in Newcastle that could build the spheres for the bell and decompression chamber. I was having some cash-flow issues at the time because I was temporarily in between projects, but I did have a signed contract with the oil company (Gulf). The guys at Vidor were willing to take a chance on me, carrying me for a few payments until the operation started to pay. They knew I was a good risk; plus, it was exciting for them to build a deep-water diving bell.

As it turned out, we had a blast working together. We got along famously and genuinely liked one another. They drove Bentleys, drank scotch, wore suits, and loved to have fun. How could we not get along?

Fun aside, there was a lot riding on this diving bell system. If not designed and fabricated correctly, it could be a disaster. Let me explain what the system is. Diving bells are dangling chambers hung under their support vessels and connected by cable and air lines. In 1973, diving bells were the acknowledged workhorses of the industry (and they still are, for the most part), with good reason: Divers can work outside a bell longer—more than twice as long as divers from a submersible—because heat and the breathing mixture (air or helium/air mix) come down through an umbilical from the ship. There is a catch, though, and this is where the potential danger lies. The threat to divers working from bells is that the ship will drift off station sometimes, as a result of being in the water, and that can cause dragging and bouncing of the bell along the ocean bottom. Even worse, it can result in dragging the bell toward something hard enough to sever lifelines. An anchor cable once sheared through a bell's lines, killing the diver. Broman International had a perfect record: no fatalities and no serious injuries. I had no intention of changing that; I liked my top rating with Lloyds of London. Even more important, my crews were like family to me, and I was not about to let my guys get hurt on a rig.

The next problem to overcome was logistics: we needed to have the bell system built and shipped to Darwin in thirty days, and I needed to have someone oversee the building of the bell because I couldn't stay in Newcastle, so far away from my daily operations. I hired a brilliant Austrian, Max, who had immigrated to Australia, and I made him my diving superintendent for the *Navigator* job. He was to run the entire operation, and I also put him in charge of supervising Vidor's construction of the bell system.

When I told him what his duties would be, he said, "That's crazy! We'll never make the deadline." He also reminded me that he had never built a diving bell system and didn't have a clue how to do it.

I said, "Well, just try. I'll be there. You're not building it, you're just supervising Vidor. They shouldn't have a problem with it."

Max wanted the diving superintendent job, and he wanted to work for me, so he agreed. He knew he was agreeing to a lot. I knew it too. Not only did we have to get the diving bell and decompression unit built, we had to take the equipment across Australia. Huge semis trucking these enormous yet delicate pieces of deep-water diving equipment all the way across Oz. But, miracle of miracles, we got it done. The Broman International deep-water diving bell system was designed, built, and delivered to the *Navigator*, all in thirty days' time. That included getting all the parts sent via air freight from Houston, Texas, too! That was the first diving bell ever built in Australia, and it was built by Jim Broman—another first.

Max proved to be an incredible diving superintendent, the best I have ever had. I had never trusted anyone besides myself when it came to work, but he became my go-to guy in no time flat. When given a task, he just got the job done. Kind of like I'd always done. I respected that. As a diver, he was very smart, and he was a powerhouse: about six feet two and built like Arnold Schwarzenegger. He was blond and blue-eyed, loved to work, but also loved music (he played the guitar, sang, and was very talented). I took him to the States to meet my manager in Lafayette, Louisiana.

We had pulled off a miracle but had no time to waste. The diving bell and decompression chamber had to be installed on the *Navigator* as quickly as possible because time is money in the oil business.

The bell and chamber were en route, and the rig was already in the harbor, just waiting. That translates to "losing money"—upwards of a million dollars a day—in the drilling industry. And oil companies do not like to lose money. I had been on the phone calling the small stations along the dirt road going across Australia, asking if they had seen a diving bell system on a semi passing through. Of course, I would then have to explain what a diving bell was. We finally got word that the truck was about two days' worth of driving away, which made us two days late and two million dollars short. A million-dollar-a-day operation shut down, and I was going to be blamed for it.

I lucked out. The rig's first mate was lost, drunk in Sydney and missing from the ship, so the *Navigator* couldn't sail. But the pressure was still on. I had to get that bell system as soon as possible or I risked losing the contract.

Finally, forty-one hours of nonstop driving later, the diving bell system arrived. Now a new big problem arose: how in the hell were we going to get the system out to the harbor and loaded on the rig?

I had searched for a crane big enough to lift the system and reload it. (Remember this was Australia, not an American port with lots of big equipment on hand at all times, so it took some improvising.)

I decided to try using landing craft designed for carrying vehicles (LCM). They had become prominent during World War II, when they were used to land troops or tanks during Allied amphibious assaults. I found three LCMs, tied them together, and mounted a crane in the middle one. Each side could float, so when the crane picked up the bell system with the attached decompression chamber, it was quite risky. But it was the only option I had.

There we were at the rig in the harbor, with three landing barges tied together with a crane in the middle one lifting the bell and chamber as one unit. I was giving the signal to the crane operator. The engine on the crane stalled twice, and the crane operator panicked, landing the bell and chamber backward on the rig. We couldn't pick up the unit now; we had to jack it up on the rig and turn it around, inch by inch.

The oil company wanted us to make a dive as soon as we were on location with the bell. The first dive was close to 287 feet. We couldn't get any air or gas to the bell through the manifold. We tore it down and discovered that soft solder was plugging the lines, blocking all air and gas going through it. What a mess! Needless to say, we couldn't use the bell, so we had to make the dive in hard hat. It was very deep, so I made the dive myself. The oil company was satisfied that we could handle all the necessary dives and also that we would get the problem with the bell fixed. Making that dive sealed the deal for me. It was very risky—new crew, new contract, new ocean, and very deep.

Although it started out dicey, it ended up being a great operation. The crew that worked on the *Navigator* was the best deep-water crew I ever had. I never had to fly out to deal with emergencies; they handled every dive they had to do all on their own. That first hard-hat dive was the only one

I had to make on the *Navigator*. The rest of the crew were Austrians who had immigrated to Australia, just like my superintendent, and they were incredible divers. Once the bell was in place, they made some extremely deep dives (as much as 460 feet!). Actually, when I heard about that dive, I did go to the rig to talk to them, not because they couldn't handle it, but because it was very dangerous to go that deep to make major repairs, and I didn't think it should be done in those depths.

I'd risked my life during extremely deep dives on many occasions, but this was more than even I was willing to do. My relationships with the other oil companies were nothing like the mutual respect I'd had with Phillips. Yet another factor that led me to consider leaving the rat race. With each passing day, I moved ever closer to my ultimate—and inevitable—decision.

Two Beautiful, Sexy Girls in Melbourne (1973)

Broman International was now headquartered in Sale, Victoria, Australia. Our business office was in Melbourne, and our field office was in Sale. This enabled us to handle all the work in the Bass Strait.

I was in Melbourne one day, having a meeting with my accountant. His receptionist was a beauty—nice body, very sexy, great Aussie sense of humor. She was a lot of fun, and we hit it off immediately.

"There's a party happening tonight," she told me. "Would you like to go?"

I accepted her invitation, got her phone number and directions to her flat, and headed to pick her up at the appointed time. I drove my van, which was fixed up with a king-size bed that covered the whole back of the vehicle. The bed could be folded up as seats, but that only happened rarely (if ever!). There was also a sink with running water, a sound system, and a bong.

She loved it! On the way to the party, I stopped the van, asking her if she wanted to check out the back. She laughed and leaned over. We smoked a joint, started making out, and ended up making love in the van and skipping the party altogether.

I dated her for a while after that first night. We really liked each other. It was very nice while it lasted.

It took me a while to get used to Melbourne—and my house in Sale too. They were both so different from the tropical Darwin. But I liked my house and offices.

The Melbourne coastline really is beautiful, and some keen surfers even travel to the beach at dawn to catch waves. By 9:00 a.m., they are at their desks, ready to work. Even nonsurfers love the beaches in Melbourne, which provide a much-valued escape. Phillip Island is not far from Melbourne, and it has become quite famous, with its sandy shores that are home to thousands of fairy penguins, bringing tourists galore every year. Some lovely, isolated beaches and good surf grace the southern coast.

I was in the city of Melbourne one day, and I saw this incredible, young Aussie girl window-shopping. I was hypnotized by her; she was so intriguing and beautiful, in a rich, classy way. No makeup but in fashion with the new natural look popularized by the hippies at that time.

I just followed her from window to window, trying not to be obvious, but she seemed curious. A silent vibe passed between us, and then I got the courage to go up to her and introduce myself.

Her initial reaction was a fear-filled expression.

I quickly said, "Please don't be frightened or offended. I am an American. I want to meet you, but I don't know how."

The fear faded from her lovely face, and she laughed, a small, throaty chuckle. "Well, it looks like you already have," she said.

I told her my name and asked if she would like to talk and have a cup of tea with me. She hesitated, but I put on my most humble boyish face, and she gave in. We stood talking for a few minutes.

"Please let me buy you a cup of coffee or tea," I said.

She seemed wary but also curious, and she agreed to have tea with me.

We went to cool little sidewalk café, and I told her all about my diving company and a little about me. She told me a little bit about herself, and she started to warm toward me. It seemed like she wanted to trust me but resisted.

I asked her to go out with me that night.

She thought about it a while, and then she agreed. So we had a date for that night. Wow!

I went to her house that night and met her mother. It was a beautiful home, and her mother was very nice. We talked and laughed for a while. The daughter was leaving in three days to go walkabout in the hippie movement. I was so glad to have met this beautiful girl, even though she would only be around for a couple of days.

After talking to her mother for a bit longer, we went out to my van, smoked a joint, and started making out. It was nice; we really bonded.

"Would you want to travel with me?" she asked.

She was so sweet, and it was very tempting.

I told her that I would let her know, but, regardless, we would see each other before she left. I then tried to get her to delay her plan, but she wouldn't budge.

I couldn't go with her—I had way too much going on with my company at that time—but it would have been very cool. Such a shame. I often wondered what might have happened if I had gone with her. Truthfully, I was very close to saying yes and going with her; that could have been my next moon pool, and then all the rest might have played out differently, including moving to Cape Trib.

But that didn't happen. She left, and I stayed. We did have a couple of great days and nights together, though. She was an incredible lover for one so young.

Meeting Ali, the Love of My Life— Long Beach, California (1973)

I went to the States on business. Peat, Marwick, Mitchell and Company was doing an audit on my company because I was selling half of it. And I also had to look at diving bell equipment in Houston, Texas. We were always looking at new bell systems to use on jobs we were bidding.

I had some free time in Long Beach, and I was ready to find a woman to date—or several different women, if that was in the cards. I called a friend of mine to see if he could hook me up with someone.

At first, he said no. He always did that; he didn't want me moving in on his harem. But then he thought of this girl who was best friends with a girl he was dating. She was a fox, he said, but she didn't like him; he wished she did, but he knew he never would stand a chance with her. (He was still married but in the middle of a divorce, and the girl he was dating was just eighteen.)

Anyway, I said, "Fix me up, and we'll double."

He agreed that would be cool, so we set the time and date to meet at the newest and coolest bar around, Charlie Brown's in Long Beach.

The night of the date, he called me to say that he couldn't go. His wife had gone ballistic: slit all the upholstery in his new Corvette and threatened him. He just wasn't in the mood to go out. But he did call his girlfriend to tell her that I would meet her and her friend at Charlie Brown's. He'd assured her that they would have a great time with me; I was sort of a celebrity, living in Australia, owning an international company, and working in all parts of the world. They were excited about meeting me.

My friend's date, Kiera, told her live-in boyfriend that she and her girlfriend were going to meet me, and he thought that was cool. Turned out, I knew him too: he'd been one of my fraternity brothers. He had a boat that he albacore fished with, and he spent a lot of time in Mexican waters; that was his love, even when we were kids.

Well, finally, it was time to meet them at Charlie Brown's, so I drove there and went to the bar. I was looking for a drop-dead blonde (that was Kiera, my friend's girl.) I look very international, wearing a cool corduroy coat that I'd bought at the Inn Shop in Sydney. (I bought all my clothes there.) It was summer in Australia, so I was very tan. I looked good: a blond, blue-eyed, suntanned, successful entrepreneur, exuding confidence.

I didn't see any knockout blonde. I went to the men's room, and when I came out, I passed this stunning, black-haired little fox on her way to the ladies' restroom. She was exquisite, in a subtle way, very stylish and with a perfect body. She wore cool glasses, looking like a successful businesswoman. What a good-looking fox.

I returned to the bar, and this time I spotted an incredible blonde with a knockout body. This had to be Kiera. I went up to her and humbly introduced myself. She was blown away, very attracted to me. She could hardly talk. It was cool talking to her for a few minutes. The little, black-haired fox was still in the head, and I kept an eye out for her while Kiera and I talked and laughed.

The little, black-haired fox came back to the bar a minute or two later. She was Kiera's friend; I'd actually been set up to meet the hottest woman I'd seen in a long time. Maybe ever. I couldn't get over it. Not just because she was so stunning but because I knew in that instant that the love of my life had arrived. She felt it too. I almost fainted, and so did she. There was just this incredible, instant connection. It was like nobody was in that bar but her and me. (Kiera, the blonde, was incredible, but she couldn't hold a candle to my little fox. I liked looking at Kiera, but the new woman in my life held all my attention.)

Anyway, there I was in this hip bar, with two gorgeous women, both of them young and very cool. We talked about everything and laughed and laughed. They were very impressed with me, thinking I was so international in my style and personality.

The black-haired, little fox was named Ali. She loved my clothes, and we had a great conversation.

After a couple of drinks, Kiera told me about an old friend of mine who now owned and ran a really successful bar for the college crowd's hangout. So we went over there, and it was wild and so much fun—a great band, lots of draft beer, and high energy. It was so cool to see my old friend again too. He felt the same way.

My friend (the owner) treated us like royalty. I danced with both girls. (Kiera was a real knockout, as I've said, and I have never missed a chance to dance with a beautiful girl). But Ali and I were already falling in love. If she weren't around, I would scheme big time on Kiera, but Ali was there, and I was glad … it was better to be with her than to hit on anyone else. When we slow danced, it was incredible. Her breasts pressed against me, and I felt her nipples. They were so hard, it was incredible. She was so turned on, she was almost trembling. I pressed my hips and gently ground her. We moved with the beat and rhythm of the music, glued to each other, just like in high school at Friday-nighters when I slow danced to doo-wop music. My little fox seemed to be having an orgasm in a smooth and quiet way; I could have them that way too. Very intense, very passionate. I didn't try to kiss her. I could have; she was ready to make out, she was so hot.

Closing time arrived, and I drove the girls back to Charlie Brown's. We got out of my rental car, and I walked them to their car. I didn't try to kiss Ali or Kiera good-bye. I gave them each a polite but friendly hug and told them what a great time I had. I did get Kiera's number, using the pretense of getting in touch with her live-in boyfriend, Cody, my old frat buddy. I got back in my rental car and drove to my motel.

Next day, I called Kiera. We talked for a bit, and then I asked the scoop on Ali. Kiera told me that Ali worked as a clothing buyer in the LA garment district. (That was how they'd become friends, even though Ali was a few years older than Kiera. Kiera worked in an upscale, women's clothing boutique on Rodeo Drive, and she met Ali through her job as a buyer.) Kiera also related that Ali was divorced and originally from the Midwest. The two of them were best friends, so I asked Kiera if she thought Ali would go out with me. I was elated when she told me that Ali was extremely attracted to me, and Kiera thought that if I asked Ali to go out with me, she definitely would.

Kiera gave me Ali's telephone number, I told her to tell Cody I'd catch him later, and we said good-bye.

I waited a day before calling Ali, and when I did, her low, husky, sexy voice just floored me. I hadn't heard it that well in the bar with all the noise. I couldn't believe how sexy she was. We talked for a while, and I asked her out on a date. She accepted, and that was the beginning of an incredible part of my life. A huge moon pool. I was going to make an extremely deep dive. Watch out!

We arranged to meet at Kiera and Cody's house, which would also give me the opportunity to get together with my old frat brother. Kiera and Cody had an adorable, classic hippie house in Seal Beach. It was right out of the *Whole Earth Catalog*. They had no neighbors, a perfect view of the ocean, the beach, and the sunset. Kiera, just eighteen, worked at an exclusive women's clothing shop right on Rodeo Drive in Beverly Hills. Cody owned a nursery called Growing My Way, right off the Pacific Coast. It was very cool. He was always cool, very quiet but sure of himself. I'd always liked him.

As soon as we saw each other, Cody and I immediately reconnected. (I eventually gave him one of the portholes I salvaged off the *MacDhui* in Port Moresby. I didn't often give away precious artifacts like that, but he was so great … a really one-of-a-kind person. He loved the porthole as much as I knew he would, so it went to someone who appreciated it as much as I did.)

Cody broke out the pot, rolled a joint, and we got high. Ali had not arrived yet, but we all smoked another one together when she did get there, and she got high too.

That little house was magical.

At last, Ali arrived, my little fox, designer-perfect and so sexy, with her thick, jet-black hair and husky, throaty voice. She had a beautiful body too: just tall enough but not too tall. Her skin was perfect, and her white teeth gleamed. She was so cool. Amazing. Exquisite. Yes, I was smitten and totally in love.

There I was, in Southern California where I'd grown up, spending time at the house of a former frat brother and his gorgeous girlfriend (who was also seeing another old friend of mine), and getting to know the woman I already knew was the love of my life. It was very surreal. I felt like I'd come full circle. I had already lived all around the world, doing exciting things and chasing beautiful women, but I felt like all I really wanted, all I'd ever searched for, was right where I'd started out in the first place.

Back to Ali. As soon as she walked in the room, I knew she was the one. I felt it even more strongly than I had the night before in the bar. And I could tell for sure now that she felt the same way. Kiera looked like she was blown away by Ali's and my encounter: it was obvious that for us, there was nobody else in that room. The chemistry and connection between us were overpowering, just like our first meeting at Charlie Brown's the night before, only more intense.

Cody lit up another joint, and we all settled in for one of the coolest evenings I'd had in a long time. It was enough to just be there with Ali, some primo pot, and our perfect chemistry. We got loaded and laughed and talked, even though Kiera and Cody were there the whole time. It was as if it was just the two us, a preview of what our relationship was going to be in the future: intense, passionate, exciting, and open. Her husky, low, throaty voice was so sexy. I could listen to her talk all night long.

I asked Ali to go to Mexico with me. I wanted to leave the following morning. I had time for a side trip before my business was done and I had to go back to Australia. Ali wanted to go with me, but she had to check in at work. She promised she would let me know the following day, after she confirmed that she'd be able to take a few days off.

"I'll call you tomorrow," I said. "I'll put off leaving till I hear from you."

When I called her, she said she had gotten the time off.

"I'll pick you up right now," I told her.

We headed for Mexico in my rental car. First, we picked up some of the best pot I have ever smoked (from Cody, of course.) We cruised down Pacific Coast Highway 1, my old stomping grounds. As a kid, I loved chasing girls there—or, better yet, I loved when they chased me.

We drove down the coast, stopped to light up, put some music on, and tripped on each other. I was crazy in love with this girl. I kept looking at her, thinking about how moist she would be. Her thick, jet-black hair was blowing all around her in the wind streaming through the car as we drove along. Oh!

We stopped at a park near the ocean in San Diego before crossing the border, and then we headed into Mexico. We had to go through Tijuana before getting to Ensenada. This was the cesspool of Mexico, but we didn't care; we were together in another world of fantasies about each other. I put on my international charm, talking about my life in Australia, my diving company, my travels around the world. She was hypnotized.

We kept talking nonstop, smoking a few more joints along the way. It was wonderful. We both were hooked on each other, madly in love. I didn't have time to take her to Puerto Vallarta or Cabo San Lucas, so we would have to settle for this quick trip. We really just wanted to be together.

We finally got to Estero Beach, and I got us a beautiful room. We showered and changed, and then we went out for dinner and listened to music at a club. At this point, we hadn't even kissed, but the passion was almost unbearable. We were so turned on that night. We danced to a Mexican band, and I couldn't keep my hands off her.

We returned to our room to go to bed. It was a king-size bed. Ali spent time brushing her teeth, washing her face, and so on; it seemed to take hours. Finally, it was my turn to use the bathroom. I was very nervous. When I got out of the bathroom, she was in bed, with a small light on. I slid under the covers next to her but still not touching her.

And then we touched each other gently, and we kissed sweetly and quietly. It was so passionate. Breathtaking.

I was still nervous, but she pulled me in. We made amazing love. This was my soul mate. I was the happiest I have ever been.

After a few days, we left Mexico. We made love every chance we could get during our time together. We were so in love with each other, so turned on sexually. I couldn't bear to think of leaving and going back to Australia without her. But we still had a week to be together, and we made the most of it.

On our last night in Mexico, we went out and then came back to our oceanfront room (very Mexican but nice). Ali went into the bathroom, brushed her teeth, washed her face, and did whatever else women do before they go to bed. I got into bed, and she slid in next to me. We started to make out and make love, and it was the best. She was so passionate, and she just loved me the right way. Always.

My time to return to Australia was coming fast. We had been together every day and night since the day I'd first called her for a date. We drove back to California. I had one more day with Peat, Marwick, Mitchell and Company, the accounting firm auditing my company's books. (My meeting with them was the main reason I was in the States. I had to get that audit done in order to sell half of my company, and I needed the money I would get from that sale to continue operation. I'd already met with my friend Wyatt's father in Wilmington, gone to New York, then to Louisiana to meet with his uncle, and then to Houston to look at a new bell system. Long Beach was my last but most important stop.)

Ali and I decided to drive up to San Francisco and Sausalito after I finished up with the auditors. Kiera wanted to go with us, just to hang out. We didn't mind, so we told her she could come along if she would do some of the driving. We headed for San Francisco.

While we were driving, I thought about all that I'd done on this trip to the States. I was going to sell half my company (to Brambles Limited of Australia—more about that later), and Wyatt's father had introduced me to his brother-in-law, David Foster, an up-and-coming attorney in Louisiana (he would later become a judge). David became my lawyer. He was on retainer; I paid him every month. It was exciting but scary. These were big changes for me. I knew it wouldn't be long before I sold the company completely. I just didn't want to be stuck in the rat race anymore. I was quickly morphing from a brilliant, young entrepreneur to a brilliant, youngish hippie, wanting to drop out, smoke pot, and live in the rain forest in North Queensland Australia. (I hadn't yet seen Cape Trib, but I knew about it, and I loved Rosebud Farm in Kuranda.)

In the middle of all this, I met the love of my life, the woman I knew I was destined to be with. And that was so unexpected, it blew me away. I keep describing how deeply in love we were. And we were! It was the kind of love where every moment together is beautiful and exciting and passionate and fulfilling. It's so magical. You have this perfect sex, the greatest ever. That's the way it was with Ali and me: all-encompassing.

My black-haired, little fox from the Midwest was a wholesome all-American girl. She had played the bass drum in the high-school marching band and dated the high-school quarterback. Now she was stylish and successful and so very sexy. She was perfect for me. I can't even put into words just how crazy about her I was.

Anyway, all the way to San Francisco, we got Kiera to drive so we could make out in the backseat. All the way across the Golden Gate into Sausalito too. Kiera didn't mind. She knew how Ali and I felt about each other.

That last week was wonderful. We spent every day and night together, making love every moment we could.

In the meantime, my second in command had come over from Australia to meet me before heading to Houston to make arrangements for sending the new diving bell back to Australia. I'd bought the bell while in Houston, but the shipping arrangements still had to be squared away. When he saw what was going on between Ali and me, he was concerned. I couldn't blame him. But off he went to Texas, and I set thoughts of business aside, focusing only on Ali.

The day of my departure arrived—and far too quickly—and so I had to say good-bye to Ali. She went with me to the airport in a cab. We made out the whole way there, so deeply in love and so sad to be saying good-bye.

I checked in at the airport, and they said I was late and my plane was already on the tarmac getting ready to taxi. I could not miss this flight; I had huge meetings scheduled in Australia, and I needed to get back. My whole company deepened on it. But, at that moment, I had only one thing on my mind: Ali. They had a limo drive us out to the tarmac, and they let Ali come with me.

Ali and I said good-bye, both of us heartbroken.

I couldn't believe all the different things I was feeling and going through. On the business side, it was a dream come true: I was about to take over all the Bass Strait diving work and all of the platform work on the maintenance contracts pipelines, along with the *Glomar Conception,* the *Navigator,* and now work in Melbourne and Sydney, plus Cabinda, Africa. But now that I had it all, I wanted a change; I wanted to sell the company and move to the beaches and rain forest of North Queensland. To top it all off, I had fallen in love, and she had pushed all these warring thoughts straight to the back of my head. All I really wanted was Ali.

No matter what I did, there were going to be some angry people. But the only one I really cared about was Ali, my gorgeous, sexy, little fox.

My Love Comes to Sale, Australia (1973)

I called Ali from Australia and asked her to come live with me. She felt the same way I did: totally in love. But she wasn't sure about the move.

I knew I couldn't be away from her for very long; a day was too long. Within another couple of days, I had called her, told her to quit her job, and sent her a ticket to fly to Australia.

I'd also made up my mind about business: I was going to sell Broman International and move to North Queensland. I was dropping out. I had decided, once and for all. It was a relief.

I explained all this to Ali over the phone. She agreed to come to Australia, so I sent her an airline ticket. Ali flew to Australia, and I met her in Sydney. We took the scenic train from Sydney to Melbourne, through the Snowys. We rented a car and drove to Sale, where my field headquarters were.

Let me back up to explain that my whole company was in an uproar when I brought Ali over. I was completely in love, and I was going to sell everything and move up to Queensland to start a new life as a hippie bushman. They felt their livelihoods were in jeopardy, and they were understandably angry and upset.

I assured them that their jobs were secure and they could carry on with the new owners, but they still were not happy.

Ali was all that mattered to me now. I wanted her to be happy, and I knew I couldn't be happy without her. My employees would find a way to go on, and it was going to have to be without me.

Selling to Brambles of Australia (1973)

Brambles Limited was my partner by this point, and they had opened a Singapore office. Brambles wanted me out because of Oceaneering. They made a deal to get me out, and I let them.

They never could have done it if I hadn't wanted them to. I could have bought Oceaneering with the backing I had at that time. I knew the owners, and with the right amount of money, they would have just sold to me, just as they'd bought California Divers/Divcon, and just as Divcon had bought International Divers.

I eventually sold my remaining interest to Brambles (which was, I believe, the fourth-largest public company in Australia at that time). They were big and powerful, but they never wanted to give me credit. I didn't need it; I got my own. I was surprised they had such a wimp representing Oceaneering. (Esso couldn't stand him.) I don't think he was ever a diver, just a salesman. This guy was just like the phonies I despised, and still do. They didn't have the balls to make it as deep-water divers, so they stayed as office-manager types, never making a single dive.

I allowed the sale for several reasons, some business and some personal. I've already described them at length. The main reason why I was okay with Oceaneering taking over was that all my divers would still be employed, which would not be the case if I just shut down the company.

Here's how the sale went: I knew that Brambles was going to try a takeover; they owned 51 percent, and I owned 49 percent. That gave them the power of being the majority shareholder. A big meeting was arranged, and they called me to come to Sydney. We met in their corporate offices, and the head man for Brambles got up, stood behind the table, and opened the meeting by firing me as managing director of the company.

I had already known this was going to happen, so I was prepared for him, but I decided to manipulate him, anyway.

"Fuck off!" I told him.

He took off his jacket like he was going to punch me. I jumped up from my seat and headed for him. The security guards restrained me, removing me from the conference room.

That wasn't the end of it. I still had a tremendous amount of power as a 49 percent owner. The law protected me as a minority stockholder too, so the meetings that followed were with the board of Brambles and my attorney, the brilliant David Foster.

Captain Sir John Williams—Sydney, Australia (1973)

I didn't know it at the time, but I had a guardian angel by the name of Captain Sir John Williams. This man was very famous and powerful in Australia. He led the team that salvaged the gold off the *Niagara*, one of the most famous and spectacular salvage operations of its time. There were eight tons of gold that went down with the ship. The *Niagara* hit a German mine during the war, and it sank in 398 feet of water. In 1941, Captain John Williams and a diver, Johnno Johnstone, used a barely seaworthy ship, the *Claymore*, as the salvage vessel to get the gold off the *Niagara*.

At that time, Sir John represented the largest shipping company in the world: Pacific Orient Lines (P&O). He also served as chairman of the Australian National (Shipping) Line. He had been knighted for his services to Australian shipping. This incredible man had powerful credentials. He represented P&O in the buyout bidding for Broman International. Sir John worked hard all his life, he loved shipping and the ocean, and he was another incredible Australian I was proud to call my friend.

He came through for me when Brambles attempted a hostile takeover. Anyway, because Sir John led the bidding against Brambles, it turned into a power struggle between Brambles and P&O, the largest shipping company in the world at that time, and much more powerful than Brambles.

Sir John did this as a favor to me. He was an adventurer at heart, and the safe door of the *Niagara* hung in his study at his home in Melbourne. As chairman of the Australian Coastal Commission, the most important government body for shipping and anything marine in Australia, Sir John could make things extremely difficult for anyone in any sea-related business, if he chose to. Brambles did not wish to make an enemy of Sir John.

Fortunately for me, Sir John had great respect for me. He admired the fact that I'd started my own deep-water diving company at such a young age, operated internationally, and worked hands-on. My company's reputation in the deep-water diving industry was impeccable. He found that impressive in one so young. He knew about the deep dives I did; we talked about them during our meetings at his home in Melbourne. He'd asked me to deliver all the accounts receivable and debts documentation to him personally, and I did. That was a smart move on my part and a gracious one on his.

I was with Ali in Australian Square in Sydney when I signed the final paperwork for the sale of Broman International. It was my choice to sell. But it was still sad. Ali and I cried as we sat together.

My final choice to sell, separate from my personal reasons, was because of Captain Sir John Williams. Through P&O, Sir John offered to buy out Brambles in a hostile takeover, but I would have to commit to a seven-year contract with them. He gave me the vehicle to keep Broman International. Remember, when I quit International Divers, they had just been bought by Divcon, which then became the largest outfit. Divcon then sold to California Divers, which started Oceaneering. They did my deal with Brambles. I didn't have to sell; I was offered unlimited money for expansion as the minority shareholder. And Sir John had it lined up with P&O to do this. It was the deal of a lifetime. But I didn't do it.

Why didn't I do it?

For all the reasons I've already described: I was way too much into pot; I wanted to drop out and be a hippie; I was bored, and my company, though at its best, no longer offered me the challenge and excitement I craved; I had met Ali, the love of my life, and I wanted to spend all my time with her.

So I turned it all down to jump into a new lifestyle to be a hippie. I had created an international deep-water diving company, the best the industry had seen up to that time. My career in the offshore oil industry was just getting started. But I let it go. I had to. If I wanted the new life I kept dreaming of, I had to let go of my old life first.

In a word, I was done. But I would always be grateful to that great man, Captain Sir John Williams, for stepping up for me and giving me that choice and that chance.

My crew at Broman International and I were the best professionals in the business, so it was heartbreaking to leave, but that little voice inside me said, *Job well done.*

When the sale was announced by Brambles, the divers threatened to strike. Australia had extremely powerful unions that could and would shut down the whole Australian oil industry. I contacted them and personally called them off. I had an excellent reputation with them; I had been a union man at one time. And they always treated me fairly. Plus, their divers were my brothers who risked their lives with me, traveled the world with me. My divers were family to me. It was sad to say good-bye to my company, but that sadness was mixed with relief. I was relieved to no longer have the responsibility of owning a deep-water company, and freeing that burden from my shoulders liberated me for my next adventure, my new lifestyle.

I had dived into my next moon pool at last. You already know what happened in Port Douglas and at the cove in Cape Tribulation, my best moon pool of all, with Ali, my love. The moon pool after that was the flood in Cyanide Creek that destroyed my Land Cruiser and nearly drowned me. You already know about that one too.

Let's move to my next big moon pool after Australia. It was in Long Beach, California. Journey with me across the wide and mighty blue Pacific, and I'll show you exactly what happened.

PART IV

Moon Pools in the Pacific—Southern California; Japan; Taiwan

After I sold Broman International, I dropped out of the rat race at last. I've already shared the details of the short time Ali and I spent in Port Douglas, as well as our magnificent life together at our paradise cove at Cape Tribulation, nestled between the tropical rain forest and turquoise waters of the Coral Sea, with our closest neighbors being wild boar and the denizens of the Great Barrier Reef.

Those were incomparable moon pools—especially my time with Ali, the love of my life.

My tropical paradise ended during the flood in Cyanide Creek: my Toyota Land Cruiser, an unparalleled bush vehicle, was totaled; I nearly drowned. That was another huge moon pool, as big as my many moon pools during deep-water diving, both literally and figuratively. It's amazing how many times an experienced diver and surfer like me, a boy who literally grew up in the ocean, could nearly drown. And yet it did happen.

My next big moon pool, after all my many moon pools in Australia, happened closer to home: Long Beach, California, the part of the world where I grew up. The waves of California had been my training ground— gigantic swells of sapphire water that carried me toward my destiny as a diver.

You'll recall from part I that I was only crossing Cyanide Creek because of a phone call I'd received, one so urgent that I had to return to the States. I had to save a piece of property I owned on the California side of Lake Tahoe.

Anyway, there I was, in California, where I'd started out. I'd felt that way when I met Ali too, that I'd come full circle. Moon pools are deep, so the full circles they take you to are more like spirals than disks; you come back to where you started time and time again, and in between you go up and down a lot. You go up and down and round and round that spiral many times before the lesson of the journey is clear. It is a wild and magnificent ride.

This moon pool in Long Beach was different from the others. There was no imminent danger, no do-or-die situation, no real risk at all. It was simply that being in California again after all that had happened to me in my travels throughout the world—Southeast Asia, Africa, Australia— caused me to reflect on my life, to feel that I've-come-full-circle feeling that I described. And it was an incredible, indelible moment.

Where do I go from here? What do I want? Who am I?

I realized, as those swells pulled me under all over again (figuratively, not literally, this time), that I didn't know the answers to any of those questions. Maybe I never really did, but I always *believed* that I did. It shook me to the core. I had now been a deep-water diver, an entrepreneur, a hippie, a military man, a world traveler, and a lover of women—and I had been successful in each of those roles—but I still had no clear, true sense of the total essence of myself.

The only way to go forward was to go back. So that California moon pool transported me to another one. A big one. A big moon pool in big waves. Much bigger than I was as a child. And then those childhood recollections led to other Pacific moon pools in Japan, Taiwan, and throughout the Far East while in the military.

Remember, that's what moon pools are: reflections. Of clarity and beauty, of wisdom and tranquility, of danger and fear. And those reflections also help us seek and find the power and courage we have within, the stuff that enables us to surmount the challenges we face and to emerge stronger.

Life after Australia—Long Beach, California (1975)

After returning stateside because of the Lake Tahoe property issue I've already described, I returned to Long Beach. I was sitting in my dad's shop one day amidst all this diving equipment. It was just like I remembered from when I was a kid: the wet suits, the diving dresses[1] hanging like dead bodies with ropes around their necks, the line of copper and brass hard-hat diving helmets gleaming in the sunlight, every make and brand of diving gear displayed. Surrounded by all the stuff I'd grown up with, and subsequently spent my whole life with, my emotions ranged the gamut. It was at once enlightening, fulfilling, and a bit overwhelming.

I had come full circle.

I found myself regrouping and reflecting on my many moon pools up to that point. Wow, what a journey!

Growing Up in the Waves and on the Beach— Southern California (1944–1956)

My dad was in the navy, stationed in Guam. He was honorably discharged to Treasure Island (on San Francisco Bay), shortly before the Japanese attacked Pearl Harbor. That attack was devastating, as everybody knows. Patriotism ran high afterward; my dad, like many other men at that time, wanted to defend his country even though he'd already served, so he reenlisted.

I was born in 1942, in Richmond, California, right near San Francisco Bay. Shortly afterward, my mother relocated to Southern California, living in one of the projects that the navy provided for the families of servicemen. During what remained of World War II, my mother and I lived in that project. Our neighbors were mostly poor people and servicemen and their families.

I was very young when we lived in that project, not more than two or three years old, but I have some vivid memories of that time, the clearest of which are of all the black people who also lived in the project. I absolutely

---

[1]   A diving dress is a waterproof, one-piece suit made of canvas and rubber that entirely covers the wearer, except for the head and hands.

adored them. They were so kind to my mom and me. I felt so safe with them.

I can remember going into one of the public bathrooms, and this black man we knew came in after me because my mom had asked him to watch out for me.

"Jimmy?" he called while I was still in the stall. "Did you wipe?"

"Yeah, I did."

"Okay, that's a good boy. You come out now."

I came out, returned the big grin he gave me, and went outside to play with the other kids. I felt conscious of how different I looked from the kids who were my friends. I had blond hair, blue eyes, and an olive complexion (usually suntanned). My friends were all black kids. Sometimes I wondered if they thought I was weird, like an albino or something. But they didn't. (Or, if they did, they never made me feel weird.) I loved them, and I know they loved me too. I thought they were beautiful. I had so much fun and felt so comfortable with them.

From my earliest memories, I loved the water. I swam like a fish, always going beneath the surface—that was my peaceful place. I enjoyed the solitude and perfect tranquility beneath the surface, but I also loved the joy I felt laughing in the sun. I was fun-loving; my mom saw to that.

The beach was wonderful. I'll never forget my childhood summers. To this day, I can still taste the hamburgers and cheeseburgers, the french fries, the malts. That was our big lunch treat. If we got tired of chocolate malts, we'd have vanilla. Those beach foods were the best.

We'd lie on the beach and feel the warmth of the sun and the sand after being in the water all day, swimming and body surfing.

My mom would always yell, "Jimmy, don't go out too far!"

But I would always push it. One day at Huntington Beach, a big breaker came up. I went out to catch that big wave, and it sucked me under, and it rolled me, and rolled me, and rolled me until I was just about out of breath. (You'll remember from part III that this was when I almost drowned.) The force and power of that wave were unbelievable. Finally, it released me, washing me up on the beach. The lifeguard was there when I came to. My poor mom was in hysterics.

That lifeguard saved my life: he rolled me on my side and pushed the water out of my lungs. At least that's what my mom told me afterward.

I don't remember the rescue; I only remember the wave. I'll never forget it: rolling around and waiting to come up out of that wave. It was like an endless somersault, but with a thousand tons of pressure on top of me. The power of water is incredible.

* * * * * *

I realize now that my experience with that wave shaped me and all that I would do in life. Someone else might have become terrified of the water and never gone anywhere near it again. Not me. I knew I was destined to spend my life in the waves.

Of course, my dad's being a deep-water diver influenced my comfort in the deep. Fear was not an option. Diving chose me more than I chose it.

More than just my destiny, diving gave me everything I had as a kid. My dad made a great living as a diver and was always a good provider. My younger sister and I had everything we wanted, and we could do everything we wanted.

We always lived in beach communities: Redondo Beach, San Pedro, Manhattan Beach. In a lot of ways, my dad was a big fish in a little pond. We always had more than our neighbors. He drove a brand-new truck, always black, and he traded it in for a new one every two years. My mom usually drove a new T-bird. (Her '55 Buick Century was an exception. She got it because she knew I was going to be driving soon.)

Mom always went first class and made sure we kids did too. We always had all that we wanted; Mom saw to that, but she also taught us how to be mannerly and respectful. She expected us to appreciate all that we had and to share it with people, especially those who had less than we did.

When I got a little older, we moved to Long Beach. We hung out in Belmont Shore, the best little waterfront community in that area. It had a bay called Alamitos, and it had a place called Naples, which was made up of canals with little bridges going out to the bay and onward to the jetty and the ocean. (I loved that place so much that I lived on a houseboat there when I returned from Australia.)

* * * * * *

I had a wonderful childhood. I adored my little sister, Artie, and she idolized me just like all little sisters idolize their big brothers. I drove her crazy, though. There was one time when she was babysitting and I snuck into the house and jumped out at her while she was watching TV. Scared the daylights out of her. Literally—she passed out from fright. I saw her eyes roll back in the sockets, and I freaked out. I ran all the way home to get my parents. She was okay, but I felt awful. She still adored me even after that. Artie was just like our mom: beautiful, kind, and forgiving. My dad and I were lucky. I always appreciated it; I'm not sure he did.

My dad was the opposite of my mom. He was tough. That was good in some ways, but not in others. After I'd been to a birthday party when I was about five, he told me that everything I had really belonged to him. (He wasn't trying to be mean, just showing me who was boss, and only because I refused to go to bed at my appointed bedtime.) I just couldn't stand it, probably because I knew it was true. Anyway, it just set me off. I hated not being in control, even at the tender age of five. So I stripped off all my clothes, and I ran out of the house. Stark naked, I hid behind a bush, praying that my mom would come find me. Soon. All the while, I hoped none of my friends would see me. But my anger was stronger than the fear that my friends would see me hiding in a bush, buck naked.

My mother did find me before long. She held open a soft blanket and wrapped it around me, pulling me into her arms. "He didn't mean it, Jimmy," she said softly.

That was my mother. Soft. Kind. Loving. Just as I've described her all along. She was the single best thing about my growing-up years. I unequivocally adored her.

I drove her to her wits' end more often than not. I've already told you about how I almost drowned in the ocean because I didn't heed her warnings. I had lots of other adventures that drove her to distraction too, though. Like the time my cousin Tommy and I were riding our bikes and we decided to play a game. It was a rural road in a desolate part of Compton, all vacant fields with big tumbleweeds that we could hide behind. We would shoot out in front of cars, just to see how close we could come without getting hit. During one such extremely daring attempt, my foot slipped off the pedal when I was right in front of this car. The driver was an old black man, going about fifty miles an hour. He slammed on the brakes just as the car hit me, and I went flying. I was thrown thirty-six feet straight up into the air. When I landed, the bicycle followed, and the handlebar stabbed me in the back, going in deep (a good few inches). I was pinned to the ground, with the handlebar stuck in my back.

That poor driver was beside himself, saying, "I never even saw the kid! He came from out of nowhere!" It was true; I had. I admitted it, though. There were no charges filed, and my dad had to pay all my medical expenses.

At the hospital, they put a rubber tube in the hole in my back in order to drain it. And then, just as it was starting to heal, Tommy and I were wrestling, and I fell back on a corner of a piece of modern furniture, reopening the wound. It did finally heal, but that place is still tender to this day.

Aside from my adventures, my growing-up years were typical. Little League, Pony League, Pop Warner, school dances, summers on the beach, fishing (which I especially loved to do with friends, my dad's diving buddies). I was a teenager when rock and roll was going mainstream, in the 1950s. I learned to jitterbug and do all the popular dances, and I have been a great dancer for my entire life. There was no better place and time to grow up than Southern California in the fifties. It was the best. The beaches were fantastic, clean and beautiful all the way down the coast to Mexico where the avocado ranches and orange groves met the beaches. We were close to Disneyland. The mountains were only an hour away by car: Big Bear, Crestline, Lake Arrowhead. We were just below the Mohave, before Palm Springs, inland from Hollywood, and not far from Santa Barbara. That was our territory, our playground.

I was very popular and had a lot of friends. I enjoyed the status. I had the same girlfriend, Cozy, from seventh grade all through high school. She was class president every year. But I was always me; even then I dated every girl I could while still going with her.

We were so hot for each other. We fought, broke up, and got back together all through that time. Our making out was the best. I totally loved her in the way that you can only love your first love, the one you never really forget or get over.

Of course, my childhood and growing up were not perfect. My dad was crazy, as I've described. He could be a jerk a lot of the time. My mother always tried to smooth things over, to make things good for my sister and me. I teased and terrorized my sister, just like all older brothers do, but I looked out for her and protected her too.

For the most part, my growing up and adolescence were ordinary. I played baseball and football. I always made first string, but when I got older, I wasn't motivated to leave the girls and the beaches to go to practice. I hit one fantastic home run in my life, and that was as an adult. (You'll remember this from my baseball playing in Darwin in part III.)

My teen years were filled with many memorable moments, though, as you'll soon see.

Car Club and Frat Life: The Outcasts and Lam Sig—Southern California (1957)

I started driving when I was fifteen, and I was part of a car club, the Outcasts. We would meet our girlfriends down at the beach. I was always trying to impress my friends and all the girls, and I started to swim across the bay one time. I actually ran out of breath before I got to the edge, and I almost drowned. (Yes, another one of the many times!)

It was a big thing at that time to swim across the bay. I took that chance. Nobody else did. That was just the way I always was.

Being a teenager in the fifties was great. I loved every minute of it. It was even better that *Grease* or *Happy Days* made it seem. There was nothing like growing up in Southern California at that time. I've said it before, and I'll say it again: it was the best!

In 1957, I drove around in a jet-black '55 Olds. It was on a channel rake (really low in the front and a little higher in the rear), with twenty-inch glass packs; mufflers that gave a cool, mellow gurgling sound when idling, and slow roar when you took off; flipper hub caps; an angora mirror warmer and angora ("fuzzy") dice hanging from the rearview mirror. It was the epitome of cool. The coolest car in the Outcasts' club.

We would drive down to Tijuana and get tuck-and-roll upholstery cheap, real leather. (All the pin striping was done by Barris & Roth, famous pin stripers from Bellflower, the town next to Long Beach.) My girlfriend's name was painted on the dash: Cozy's Carriage. My beloved 45 record player was mounted under the dash. I always played 45s or had the radio on, listening to Johnny Otis or Hunter Hancock or Wolfman Jack.

Cruising to Hody's, a drive-in with all-girl car hops wearing short shorts, was one of our favorite pastimes. It was right off Pacific Coast Highway 101, Long Beach, California. Of course, I always had my colors flying in the rear of my car, my club plaque proclaiming "the Outcasts." It was so cool.

We had the Southern California lifestyle—the beaches, the ocean, the mountains, the deserts—and we also had Hollywood, so we could take our cars, cruise down Sunset Strip, and then come back to the beach. We went into Cobra City, where we used to meet what we called "Valley Girls." And that was like going to a foreign country. We were the "beach guys," which gave us more points with the girls from the valley. What great times those were.

We would come in cool, meet new girls, and have all kinds of fun. Sometimes our girlfriends actually followed us in their cars. We would cruise Hody's, and one of the guys would look toward the car next to us and say, "Guess who's following us, man!" It would be my girlfriend with a carload of girls, or it could be another girl cruising with her sorority sisters, an older girl who had a crush on me.

The soundtrack to it all was doo-wop, that iconic style of vocal-based rhythm and blues from the 1950s and early 1960s. Who doesn't love that music? I can't think of songs better to listen to while falling in love for the first time, making love for the first time, coming of age, and discovering what life is about.

Doo-wop songs featured both fast beats and slow beats, so it was great music to learn to dance to also. "Sh-Boom," "Sincerely," "Earth Angel" (my favorite slow-dancing and make-out song), "Only You," "Why Do Fools Fall in Love," "Little Darlin'," "Since I Don't Have You," "I Wonder Why," "There's a Moon out Tonight," and the list goes on and on. (Some of these songs were from the mid- to late 1950s; others were from the early 1960s. To me, though, all those songs bring up the memories of being a teenager during the best time and in the best place in the world.)

We danced to doo-wop as teenagers, we made out to doo-wop too, and we spent our weekend nights cruising in our lowered cars. We had a lifestyle like no other. Guys in car clubs had the best access to beautiful girls. We always had all the girls we wanted. I loved being in the Outcasts. Our club was started by five guys in Long Beach. I was the seventh member. We were a small but elite club.

We had clothes that were the most stylish. (I was always awarded "best dressed" every year from junior high through high school.) We took our dates to dances at Disneyland, but we would also throw our own dances, real first-class affairs with shirts and ties. Sometimes we made them casual. Either way, they were so much fun.

* * * * * *

The summer between junior high and high school was great. I was fifteen and already driving, as I've mentioned. Up until that summer, I drove my mom's '55 Buick Century, a three-tone-blue, two-door, very cool car, with electric windows and an automatic transmission.

It was the fastest car around. We would go out to Ball Road, near Knots Berry Farm and Disneyland, and have drag races. I dropped two transmissions racing, but those were the only races I lost. It was deceptive: that road looked so straight! Hotrods and race cars would line up there. I was in a stock car with an automatic transmission, and I wiped everybody off the strip.

Not long after that, I got my own car, the '55 Olds I described earlier.

The summer between junior high and high school was also the time to pledge for a fraternity. I wanted Lambda Sigma (Lam Sig). There were alumni who wanted me in and a few who didn't want me. I was cool with it. I got turned down the first time out, but the second time I was accepted to pledge.

Pledging was a bitch and very cool all in the same time; sometimes they would have a joint meeting with a sorority during pledging. All the pledges had to obey any order from a member. Some of these orders were cool; others, not so much.

Oftentimes the order was to take one of the sorority sisters on a date. I was even ordered to make out with some of them. There was one girl whom I particularly remember; she was a senior, and I was fresh out of ninth grade, just going to be a sophomore. I felt really cool to be with an older girl. She was a slim, sexy, black-haired wild thing. That girl was so hot! She wanted me at any cost, and she told a Lam Sig member to order me to take her out. I was thrilled, needless to say. Our first date was intense. She broke out a bottle of thunderbird wine, we made out, and she wanted me to make love to her. I did, and she was a great lover.

So much for the pleasurable orders during pledging! Most of the orders *didn't* involve having sex with gorgeous sorority girls. In fact, the things the members made us do were downright humiliating, degrading, and even painful. There was the egg scoot, where we had to strip down naked and sit on the floor, put an egg between the cheeks of our asses, squeeze tight, and then a member would say, "Go!" We each would scoot down to the finish line, trying to win the race. Eggs would break all over the place, and it was a mess. The winner would get privileges, such as no swats.

Next was the elephant walk. The members said, "Time for the elephant walk!" When none of us knew what that was, they said: "Form a circle, get naked, then take your right thumb and stick it in the asshole of the guy in front of you. Take your left thumb and stick it in your mouth, and walk around in a circle, all of you connected, until we yell, 'Switch!' Then, you pull your right thumb out of his asshole in front of you, take your left thumb out of your mouth at the same time, put your right thumb in your mouth and your left thumb in the ass of the guy in front of you. Got it?"

We got it, but we all refused to do the elephant walk.

The egg scoot and elephant walk were part of Black Tuesday. After that came Hell Night, the last night of pledging. If you made it through Hell Night and survived, you got to be a brother, a Lam Sig member. Obviously, getting through it was hard.

A member picked up each pledge, bringing us to Huntington Beach, in front of some oil wells along the coast, right on the beach oceanfront. Down on this isolated part of the beach, we each had to strip down naked. And then the torture started: they swatted us with these paddles that stung like nothing else I have ever felt. Afterward, they forced us to go out to the ocean. The saltwater rubbed us raw after the swatting.

One of the members had a jar filled with a warm substance that we were supposed to drink. "Gargle it," they told us.

It was horse sweat that they had sponged off the horses at the riding stables where we went for hayrides and horseback riding. Of course, they didn't tell us that it was horse sweat until after we'd gargled and they had commanded, "Swallow!" As that warm horse sweat went down our gullets, we all retched and puked. After that, they told us it was really just saltwater. And it was. But when they told it was horse sweat, our guts turned inside out, and after you've been swatted like that, you get sicker than you ordinarily would. We all puked out our guts.

But the cruelest of all was yet to come: Sloan's liniment poured down the rectum and over the testicles. I have never felt pain like that in my life, before or since. It burned, along with the sand and salt already covering us from head to toe. It rubbed our balls raw. Then we had to travel ten miles home, stark naked.

Was it worth it? Believe it or not, yes!

One of the guys went out to the ocean and never came back in. He swam down the beach and walked home naked. He couldn't handle it; he was known as a coward because he quit. Nevertheless, he scared the shit out of the members. They had a missing person who could be dead, drowned, and they had to call the police, search parties, the whole deal. When they finally found him home in bed, they were relieved. No more Hell Nights after that. Plus, he was let in the frat, forgiven, and shown mercy. He was a very cool guy; he just couldn't handle the abuse. It was very rough. My balls peeled for two weeks. I said it was worth it because I loved being a frat brother. But by now you know I am a wild man. My thinking it was worth it doesn't mean the average person would agree.

Coming of Age—Southern California (1956–1959)

There's one thing that made childhood, junior high, and high school great for me, and this story wouldn't be complete without my acknowledging it. Or should I say without acknowledging her. My mom. I've already shared how much I loved her. But not only was she an incredibly good mother, she was also so cool, and all of my friends loved her. We went horseback riding, we had hayrides, and she would always invite my friends and pay their way. She actually took us to opening week at Disneyland: Sunday, July 17, 1955. How awesome is that!

Better than that, though, she really loved all my friends. All kids, even teenagers. They loved and trusted her, told her things they couldn't tell their own parents. What a blessing she was to them. And to me. What a mom. I was and am so blessed.

My friends and I were girl crazy, and as we got older, we had make-out parties. All that passion building up needed to be released. The parents let us have these parties. (I always had a feeling my mom was instrumental in this because she really understood teenage boys, but I never did find out for sure.) Anyway, the parents would be in the other room, and they gave us privacy. We would make out for three or four hours, after which time we were pretty turned on. Okay, very turned on. And then we would switch partners. I would always end up making out with every girl in the room. It was great, so much fun.

I remember one party when I about was about fourteen. I was making out with a girl, and we were very turned on. We started rubbing on each other, and she was so hot grinding back and forth. Well, it happened to both of us. At first, we were surprised. There I was, coming in my pants, and she was coming in hers too. The front of my pants was all soaked, and so was hers. We were all wet in front, soaked through, and it felt so good.

I didn't realize exactly what had happened until I got home and replayed it through my mind. I had an orgasm! I grinned to myself. I had never felt anything so good. I knew at that moment that this was going to be my biggest quest in life, not just for myself but for the woman I was with, to feel her have orgasms with me and love me.

That was a defining moment.

* * * * * *

So that was my childhood and adolescence—beaches, doo-wop, fast cars, making out, falling in love. There was also Disneyland, hayrides, and horseback riding. The frat (Lam Sig), the car club (Outcasts), and drag racing. (When I was younger, we also had soapbox derbies, which were so much fun. Even though I almost got my throat cut by barbed wire during one race down a hill so steep that it was more like a cliff. Those wooden cars that dads helped some of the kids build for the derbies went so fast; they were unbelievable. It was a miracle I didn't get killed in that one race, but then again, that's just how I roll.)

But it wasn't all fun. Car clubs and drag racing gave rise to what we called "rumbles" (think of *West Side Story*), or what today would be referred to as "gang wars." It was rough, and it got very ugly. I dropped out of high school and was actually in a gang. I felt ashamed, but I was also lost, and I didn't know how to get out of the mess I had made. My mother was devastated, and that made me feel even worse. I had vowed to protect my mother and my sister after my parents divorced when I was sixteen, and I felt I'd failed.

I knew I had to do something to straighten out, and I felt the only answer was to join the military. Best decision I could have made at the time.

My fights during the gang wars took a toll on my poor, beautiful, kind mother. She was crushed, hurt to the bone, so embarrassed and ashamed. She hated violence. The pain I caused her did get to me. So I joined the air force, breaking family tradition by not joining the navy. But that was what I always did: break traditions. My whole life, I did what I thought was right; I paid the consequences, and I also reaped the rewards.

My cousin Tommy was joining with me. We'd been close all our growing-up years, even though our personalities were completely different, and we were always getting into all kinds of trouble, as I've described. Joining the air force together was going to be great! Neither one of us could wait.

I was about to dive into a new moon pool. I made the right choice. I knew it the moment Tommy and I got to the train station in LA. We were headed for San Antonio, Texas. I knew that my real life was just getting started.

Air Force Boot Camp—San Antonio, Texas (1960)

I was just seventeen when I joined the air force, but I only looked about fifteen. Hundreds of other kids and young men were at that train station with Tommy and me, people from all backgrounds: rich and poor, black and white, and Latino and Asian too. It was the biggest mix of different kinds of people I'd ever seen.

My dad came to see me off, even though he and my mom had already split up. And Mom and some of my aunts (my mom's sisters) were there too. My poor mom was heartbroken that I had enlisted; she loved me so much, and she was very worried. I felt bad about that, but I knew that joining the military was the right choice for me, the only option at that time. I never regretted it, and I never looked back.

As we were getting ready to board the train, one of my aunts gave Tommy and me each a pint of whiskey. She winked at us, and we smiled at her.

Tommy and I shared a room on the train—if you could call those compartments "rooms." We started drinking the whiskey as soon as the train pulled out of the station, and we got pretty drunk. The curtain on the compartment window caught fire from a cigarette, and we had to put it out. It never took too long for drama to start if I was around!

Soon afterward, I ended up in a card game. I have played poker for money since I was ten years old, so I won a couple of hundred bucks. There was a civilian in the game, a Texan, who got mad and wanted to fight. Fortunately, that didn't happen. The guy was outnumbered by a thousand air force recruits, so he thought better of it.

I was two hundred bucks ahead at the start of my journey to basic training, so I was pretty happy. Beyond that, I was excited, eager to serve. Don't get me wrong; I am still glad that I served, but the feeling was different in those days. We were all patriots, and anyone who returned home from military service still received a hero's welcome at that time. That wouldn't change until Vietnam, several years later. My time in the military was still pretty much the way it had always been. I had the best life in the military that a guy could ever hope for, but, of course, I had no idea what I was in for. None of the other recruits did, either. No recruit ever does; that's the whole purpose of basic training.

* * * * * *

When that train stopped in San Antonio, Texas, we got off, and as soon as our feet hit the ground, basic training started. In that first instant, we didn't even realize it. We were in for a rude awakening, which we did realize soon enough.

A drill instructor (DI) met us. I will never forget the way he looked and acted: he wore starched fatigues and wielded a baton, and he yelled and barked orders to us as we got off the train.

Mind you, Tommy and I were each suffering from a massive hangover, courtesy of my aunt's gift of whiskey. We had spent two days traveling on the train, wearing the same clothes as the day we'd started, no shower, plus the hangover effects. It was not the best of all days.

As we unloaded from the train, the DI had us line up. He walked up and down in front of us, looking at us with contempt.

"All you recruits are from California," he said. "I've only seen two things that came from California: hotrods and queers. And I don't see any tailpipes on any of you."

That was our introduction to the air force.

They loaded us on buses that took us to the base. As the bus entered the base, I have to admit I was impressed and excited and apprehensive too, seeing all the troops marching. These were real men in military uniforms. Real members of the US Air Force. It was awesome. For a brief moment, I felt proud. I had no idea how brief that moment would be.

Next, we were taken to the barracks. The DI told us to each pick out a bunk. I picked a top one, and Tommy picked the one next to me, also a top bunk.

The DI shouted, "Empty your wallets of all personal items—pictures of girlfriends, family, and so on."

I took my stuff out and placed it all on the bunk.

The DI came straight over to Tommy, picked up his wallet, and found a picture of his girlfriend in a bikini. He grabbed Tommy and slammed him against the wall. "I just told you to take everything out of your wallet, including pictures of family and girlfriends. I said 'everything,' didn't I?"

Tommy had just had the crap scared out of him. He couldn't utter a word in response, correct reply or otherwise; he was in shock.

Before the DI could even react to Tommy's lack of response, I started laughing. I just busted up; I couldn't help myself. The scenario looked just like the ones in the movies; Tommy looked so shocked, it was comical. (Besides, that's the way he was, comical without even trying.) Anyway, to me, in that instant, it didn't even seem real. It truly was just like a movie.

Reality hit me quick enough, though. The next thing I knew, that DI had me in a chokehold, slamming me against the wall. I stopped laughing.

The full reality hit me in the next few seconds as I understood what we were in for. All I could think was, *I am signed up for four years of this!*

But that was just the way it was. The air force controlled my life for the four years that followed; they owned me. In the beginning, I was almost suicidal. Basic training was all but unbearable for a seventeen-year-old who had never been controlled before.

I didn't know this then, but the DI's job was to take everything out of our heads—our habits, our pride, everything that we had at home—empty it all completely and then refill it with the military: taking orders, obeying commands, submitting to authority, and doing things the military way.

Suffice it to say that the pride I'd momentarily felt upon entering the base vanished, at least for a while. I would learn to feel proud again while in the air force, but it would be proud in the military way.

It was a huge adjustment—an enormous moon pool—and I had only just jumped in, barely broken the surface. There was a lot more learning to come.

* * * * * *

The first morning on base, the DI woke us up at three thirty in the morning. It was still dark outside. He turned the lights on in the barracks, walked around, and rapped the iron bunks with that baton.

We stayed in our civilian clothes for two more days, while the other troops kept marching past us in their uniforms. By that time, we were dying to get our uniforms so that we didn't look like new recruits (and also to have some clean clothes).

Finally, we got to go the big, white elephant (that's what they called it), where we would get our haircuts and then be issued our duffel bags, uniforms, brogans (combat boots), fatigues, socks, underwear, toothbrushes, etc.

The first stop was the barber for our haircuts. Or should I say head shavings. I had this beautiful head of thick, blond hair, and the barber shaved it all off. I now looked like Elmer Fudd! My ears were sticking out, and I could barely take it. That was my last moment of vanity in the military. It was a rough moment, feeling homesick and humbled, but that was the purpose of shaving our heads: it eliminated any last vestige of individuality. It was hard, but we each had to get through it, and we did.

After that, we each got a duffel bag. We went through the line, got our brogans, three sets of fatigues, socks, underwear, toothbrushes, etc.

Everything was "Government Issue" or GI, that's what those letters stand for. Last, we got our uniforms, and then we went back to the barracks.

We put on our uniforms, and then we went outside and started marching, going through the whole process of basic training, which is basically marching and parades every day. We had shorts, a gymnasium, and boxing matches. We did everything to start getting us in shape.

The DI took all our strengths and eradicated them, starting to make us all the same. Blacks, whites, Latinos, Asians—it didn't matter. There were no racial lines. There were no class divisions whatsoever; no rich or poor, no status of any kind. We were all the same. This was what brought us together. It formed an unbreakable bond between each of us and all of us. We were brothers now, all with the same problems. We needed to survive this basic training, and in order to do that, we had to help one another.

Tommy and I made new friends quickly. One of our best buddies was Freddie, a black guy from Watts in LA. We were also friends with several Latinos from Compton and East LA. Some were gang members, but that didn't matter; we were going to be brothers now regardless of our backgrounds.

Tommy kept me in stitches all through basic training. Like I said, he just was comical; I don't know how I would have made it without him there to keep me laughing. I would have gotten through it, but it wouldn't have been the same.

When we marched, the DI made us sing. The songs, if you want to call them that, were ridiculous:

> Lift your head and hold it high,
> California's passing by.
> Sound off: one, two;
> Sound off: three, four.
> Sound off: one, two, three, four!
> California's passing by.

When the DI wasn't within earshot, Tommy would do hilarious takeoffs. If the DI heard him, he would yell, "Spark! You are making a mockery of this training!" And then he would throw pebbles at him. The DI called my cousin Spark because he was always bouncing around, laughing, and making the rest of us laugh. It was just natural with him, which made it even funnier than it would have been with someone who really tried to be funny.

Like when we were in the chow hall and we were supposed to eat a "square meal." That meant, as the DI had trained us, "Lift your spoon up till it gets just across from your lips, then move in, take a bite, and move back out." That was a square meal. Imagine eating a square meal with a guy like my cousin. Hilarious.

We needed the comic relief in basic training, we really did. We had to make our beds so that the DI could bounce a quarter off of them. We each had a footlocker to roll all of our clothes into; they had to be rolled perfectly, and if they weren't rolled perfectly and separated perfectly, the whole squadron got penalized. If you messed up, and the whole squadron got penalized, there would be a blanket party; that night, the guys in the squadron would come over with a blanket, throw it on you, and then beat the crap out of you. So that was all the stuff that was going on. Some of the guys got dishonorable discharges because of it. They couldn't handle the discipline, or they were so homesick that they couldn't handle the military at all. They would pee in the bed, do anything to get kicked out and sent home.

But back to eating square meals with my cousin. I remember one time in particular. I was sitting in the chow hall, and Tommy started making me laugh. As usual, he was not even trying to; he was just so naturally comical. Watching him eat a square meal was one of the most hilarious things you could imagine. I leaned back in my chair, I was laughing so hard. I didn't think our DI or any of the drill instructors or sergeants were around. So there I was, leaning back in my chair and laughing hysterically. Next thing I knew, I got smacked across the head. Then I heard, "Broman, push-ups! One arm."

I knew the drill; that was my standard punishment. One day I'd been showing off in the barracks, doing one-arm pushups like my dad had taught me. The DI had seen me, and that was it: every time I got in trouble after that, he had me do one-arm pushups.

My bout of hysterics resulted in worse than the standard protocol, though. He also made me do many laps that whole night, the whole works. It was constant stuff like that whenever they caught you doing something that was out of the structured discipline. Cleaning the latrine and toilet with a toothbrush was a favorite.

* * * * * *

The punishments really didn't have that much of an effect on me. I mean, I got the message and I understood the importance of the discipline, but every once in a while (okay, more than every once in a while), I had to act out. I couldn't help it; I just had this rebellious streak that I couldn't contain.

There was one episode in particular that is worth mentioning. I'll never forget it. We had to shave every day as part of our routine, but I didn't need to shave. I didn't even have peach fuzz. None of that mattered; we each had to shave whether we needed to or not.

Remember the morning ritual: The DI woke us at 3:30 a.m. every day, turning on the lights and rapping the metal bunks with his baton. After jumping a foot or so in the air, we each made our bunk, showered and shaved, and had to be outside the barracks at 4:30 a.m., sharp. We'd line up every morning for inspection. The DI checked each of us and our uniforms while we stood at attention outside, and then he went into the barracks to check our wall lockers, our footlockers (to see if all our clothes were rolled perfectly), and our beds (to see if they were made perfectly, and if he could bounce a quarter off them).

This one morning, I just didn't shave. I'd been shaving all along, but no one could tell if I did or not. I just didn't have any beard; I still had a baby face.

The DI shouted, "Airman Broman! Up front!"

I stepped out to the front of the whole squadron.

He came right up, maybe an inch from my face, and looked at me, just staring at my face. "Did you shave this morning, Airman?"

I said, "No, sir."

He said, "Why not, Airman? You know you're supposed to shave every morning. Is that correct, Airman?"

I said, "Yes, sir."

He said, "Then why didn't you shave?"

And I said, "Somebody stole my radio, sir."

He looked at me like I was crazy. "What the fuck do you mean, somebody stole your radio? You don't have a radio."

I said, "I know, sir, but somebody stole my radio."

He said, "Well, what has that got to do with not shaving?"

I said, "Well, sir, my razor was on top of the radio."

The whole squadron burst out laughing. It really was hilarious. I had really pulled one over on him.

The DI went ballistic. Boy, did I pay. It was severe for two days straight. But it was so worth it.

* * * * * *

We did have a lot of laughs during basic training, but most of the time we just worked our butts off. It was hard, grueling. Most nights, we were exhausted before our heads even hit the pillow. But we got through it.

Before we knew it, it was time for our bivouac. Bivouac was a test we each had to complete prior to finishing boot camp. It was a culmination of all the training that we had done with physical exercise and guns. We had to do a long night march, bivouac, and then the obstacle course. And that was it. Upon successful completion, basic training was over. This would mean that we each had passed and graduated, after which time we would go on to different tech schools for training in our respective chosen career fields.

Tommy and I were teamed up. We got to the first obstacle. The first thing we had to do was get on a rope and swing across a river. (It wasn't really a river, just a stream of water that was supposed to be a river.) So I grabbed the rope, swung, and landed on the other side. I swung the rope back across the river for Tommy to catch, and then it was his turn to swing across. He grabbed the rope, swung across, and fell in halfway. So there he was in the water, with his pack and wearing his full uniform. He was soaking wet, but he had to get up and go to the next obstacle.

Next, we had machine guns shooting over our heads while we crawled under barbed wire. We made it through that, but it was rough, crawling on our bellies through the dirt. Tommy was wet, so the dirt turned to mud. Now he was covered with mud from head to toe, and he looked like a big chocolate bear.

The next obstacle was called the "gas house." It was filled with tear gas. We had to hold our breath, go through this door that was more like a window, and then crawl out through another window on the opposite side. Tear gas is horrible, worse than smoke. The DI was watching the entire time. So, I went through the house, came out, and waited for Tommy. He was right behind me going in, but I never saw him come out. I started to panic. I thought maybe he passed out in there or something. But, sure enough, he had gotten out. He must have gone through a different window or something because I saw him farther on, crawling some other obstacle, still looking like a huge chocolate bear. Well, I couldn't help it, I burst out laughing. He was so comical without even trying. What a great guy.

I raced ahead to catch up with him, and then we hit the next big obstacle: a brick-walled area with flames shooting out of it. This was called the "flamethrower test." We had to run through the area with the flames, staying straight on this line. If we moved off the line, we'd be burned by the flames to the right or left of us. Needless to say, when Tommy came out, he was a sight. The flames had singed off every bit of his eyebrows, and his face was all red. That really did it to me. I just started laughing hysterically, rolling around on the ground. I got in trouble, but I just couldn't help it. Leave it to my cousin! Somehow, he didn't run like the rest of us, and so he got singed. It was unbelievable. Fortunately, though, the DIs loved Tommy because he was so comical and because they knew he didn't try to be comical; it was just him.

Anyway, we got through the obstacle course, and then, finishing our long night march, we graduated. We made it through basic training.

And then, in the next day or so, we received our orders. Those orders devastated Tommy and me because we had joined in the buddy plan, and so we thought we'd end up going to our tech schools together. And be together for the whole four years. But they had lied. Our moms even tried to complain to the air force (we were only seventeen, remember), but it didn't do any good. We had taken the same career field and everything just so we could be together. So much for that.

Tommy's orders read for Chanute Airbase in Champaign, Illinois; he was going to be in B-52 bombers. I was stationed at the Amarillo Air Force Base, which meant I was staying in Texas; I was to be in a fighter squadron on jet fighters. So, he went to bombers, and I went to fighters. Jet fighters was what I wanted, but I wanted my cousin to go with me.

It was a sad, sad night for us when we got our orders. We got ready to split up from our squadron, but it was hard. We were a team by that point, brothers, a family, and many in the squadron didn't have close family ties. We had gone through all of basic training together, made it through together, and now we all had to go our separate ways. We were closer to one another than any of us had ever been with our friends at home, all because of the hardships we'd endured together through basic.

But that separation was part of the training too. We each were learning how to be a man. That's what basic training was. It was great part of my life, really, because it changed me; it gave me some discipline and direction, and I needed it. As I mentioned briefly, my parents divorced when I was sixteen and still in high school. I kind of lost my way when that happened. It really messed me up.

A lot of kids I knew went to college, but during the first year of college, most kids just missed high school, their friends, and their families. It was easy for them to fall prey to drugs and other dangers. Basic training was better for me because it took all that crap I was carrying around, beat it out of me, and rebuilt me. In a way, being in the military protected me. I had to obey orders, yes, but they also fed me and housed me and gave me some spending money. Most important of all, I had to grow up. It gave me discipline and direction, but, more than that, it saved me.

It was cool too. I loved marching with my squadron, being part of a team, counting on one another and learning how to be proud, but in a military way. Sometimes I changed the lyrics in my head while we were singing our marching songs:

> Lift your head, and hold it high;
> Jim Broman is passing by.

* * * * * *

The day came when it was time for our next step: tech school. We'd gotten through basic training, and now it was time to specialize in the career fields we'd chosen. Tech school was the place where we did that.

As I said, I was in fighters at Amarillo Air Force Base, and my cousin Tommy was stationed up in Chanute on bombers. I stayed in Texas; he went to Illinois. We'd always been close and grew even closer during basic. The separation was rough on both of us, but we got through it. The career training we would receive in the military was the reason we'd joined up in the first place, so neither one of us was about to mess it up. Not on purpose, anyway. With my rebellious streak and Tommy's hilarity, it was always anybody's guess what might happen.

I had wanted the fighters from the beginning, and I was happy I got it, even though Tommy and I were split up. As it turned out, I liked the fighters even more than I'd expected I would, partly because it fit perfectly with my natural style. If I'd had my high-school diploma, I would have been in air-sea rescue because of my background in both diving and athletics. I could be transferred if I reenlisted and got my GED, but that was another story.

When I finished tech school, I would have a tremendous amount of responsibility, anyway. I was ultimately responsible for an F-100 Super Sabre fighter-bomber jet in Japan, and when it went over to South Korea, it was loaded with a nuclear weapon. That was my airplane. My name was painted on the side of it, along with the pilot's name. So, it was a pretty awesome responsibility. I'll get to all that a bit later. In the meantime, let's get back to tech school.

We didn't get to go home after basic training; we shipped out to tech school right away. I went straight to Amarillo Air Force Base. I started in jet mechanic fighter school, and all of us were called jet mechanics, but we could specialize in electronics or engines or a whole bunch of other things. I did well in all of them, and I ended up a crew chief. That was always my style, to be in charge.

I'm getting ahead of the story again. Let me back up a bit. When we arrived at the base in Amarillo, we had to wait. There was a waiting line for the classes to open up. So we were all concentrated in an area that was just waiting to process us to go through school. That meant every day that we were there wasn't getting us any closer to getting home. You had to go through the school before you could get your leave to go home, so every day was just depressing. The most depressing part of it was that other guys just like us were in charge of us. These guys had been there longer than we had, but they weren't sergeants or other noncoms, they were just like us, waiting to go to school. The power really went to their heads, and they were jerks about it, excessive with discipline and that kind of thing. Those guys were lowly grubs like we were, airmen and nothing more, but they were meaner than any staff sergeants or anybody with real authority. A lot of guys went AWOL. Guys got thrown in the brig because it was harder to obey people who weren't the real thing than it was to obey those you felt okay with obeying. That was the first time I thought about going AWOL. It was that rough, totally depressing.

At one point, it looked like it was going to be weeks before I would get into my classes, and that meant even more weeks before I would get home. I got even more depressed, and I gave some more thought to going AWOL. Serious thought.

I said to myself, *Okay, I've got to get out of here. I'll just get out and go home.*

But then I thought about it some more. I knew the air force would find me, and then what would I do and where would I go? I'd be a failure. A coward. I wouldn't be able to face anybody. So I stopped thinking about going AWOL. I knew that I had to stay on the base in Amarillo, but it was hard. I was really homesick. And I also missed my cousin Tommy and all my buddies from basic training. Loneliness and homesickness combined. Not fun at all.

Finally, I did get into my class. Just as I'd done all through school, I got by in tech school, but I was not the star of the class. I passed; I made sure I passed because if I didn't, I wouldn't get to go on my leave, take a trip home, and then get stationed at my regular base. I did the bare minimum, nothing more. The tech school was harder for me than basic training was.

There was one big thing that happened while I was at tech school, though. One of my high-school frat brothers headed out to Amarillo, Texas, to visit me. While he was on the road, the engine blew up in his car. He ended up buying another car, getting the money from me (I wired it to him). Now, no one was supposed to have a car while in tech school, but I decided that I was going to have one. My plan was to have him come out, bring the car, and then we could go look for girls. That was everything to us: looking for girls. (I've already admitted to being a womanizer my entire life. My dad trained me, and maybe it was in my genes too. School and the frat reinforced it, and then the military reinforced it even more. Society at that time—the 1950s and '60s—reinforced it. Most of the young guys and older men I've known throughout my life were not appreciably different from me. I'm not making excuses; that's just the way it was.)

The car my friend wound up buying was a 1949 Packard, a four-door, very old (remember, this was 1960). It was not the cool car we'd had in mind. As far as we were concerned, it was just a big, old bus. Anyway, as soon as he arrived, we met to talk. He hung on my every word; he was so devoted to me. A lot of the other guys in high school were like that with me too. I was the leader in the fraternity. I was the leader in the car clubs. I was almost like a mafia boss to these other kids. I was Broman, "the man." (That guy in particular, though, the one who drove the '49 Packard to Texas, was devoted to me because he had a crush on my mom. At least that's what I thought. Then again, every guy had a crush on my mom; she was so beautiful, inside and out.)

We had a great time, and as I said, we weren't allowed to have cars on the base. But I was determined to have a car; I was never going to get to see girls without a car. So when he left, I talked him into taking a bus back home, and he left the car with me. Some buddies and I found a place to park it off base, very remote, where no one would ever find it. And then, when we'd get our weekend passes, or if we should happen to get one through the middle of the week, we would go off base, go pick up the car, and then go cruise around to pick up girls.

What a plan that was! It worked out great. We actually did pick up girls, a lot of them. Mostly, they were Latino girls. They were so pretty. I always loved the Latino girls; I still do. Sometimes we picked up Mexican girls. They were pretty and sexy. And sweet too because we didn't have the status that the jocks and the college guys did. We were what they called "military guys." I didn't care; a pretty, sexy girl was all I was interested in, and as long as she liked me too, that was all that mattered.

I always got along well with Latinos; they liked me, and I liked them, both the men and the women. We just connected. In high school, I would drive into East LA, the Barrios, flying my Outcast plaque and my colors in the rear window: Long Beach, California. I would pull in to their turf, a drive-in where they would hang out, and the car hops would come out, and the cars would cruise around the restaurant. I was always welcome.

The Latinos in Texas were not much different from the Latinos in California. I fit right in, and we got along great.

I ran around with another airman, a guy by the name of Hawkins, from Fort Worth, Texas. I loved that guy. Then there was Mallory, another good friend; he was from New York. We had other friends too, but the three of us were tight. We would go out, cruise, and pick up girls. Man, what a time that was. It was wonderful. I loved it. We'd go to the beer garden on our time off, and we'd talk about home and brag about all our stuff that we had and what we did, just the things that young guys do everywhere.

* * * * * *

One night, just as we were heading out on our weekend passes, we saw these posters for USO dances. We'd heard that they were the most terrible things. The girls from town would come to them. Because we were military guys, we didn't usually get the best girls, and so we were kind of hard up. Our plan was to head into town. There were a couple of girls we'd met in town who liked us. We liked them too, and we were going to see them.

I turned to Hawkins. "Let's stop by that USO dance before we go," I said.

"Man, they bring the biggest dirt bags ever to those dances."

And I said, "No, come on, let's go."

He gave me a dubious look.

But I had a hunch about that dance.

"If it's no good, we'll just continue on our way and head on into town," I assured him.

He agreed.

That would prove to be one memorable dance indeed.

We walked into this big auditorium, and we saw a bunch of girls. There must have been a hundred of them. I started looking around, and they were cute. Some of them were absolute sweethearts, really adorable. I couldn't believe it.

I said to Hawkins, "You see? Some of these girls are beautiful."

He said, "I can't believe this, man. We hit the jackpot. Where'd they come from?"

Anyway, we looked real cocky. I walked in my California way. He walked in his Texas way.

I went right up to one of these gals who was just as cute as could be. I couldn't believe it, man. I mean, she was knockout. And a turn-on right away.

I looked in her face, right in her eyes, and I said, "Would you like to dance?"

She looked back at me, right in my eyes too, and she said, "Yes."

So I turned around immediately, and my back was facing her, and I reached out my right hand, took her hand, and we walked out to the floor. When we get out on the dance floor, I reached for her other arm to take her hand and start to dance. Well, I was in shock! She didn't have another arm. She only had one arm.

Now, I'm not making fun of anybody, and for years after this I felt so guilty, but I went into shock at the moment when I realized that she only had one arm. She was beautiful, and it shouldn't have bothered me, but I just couldn't get over it. It shocked me so badly; I just could not wrap my mind around it. I swung my arm around her, and this girl had only one arm, no fake arm or anything to replace the other one. It was just like a stub up there. It was really weird.

I pulled myself together, just putting one arm around her back, and she kind of snuggled up to me while we danced. But I was still in a state of shock. I did not know how to handle this situation. I just wanted to get out of there. I looked over and saw Hawkins; he was dancing with a gal, and he was moving up and down, because the girl he was dancing with had only one leg (actually, one leg was shorter than the other one).

All the people at that dance were handicapped, brought in from town.

Hawkins looked at me, and I looked at him. We were the only guys in there dancing. I was with a one-armed gal, and he was with a gal who had one leg that was about a foot shorter than the other one. You would have laughed if you saw our expressions. Not to make fun of the people at the dance or the girls we were dancing with. What was funny was how shocked the two of us were; we thought we were so smooth, but we didn't know how to handle that situation. We didn't have a clue.

So we got out of there. I've thought about it through the years, and I wish I would have stayed there and gotten to know that gal. She was cuter than any of the other girls I was taking out at that time. But I didn't get to know her; I never even asked her name. I wasn't mature enough to handle it right. I was completely shocked, and I couldn't get past it. It just blew me away. Hawkins had the identical reaction.

* * * * * *

I finished up tech school that same year that Hawkins and I danced with the handicapped girls. I finally got my orders, and I was getting ready to go home and then leave for my first post.

Everybody was finished and heading home and then out, not just me. Some of us were stationed in the States, some overseas. I really lucked out; I wanted to go to Japan, and lo and behold, that's where I was stationed, with the 531st Tactical Fighter Squadron at the air base in Misawa, Japan.

It was the best air base over there, a small base on the northern end of Honshu. It was incredible.

I was going to be working on the F-100 Super Sabre. The F-100s were bombers that could carry a big payload, but they were really good fighters too, with GAR-8 Sidewinder rockets mounted on them, and a nuclear weapon could mount on the centerline as well. It was heavy-duty stuff.

That was where I was going to go. Plus, I got to go home first.

And, man, that first trip home was the best. I was a real hero. I was the first one of my friends to go in the military, and since I'd joined, about five or six of my other friends had joined too—the army, marines, air force, all the branches. But I was the first one to come home and to be successfully out of boot camp and getting stationed overseas.

It was so awesome. It was like God himself was taking care of me. As I look back on my life now, I *know* he was. I can see that now. I always prayed a lot. Maybe not for the right things, but I thought they were the right things at the time. Now that I'm older, I know for sure that a lot of those prayers weren't for the right things, but I still had great things happen to me. Somehow, I was protected no matter what happened to me, no matter what I had to go through. Maybe God sensed my sincerity and said something like, "He has a lot to learn, but his heart is in the right place." I feel so blessed, so I have to believe that's pretty close to what he's always felt about me.

I sold that 1949 Packard to some old guy, but then I won it back from him in a poker game. I passed it on to somebody else because my friends and I were heading out.

I missed Hawkins and Mallory and my other friends. I missed Hawkins the most; we ended up really close buds by the time we left tech school. Somehow or another, I always ended up close with certain people. That was one of my problems in life: I tried to be close with everybody, but some people just don't want to experience that. Hawkins was a cool dude. He appreciated the closeness of our friendship as much as I did. We had a good time together; we made the best of tech school. I mean, what other guys would have their cars stashed off base? Not to mention, we were the only ones who even *had* a car in tech school. It was cool, and so were we. Thanks to a frat brother who drove all the way from California to Texas to deliver a car to me. My Texas buddy and I had the car and got the girls.

What a great time that was.

Orders for the 531st Tactical Fighter Squadron— Misawa Air Base, Japan (1960)

I had changed during my time in basic training and tech school. That was a huge moon pool, and it changed me irrevocably, even though it was a very short span of time from basic training to tech school.

I went home on leave, but I was an outsider now. I never felt close to Long Beach again in the same way. I would hang with my friends, cruise around, take out girls, and all of that, but I wasn't really part of it anymore.

It was unbelievable how quickly things could change. That is something that's hard to take in when you're young and experiencing it for the first time.

I only had thirty days' leave, and then I was heading for Japan for a two-year stint. During that time, the unforgettable song "Soldier Boy" was a big hit. Remember, I was the first in our group to join the military, and so all my girlfriends dedicated that song to me. It broke my heart to leave them, and I think my leaving broke their hearts too. Still, the military was the greatest thing that ever could have happened to me. Kids my age were starting to do drugs, pot mostly. (The only drugs I had tried at that point were bennies and one joint during a frat outing at Big Bear; I would do more drugs over time, but when I was older and better equipped to handle the consequences.) Once again, I was being protected. I am a born addict, so any time I was ever around drugs or Oreo cookies or beautiful women or whatever tempted me, I would overdo it. I was always over the top, always creating drama. That was just me; it still is. You already know the way I am. My story speaks for itself.

* * * * * *

I was only seventeen when I left for Japan; I hadn't yet turned eighteen. I boarded this airplane headed for Japan, excited but a little apprehensive. When I arrived, it was not what I thought it was going to be. It never is at first, but in time, I came to see that it was better than what I'd left behind. We all have those moments; that is just part of growing up, of becoming an adult in the truest sense.

* * * * * *

I was stationed at Misawa Air Base in Japan for two years, during which time I also had deployments to South Korea and Taiwan. After my tour in Asia, I was assigned to a base in Spain, with a mission to West Germany. Consequently, at the age of twenty-one, I was already a seasoned world traveler.

While stationed in Japan, I was a crew chief on the F-100 Super Sabre, with the 531st Tactical Fighter Squadron, as I mentioned earlier.

My experiences in South Korea and Taiwan were interesting, but my favorite part of my Asian tour was Japan, hands down. Even our barracks were great: one man to a room, with a Japanese houseboy who cleaned our rooms, made our beds, shined our brogans and shoes, did our laundry, ironed our clothes, and even did our kitchen duty. (We had no KP [kitchen police]; we paid the houseboy extra to do that for us.) The base had a golf course, rental cars, a sports complex, a movie theater, a PX (Post Exchange), and the best NCOs' club with live entertainment.

Misawa was a great town, even off the base. The Japanese were fantastic; I loved their culture, especially the women (of course!). It cost me thirty-six hundred yen a month (approximately ten US dollars) to have a place in town. It was a small flat, and I paid all the expenses for my jo-san to live there in town and be with me whenever I wanted. That was all the time, of course, and I was with her as much as I possibly could be.

My jo-san's name was Sachiko, meaning "child of happiness" (幸子). She was twenty-three; I was eighteen. She enjoyed what I gave her, especially shopping with me at the PX on the base. And she gave me so much in return, far more than I realized at the time. I learned so much about sex and lovemaking, how to be slow and patient and at the same time very passionate. I was always a good lover, but I became an even better one because of Sachiko. She was trained to love a man the way a woman should, and did she ever get that training right! She was beautiful and sensuous, passionate yet gentle and delicate. My time with her was incredible in every way.

Sachiko referred to me as a "butterfly." That was what the Japanese girls called men who slept around, because they flitted from flower to flower, enjoying the perfume of each one that was sweeter than the one before it. Yes, I was a butterfly, but not because I was always searching for a sweeter, more beautiful flower; with me, it was because I couldn't resist any of the flowers—they were each sweet and beautiful in their own way, but no one more so than any other. I continued with my butterfly ways, but Sachiko was my main girl, my jo-san.

There was one girl who was the beauty of all the jo-sans. She had an officer taking care of her, but she would still party. She didn't ever sleep with anybody else, but she would go out to have fun. Her boyfriend (the officer) didn't like her to go out, but he didn't stop her because he couldn't risk the chance of losing her. Any man who saw her fell in love with her in that same instant. The officer couldn't be seen with her in public because he was married. His wife and family were back in the States. It was the same thing with a lot of the guys—officers, noncoms, and enlisted men.

Anyway, I had a big crush on this girl; all the guys did. She was exquisite. One look, and all you wanted was to sleep with her, love her, spend time with her; it was an obsession, but I couldn't help how I felt about her. She was magnificent, and she knew it, and that made her all the more desirable.

I schemed on her for about a year, and we did finally get together. We were in the same bar one night (because I had schemed and made it happen, but she didn't know that), and I ended up going home with her. She wound up falling for me, pretty hard, I guess, because she gave me her key and wanted me to be her "boy-san" (her main guy). I really would have loved that, but her boyfriend was an officer, and even I knew when I was asking for too much trouble. We did enjoy each other, though, and had a great time while we were together.

Once a butterfly, always a butterfly, I suppose.

Socializing wasn't all about women. Mostly it was, but we had some fun guys' nights too. I started a club, the Five-Thirsty-First Boys, similar to my car club at home during high school. I designed hats with the Five-Thirsty-First logo. (These were similar to the jacket patches with the Outcasts logo that we wore in high school.) I designed the logo too, which was the same as our squadron's logo, only the eagle was carrying a Nippon beer bottle in its claws, and below the image it said the "Five-Thirsty-First," instead of 531st (as in, Five-Thirty-First), and below that it said Misawa, Japan; Kunsan, Korea; Taiwan, Formosa. Directly in the very back and center, you could see the bird (a hand giving you the middle finger) to show how wild we were in the Five-Thirsty-First. The hats were beautiful, red and very cool with the logo. The pilots loved them, and even the squadron commander wore one.

We were a crazy bunch and proud of it. Those were really great times. I loved that Five-Thirsty-First Boys club.

Anyway, we had to make our own fun off the base. The nearest city of any size was Hachinohe, about a thirty- to forty-minute car ride from the base. The area surrounding the base was mostly rural and quite scenic. There was some limited nightlife, mostly concentrated around the base. That scene was where we would meet our girlfriends.

Tokyo was an hour away by plane, about three and half hours by train, and about ten to twelve hours by car.

It was exciting to be in the air force at age seventeen, especially working in a fighter squadron. To be a crew chief in charge of a Mach 2 jet fighter aircraft at age eighteen was even more exciting, particularly because my name and the pilot's name were painted on the side of the plane. It was *our* plane.

But it wasn't all fun and excitement; it was a huge responsibility. Flying our jet fighter from Misawa, Japan, to Kunsan, South Korea, with heat-seeking GAR-8 Sidewinder rockets mounted on the wings and a nuclear weapon mounted on the center pylon was a serious responsibility. We were Alert Pad C—the nuclear alert pad—and proud of it.

I was very patriotic, proud to be an American, proud to serve. And damn proud to be a crew chief in a jet fighter squadron.

The Riviera by the Yellow Sea—Kunsan, South Korea; the Beautiful Island of Formosa— Taiwan, Republic of China (1961)

"The Riviera by the Yellow Sea" was our nickname for Kunsan. We were sent on alerts to South Korea every six months. Our planes had taxied off the jacks on several occasions, with threats from the Russians (Soviets, but we called them Russians) and the Chinese. Our aircraft was always loaded with a nuclear weapon, ready to strike. Our motto was "strike and return"; that was our mission.

Our deployments to South Korea were regular: every six months, and more often if necessary. We were also deployed to Taiwan (Formosa), but that only happened once. It was a very cool assignment, though. There were no American bases over there, so we had to live off base. Of course, we found women soon enough. They were all Chinese and Taiwanese girls, sweet and beautiful. They were similar to the Japanese girls, gentle and gracious in the way that only women of the Far East could be. I was in heaven.

My Asian tour was a good time in my life. Exciting and fun, and filled with beautiful women. What was not to like?

That deployment to Taiwan was a big privilege: there were only five guys out of our squadron flying on a C-130. We were going to simulate our whole squadron flying over there.

We went on an advance party, landing at the Taiwanese base, and then we went to the hotel where we would be billeted for the duration of the assignment.

They brought in Taiwanese girls on trains to entertain us. As Americans, we were treated like royalty. Just five of us, and we had all of these women at our beck and call. I was in heaven. (Did I say that already?

Well, I'll say it again. Those girls were magnificent, and they made that experience heaven for me, and the other guys too, I'm sure.)

Security was high. We had to have an ID in order to get on base, but they didn't mess with us. They knew we were American, but any one of us could be an American spy; all of us could be spies. They were cautious and rightfully so. It was still the Cold War, after all.

I came went to the base drunk one night. Our staff sergeant from Misawa was with me. I knew what happened if you came to the base without your high-security clearance ID card: they put you on the ground and put a gun to the back of your head. Well, you know me by now. I was always losing my ID card or misplacing it. I had been out drinking, and I didn't have my ID card, so they did put me down on the deck, gun to my head, the whole nine yards.

Finally, the staff sergeant with me got back to our hotel, got the officer in charge, and got me released. Never a dull moment. There were better ways to have excitement, though—chasing the beautiful women, etc.

Anyway, back to Taiwan. It was a beautiful country. The people (the civilians, people mean) were friendly. They would smile and say, *"Ding how, ding how!"*

The Taiwanese were beautiful people who loved Americans, and they treated us fantastically well, better even than the Japanese did. (To rank the Far East Asians in order of how well they treated Americans, the South Koreans treated us okay, but not as well as the Japanese did, and the Taiwanese treated us the best of all.)

What a landscape! Water buffalos and carts and big rice fields; it was such a beautiful island, absolutely magnificent. Being there was a great experience.

We did our flight simulation on the C-130; that was the purpose of our deployment. There were all kinds of ground troops there to support the aircraft and the 531st Tactical Fighters Squadron.

We completed our mission, and then we prepared to leave, just waiting on our orders. That was a great couple of days because we didn't have any work to do. We just messed around with the girls and shopped and that kind of stuff.

Plus, we had all kinds of extra room—a whole plane, in fact. Well, I got this great idea: I bought bananas, coconuts, and pineapples, and I loaded up the whole empty plane with them. A C-130 filled with fruit! I had it all shipped back with us, planning that I'd have all this contraband to sell.

When we landed in Japan, it was snowing. I called the barracks and had a weapons carrier sent out. I loaded all the fruit on it, and then I took it to this Japanese guy in town to have him sell it for me.

The word got out that bananas, coconuts, and pineapples had been shipped from Taiwan. Well, who was in the group to Taiwan? There were only five of us who could have done it, and I got caught. I did get an honorable discharge, but I also got an Article 15, which kept me from making Airman First Class. I ended up Airman Second Class, but I still had a level 5, which meant that I was a crew chief responsible for my airplane, not just an assistant. I loved being a crew chief, so I was glad I retained my level 5.

That experience with getting the Article 15 was a turning point for me: I made up my mind that I wasn't going to reenlist. Later on, they tried to tempt me, offering to give me any career field I wanted, including flying, air-sea rescue, or whatever. But they also told me that I would be going to Vietnam in the Special Forces. I wanted to go. It would be another adventure. Actually, the opportunity to go to Vietnam was a real dangling carrot.

But I decided that the military life wasn't for me, not just because of the Article 15—that was the clincher—but I was already leaning toward getting out when my tour was up. I knew that if I reenlisted, that would mean another four years, for a total of eight years. That meant that I wouldn't make any money for eight years. I was smart and very practical; I did want to make some money. And I also wanted to control my own life. The military was great for me, and I was glad I served, but four years active and two years reserve was enough, simple as that.

I'd only served two years at that point, though, so I did still have two more to go. My first two years had been great: Japan, South Korea, Taiwan. Exciting, fun times—especially my time with Sachiko, my beautiful jo-san. I learned so much about life—and love—and, as I said, the military was truly what made a man of me. Those lessons were all invaluable. I wouldn't trade any of it, not one single bit.

Tactical Jet Fighting—Japan (1960–1961)

It wasn't all about fun times and beautiful women. Well, with me, it was always about that, at least to a certain extent. But I learned specific critical skills in the military too. Of course I did.

The F-100 Super Sabre was a fighter-bomber aircraft, top in its class. I've talked about it briefly, but I don't want to leave out any key specs. The F-100 was a sleek, swept-back-wing fighter that gave the United States a supersonic air force. Armed with a nuclear bomb, four 20-millimeter cannons equipped to fire rockets and missiles, including the heat-seeking GAR-8 Sidewinder, it was a powerful machine. With speeds in excess of 1,000 miles per hour, F-100 Super Sabres were chosen by the air force to perform throughout the world in aerial precision demonstration flights by famed "Thunderbirds," a four-man aircraft team. During these flights, the pilots performed intricate precision maneuvers at low altitudes.

I loved being a crew chief of an F-100 at age eighteen; that was my plane, with my name on it just like the pilot's. It was a source of great pride, but it was also an enormous responsibility. If anything went wrong with the aircraft, I had to oversee and supervise the work. Any electricians, armament men, or engine men working on that plane had to answer to me.

Being a level 5 was what enabled me to be a crew chief, so, even though I never made it to Airman First Class, I was still proud of my work, achievements, and service to my country. When that two-year stint in Asia was over, I felt I'd done good work, and I was ready for the next phase: the rest of my tour and then "real life" after that. At eighteen, that was how I thought of it—"real life" started at a specific point; it wasn't what had been going on all along. Only life experience can give any of us perspective and wisdom, regardless of what our individual experiences might be.

And then there was the alert pad. It was exciting when we would have a "fast-boy" (a practice alert) or an actual alert. Mine was Alert Pad C, the nuclear alert pad, as I've mentioned.

Standard operating procedure (SOP) was that we jumped in the weapons carriers, and they raced us out to the airplane. We had to get there before the pilot so that everything would be ready for him. We would start the aircraft, have it all ready, and then the pilot would arrive, suit up, and take off. (The entire process was perfectly orchestrated, down to the last detail. It was a lot like deep-water diving in that respect. So, even though I was in the air force, not the navy, my service proved invaluable to my diving career.)

I can still remember one alert when one of the pilots kicked me off the ladder because I had my hands inside the cockpit. They had secret information in there. They even had pills that they could take in the event that they were captured. Still, we were on the same side, so his reaction was strange. I never found out the reason for it; maybe there wasn't one. There was a lot of stuff that went on. Being in the military was a great experience, an exciting adventure, but it was intense too. A lot of guys couldn't handle it, even in peacetime.

The real alerts were beyond exciting, beyond adventurous. They were scary, and we were always nervous. We did our jobs, but the fear was always there. (That was also a lot like diving.) I would start the aircraft, have it ready, and then the pilot would taxi off the jacks. There were several real alerts as a result of Russian (Soviet) MIGs having threatened us. It was very serious. Scary stuff. But we would be ready to taxi off the jacks, with an armed nuclear weapon aimed for the USSR. That was pretty unbelievable.

On the serious side of things too, a lot of guys had stories to tell about their service during the Korean War. That was a brutal and tough war, with a lot of Americans lost. It's often called the "Forgotten War," but those who were there never forgot. No one ever should. All who serve earn the right to be remembered and honored.

My time in South Korea was several years after the war. We only spent about six weeks there each time, and then we went back to Japan. One of my times in South Korea was on an actual alert; the other times were fast-boys. Some of the guys volunteered to go there because they liked Korean women and they could save their money and so on.

There were some cool guys in the squadron, from all over. They had their jo-sans, and we all hung together and got along well. There were one or two guys who weren't cool, but that's just how life is; it happens in all situations and in all places. For the most part, those were good times and great experiences, as I've said.

Before I go on to my next set of experiences, I have to describe two more incidents that happened in Japan. A bunch of us guys got drunk, and we took our jo-sans to some motorcycle races by the *benjo* ditches. These were huge ditches where they dumped all of the human waste. They used honey buckets, went from house to house dipping the buckets, and then a honey wagon came to pick up the buckets and dump the contents into this big ditch. That was their idea of "sewage plants." Anyway, we were in a cab with our girls, and one of the guys, Roger, fell out—right into the *benjo* ditch, which was literally a hole filled with crap. He was submerged all the way up to his head. It was awful but hilarious!

We pulled him out, and the girls took him to a bathhouse and got him all cleaned up. The whole geisha mind-set and way of life was so great; they never minded doing things like that. (To the jo-sans, everything was about the man's comfort and pleasure. I loved that. Sachiko always did whatever I wanted. Made love whenever I wanted to, and she loved it too.) The guys never let Roger live it down, though. For the rest our time in Japan, he was always the guy who had fallen into the hole of crap.

The next incident was related to money, not crap. One morning when I woke up, the military police (MPs) were all around, announcing that we had to take all of our military pay certificates and turn them in to get greenbacks (American money) in exchange for them. That was because they had closed the whole base off; it was like a big sting operation. If you didn't turn it all in that day, the money would be no good.

Meanwhile, all along up to that point, all the Japanese shopkeepers and jo-sans and people in town held a lot of these military pay certificates. They weren't supposed to, but they just didn't get the time to trade it all in. You could always trade in pay certificates for American dollars in town. Some of them had thousands and thousands of dollars of this stuff.

Needless to say, there was a big riot outside the fence surrounding the base when the word got out. They had to use fire hoses and everything to get things under control. A lot of Japanese lost money because the military pay certificates were virtually worthless at that point. The MPs did warn everybody all along not to use those certificates in town; they had always made it clear that they had the authority, capability, and right to enforce strict limitation of pay certificates to the base. They had never enforced that rule up to that point, but that morning, they did.

So that was my two-year stint in Japan. It was a long time—or so it seemed to me at seventeen and eighteen—but it was wonderful. It was an absolutely fantastic experience, exciting and lots of fun, as I keep telling you. But can you blame me? I mean, it was glorious. Sachiko, the Five-Thirty-First Boys, the jo-sans, and all the fun times. The base had everything we needed, but we still made our little jaunts on the outside. It truly was wonderful in every way. I'm a very fortunate man to have experienced that part of the world in peacetime. It was a privilege to serve, and I'll always be grateful.

And now, on to the remaining two years of my time in the air force.

George Air Force Base—Victorville, California (1962)

The air force sent me back to California, to the base in Victorville. We actually lived in Apple Valley, five miles away, in the high desert, but the base was about ten miles outside Victorville. This started a whole new segment of my life.

I had not been stationed in the States up to that point, and the only bases in the States that I had lived in were during basic training and tech school. It was quite an adjustment after two years in the Far East, pampered by my jo-san, my other Asian girls, and the Japanese houseboy. Anyway, I made the adjustment without too much trouble, and I got used to living off base on separate rations. I ran around with all the locals, which was very unusual. Rarely if ever was any serviceman accepted by the local young crowd in the States. But I was from the beach, a native Californian, so that gave me an in.

Apple Valley was nothing like the Southern California beaches where I grew up, but it was still California. It was a great place to live, just below the mountains in the high desert. I liked it a lot.

Newt Bass was a very famous man up there; he had developed the area. Cowboy actor Roy Rogers and his cowgirl actress wife, Dale Evans, had a museum there. I guess they all liked it too, and I could see why. It was beautiful. It was just another of many times in my life when I had the blessing of being in a good place. Even though it was the desert, it was good. I love jungles and the tropics—and the water, of course—and I loved those warm, wet climates then too, but the desert was magnificent in its own way, and I appreciated that. I liked the dry heat and the wide-open spaces. And the beautiful girls. (Well, you knew that was coming!)

* * * * * *

My adventures started pretty early on. There was one big incident, a fistfight. My buddies and I were always chasing girls. As usual, I was the lead chaser. I met two girls at the bowling alley. They both worked as cocktail waitresses. One was Cat, and the other was Mia. They were really good-looking, but they were older than I was—quite a bit older, I'd say twenty-six or twenty-seven. I was twenty-one at the time. I established that both of them were divorcees with no kids. So I was in. They were two gorgeous gals.

I started dating one of them and ended up kind of taking both of them out. We liked to hang out at Riley B's, a really wild place. Cat and Mia both had danced there, and they loved the place. I liked it too; it was the place where we all went to pick up women. I went there with some of my friends one night, and Cat and Mia were there at the bar.

Mia's ex-husband, who was one of the roughest guys in the whole area, was there too. He worked for a guy who was supposed to be one of the toughest guys around also. They were called hay-buckers; they would drive these trucks to the ranches in Nevada and places like that, pick up the hay, and bring it to outlets. So, these guys were strong, tough, and wild. And one of them was Mia's ex-husband, and another one was his boss. Mia was dating the boss, which I didn't know at the time. I really had a thing for Mia; she was the one I was actually dating. Cat was good-looking too, not quite as cute as Mia, but she was sexy and lovable, and so I took her out too. Plus, she was just always there because she was Mia's best friend. (That's happened to me a lot; you'll remember from part III how I met my girlfriend Ali and how her best friend, Kiera, was always tagging along with us. It was great when she drove because then Ali and I could cuddle up and make out in the backseat, undisturbed. Gotta love a girl's best friend!)

Anyway, I was with all my friends at Riley B's, and the dance band was playing. I saw Mia and Cat move from the bar to the floor, and they were dancing with different people. I went up to Mia and asked her to dance. She started dancing with me because she liked me a lot, and we were already dating. So there we were, dancing fast and slow. She cuddled up to me, grinding against me, and her ex-husband was furious. He kept watching us the whole time we were cuddled up on the dance floor.

Later on that evening, he came up to me, right into my face, and said, "Listen, wing nut (that's what they called us air force guys), don't dance with her anymore. Don't you even talk to her anymore, or I'm going to kick the shit out of you."

He made this threat in front of all my friends. I wasn't going to take that.

All my friends agreed: "Man, don't mess with that guy. He is one bad dude."

Like I said, I wasn't going to take any abuse from that guy or anyone else, so I didn't listen to my friends. The music started playing again. My friends and I were sitting at a table by that point.

I said, "I'm not going to let that guy push me around." And I wasn't going to, even though I was a little bit scared of him.

I went up to Mia again, and we started dancing, cuddling up, and I gave her this long, passionate kiss. She kissed me back, and it was obvious to anyone watching us that she was kissing me back. And her ex, of course, was watching. She was very affectionate and a real knockout. We were both really turned on, and I kept dancing with her.

Meanwhile, her ex was furious. He kept giving me the dirtiest looks all the rest of the night—not just dirty but threatening, menacing. He kept drinking too.

The place closed at 2:00 a.m., and we all went outside. There was Mia's ex, waiting for me. He was just standing there, leaning against the wall. As soon as he saw me, he came right at me and pushed me. A real shove. I was pissed. I hauled off and hit him right smack in the nose, and we started fighting. A big crowd formed. All my friends and all his friends surrounded us, and he and I kept fighting. Well, I was winning. I just kept boxing him, really hammering him. I broke his nose, and his face was a bloody pulp. I kicked him in the balls over and over again, and he could barely stand up. He was a total mess.

All of a sudden, somebody yelled, "Cops!"

I turned to look, and before I could turn back around, he jumped on my back. I went down, and he jumped up and started kicking me in the ribs. It took my breath away. Somehow, I went under a car. My head was wedged between the tire and the car, and then the cops actually did show up. He split, helped by his friends; he could hardly walk or stand up because his balls were in such bad shape.

It wasn't all bad, though. Before he took off, Mia had jumped on his back, trying to help me. I think she fell in love with me before that night, but if not, she sure was in love with me by the time that night was over. She was my girl after that, all the rest of the time I was in Victorville.

She took me home with her that night, and she nursed me so tenderly. She was so beautiful, and she was all mine. She made love to me in the sweetest way that night; my ribs were busted and painful, but she was so gentle and an incredible lover. She had orgasms that were long and sweet and loving all the way through what was left of that night and into the morning. I didn't leave her place until the following afternoon. I lost count of how many times we made love before I left. I was blown away by how beautiful she was naked.

That was just the beginning of my time with Mia.

That night at the bowling alley, I heard from friends that Mia's ex was in the hospital. I had beaten him pretty badly, and his balls were so swollen that he couldn't move. They said he would be bedridden for a week and was in serious condition.

As far as I was concerned, he had it coming. Not that I intended for him to wind up in the hospital. I didn't, but I wasn't going to lose the fight, either, especially when he was the one who started it, and for no reason. Mia was his ex-wife, so he couldn't claim any rights, in my opinion. The long and short of it was that he started the fight, and I finished it. Maybe next time he wouldn't be so sure that he could win any fight he started.

In any case, that wasn't the end of it. The word on the street was that his boss was looking for me, and he was going to kick my ass for hurting his friend and employee, and for taking his girl, Mia. By which I mean that Mia was the boss's girl, as I mentioned earlier, but I hadn't known that at the time I started dating her.

A day later, the boss guy showed up at the bowling alley. I was there, and he called me outside to the parking lot to fight. The whole crowd emptied out to the parking lot to watch.

We met, and he was about twenty feet away from me, yelling, "I'm gonna kick your ass, wing nut!"

I called his bluff. I put my fist up and started walking toward him. I saw the fear in his eyes; he didn't expect me to take him on. As I got closer, he started to chicken out.

"Hey, man, maybe we can work it out peaceably," he said.

I said, "Fuck you! I'm gonna kick *your* ass."

That whole crowd was blown away. I had cornered the leader of the hay-buckers and made him back down.

"I don't want to fight," he said.

I charged him, and he ran. The ultimate in cowardice.

The feared hay-buckers were defeated. Jim Broman was the man. Thank you!

My friends and I ruled the town and the entire area from that point on. It was the best.

And it was better for me than anyone else: I was having a great time with Mia.

She was getting ready to find someone to marry, and she knew I wasn't a candidate. So it all worked out okay.

Mia and Cat, two incredible, gorgeous, wild women. What a time I had in Victorville, California.

The Cuban Missile Crisis (1962)

After seizing power in the Caribbean island nation of Cuba in 1959, leftist revolutionary leader Fidel Castro aligned himself with the Soviet Union. Under Castro, Cuba grew dependent on the Soviets for military and economic aid. During this time, the United States and the USSR (and their respective allies) were engaged in the Cold War, an ongoing series of largely political and economic clashes.

The two superpowers plunged into one of their biggest Cold War confrontations after the pilot of an American U-2 spy plane making a high-altitude pass over Cuba on October 14, 1962, photographed a Soviet SS-4 medium-range ballistic missile being assembled for installation.

President John F. Kennedy was briefed about the situation, and he immediately called together a group of advisors and officials known as the Executive Committee (ExCom). Throughout the two weeks that followed, the president and his team wrestled with a diplomatic crisis of epic proportions, as did their counterparts in the Soviet Union.

For the American officials, the urgency of the situation stemmed from the fact that the nuclear-armed Cuban missiles were being installed so close to the US mainland, just ninety miles south of Florida. From that launch point, they were capable of quickly reaching targets in the eastern United States. If allowed to become operational, the missiles would fundamentally alter the complexion of the nuclear rivalry between the United States and the USSR, which up to that point had been dominated by the Americans.

Soviet leader Nikita S. Khrushchev had gambled on sending the missiles to Cuba, with the specific goal of increasing his nation's nuclear strike capability. The Soviets had long felt uneasy about the number of nuclear weapons that were targeted at them from sites in Western Europe and Turkey, and they saw the deployment of missiles in Cuba as a way to level the playing field. Another key factor in the Soviet missile scheme was the hostile relationship between the United States and Cuba. The Kennedy administration had already launched one attack on the island—the failed Bay of Pigs invasion in 1961—and Castro and Khrushchev saw the missiles as a means of deterring further US aggression.

In a TV address on October 22, 1962, President Kennedy notified Americans about the presence of the missiles, explained his decision to enact a naval blockade around Cuba, and made it clear that the United States was prepared to use military force if necessary to neutralize this perceived threat to national security. President Kennedy further indicated that we were not going to tolerate this Soviet threat.

My purpose here is not to give a history lesson, just to provide a backdrop for the next phase of my time in the military. Because of that standoff during the Cuban Missile Crisis, my unit was on alert. We were deployed to Spain from George Air Force Base, loaded on C-130.

We stopped at the Azores to take a short break. We got off the airplane and went to the terminal. I lost my ID (of course!), and we had to wait in that hot airplane on the runway while they went ahead and found my identification card. Everybody was pissed at me, and there were some rumblings that I was responsible for making everyone wait in that stifling airplane with no air-conditioning.

I stood up and said, "Hey! I'm pissed at me too."

Everybody laughed, and it defused the situation.

Before long, we were airborne, on our way to Spain. Our destination was Morón Air Base in southern Spain, approximately thirty-five miles southeast of the city of Seville. Morón's massive flight line, in-ground aircraft refueling system, long runway, and prime location on the Iberian Peninsula, close to the Mediterranean and the Middle East, made the base a vital link in any operation moving east from the United States.

Seville (Sevilla in Spanish) is a beautiful city, with incredible Old World charm. The history of European cities like that is incredible, all the stone and marble hundreds and hundreds of years old. We went into the city as soon as we could, but we didn't pay much attention to the history for long. Naturally, we were looking for girls! Some nice Spanish girls, preferably good-looking ones. Like everywhere else, there were bars, and those were always the best place to find attractive girls. Flamenco dancers were all over the place. I'd never seen dancing like that. Unbelievable. And the girls were gorgeous too, with their full, ruffled skirts and castanets. Great legs, being dancers. Once again, I was in heaven.

We were there on alert, so there wouldn't be as much time for local "exploring" as there usually was. However, I was determined to spend some time wandering around the streets, stopping at the little cafés, drinking wine, and chatting up the locals. And searching for beautiful women, of course! I did get to do my fair share of all that, but the stint in Spain was more intense than I'd experienced up to that point, all as a result of the Cuban Missile Crisis, which was the reason we'd been deployed to Morón in the first place.

For starters, someone accidentally shot off a GAR-8 Sidewinder on the F-104 Star Fighter. These rockets were ready to be deployed because we were on alert; in the event that the crisis in Cuba escalated and we had to go fight against Russia (USSR), we were ready. There were plenty of troops, pilots on call, and about three crew chiefs to each airplane.

I was still a crew chief. My new plane was an F-104 Star Fighter. I loved that aircraft! It was a Mach 2, with a wing span of only seven feet. There was a pilot training program called Operation Bootstrap. I thought I might try for flight school and become a jet pilot.

My pilots all told me, "Don't do it. You'd have to spend your whole life tied to the military, at low pay compared to civilian life."

I took in what they had to say because they'd all been flying for a while and had been in the military a lot longer than I had been. Looking back now, I realize just how wise they were. All politicians use the members of our military, but how many of them have actually served? How many recent presidents have served? Barack Obama never served, and neither did Bill Clinton. And yet, they made decisions that put every member of our military in harm's way—so many have come home blind, without arms and legs, with traumatic brain injuries, with all kinds of physical and psychological wounds that rarely heal, if ever. I am talking about young people—eighteen, nineteen, twenty years old. It's tragic. It breaks my heart to think of all those sacrifices, but it also makes me grateful that those pilots gave me good advice all those years ago. I am glad I listened to them! I really only toyed with the idea briefly, anyway. A career in the military wasn't for me. I'd already recognized that and accepted it. It was fun to fantasize about being a pilot, though.

Who knows? I told myself. *Maybe someday I'll learn to fly a plane, just not in the military and not as a career.*

(In case you're wondering what happened with that, I'll tell you all about my flying lessons later, in part V.)

As I said, we had plenty of crew chiefs, and our flight chief (the master sergeant in charge) was a great guy and very cool. He gave us plenty of time off. So I got to drink wine in the local bars, sit in the cafés talking to the locals, and pick up beautiful women galore.

Spain was for me, all right. Flamenco dancers and Spanish wine were pretty hard to beat and still are.

Traveling through Spain (1962)

There wasn't that much to do in Seville, even though it was a beautiful and charming city, so we spent most of our leave time in Madrid. As the capital city, it offered lots to do, especially nightlife.

There was one night in particular that I'll never forget. I was with this one guy I knew from the base. I didn't know him that well, but he seemed okay. He was not very good-looking or sophisticated; he'd never been around the bars and flamenco places that we went to that night.

He'd never even experienced any bars at home. I felt kind of sorry for him. Anyway, we ended up in this flamenco place. We had gone there by horse and buggy (that was kind of like a taxicab over there). It was a great time, and we each had a girl with us.

We were just sitting there, and I was talking to this girl, and all of a sudden, the next thing I knew, this guy from the base decked the girl he was with. I couldn't believe it; he really knocked her out. She had rejected him, and that was his reaction.

In no time at all, a crowd of Spanish people surrounded us. I didn't blame them; they all saw what this guy did to that girl.

I was not willing to get into a fight with a mob of enraged Spaniards in an attempt to help this guy. I thought he was a real jerk for punching that girl. What kind of guy knocks out a girl, anyway? I backed up against the door as the crowd started advancing, and then I turned around and ran. The guy followed me.

The only transportation was the horse and buggy, so we yelled to the driver, "Get going!" And then we jumped in.

The Spanish mob was right behind that horse and buggy, chasing us.

We got back to the base okay, but that was one incident I wouldn't ever forget. I stayed as far away from that guy as I could after that.

The guys I usually hung around with were cool, card players and all that, but I wanted to change the group I ran with. I needed some new blood in my social life. I also wanted to travel through Spain, and I was willing to use my accrued leave time. At around the same time, I met some new guys: one from New Jersey, one from New York, one from Iowa, and one from Ohio. All of us guys started talking, and it turned out that we all wanted to see more of Spain.

I said, "Hey, let's go to the Airmen's Club! We can rent a Volkswagen bus with a driver and tour Spain."

That's exactly what we did.

The Airmen's Club (service club) took care of everything: they got us a driver and a Volkswagen bus, and they even booked all of our accommodations. Our route was going to take us through Madrid, and then to the Rock of Gibraltar, and on to Málaga, our final destination. We ended up going through a small town called Torremolinos, which changed all of our lives. It was wonderful place, a small municipality on the magnificent Costa del Sol, due west of Málaga.

We were all excited. The guy from New York was Italian, and he spoke the language, so he was our interpreter. He'd already picked up a lot of Spanish because of his Italian, so by the time we were ready for our trip, he was speaking Spanish very well.

We all got our leave, and then we were off, heading through Spain in this Volkswagen bus, with a driver doing all the work so that we could watch the scenery. It was first class all the way, exciting times, beautiful country, and so much fun. I just loved it.

I found the Spanish landscape magnificent, with its miles of endless sunny beaches along the coast and massive snow-capped peaks inland. There tends to be sunshine year-round in Spain, which is probably why the Spanish have a much more relaxed lifestyle than any other country in Europe. For example, most businesses are closed between 2:00 p.m. and 5:00 p.m. for the siesta (afternoon nap). This long break in the day allows families to get together for a good meal and to spend some time together. It's a very nice tradition.

There are bullfighting arenas in most Spanish cities and towns, and flamenco shows happen almost every night of the week. So we got to see plenty of gorgeous dancers during our traveling time too.

Gibraltar is south of Spain and one of the busiest ports of call in the Mediterranean. Sitting where the Atlantic Ocean joins the Mediterranean Sea, Gibraltar has been prized and fought over by many countries in Europe and North Africa, all throughout history. A British colony since the 1700s, it is most famous for the two huge promontories (high points of rock) that dominate its landscape, towering high above the surface of the surrounding water. In fact, the Rock of Gibraltar is the most famous rock in the world. Even the ancient Greeks had legends about these promontories, calling them the Pillars of Hercules.

The narrow stretch of water that separates Gibraltar from North Africa is called the Strait of Gibraltar. The Bay of Algeciras is on one side of Gibraltar, and the Mediterranean Sea is on the other side. (This is where the Mediterranean meets the Atlantic.) Gibraltar borders the town of La Línea de la Concepción, part of the county of Cádiz.

The long history of the place was intriguing, but what we really wanted to see was the rock! We got to Gibraltar, checked into our hotel, and unpacked. We relaxed around the hotel that evening, planning to go to the Rock of Gibraltar the following day.

And that we did. We were such tourists. The rock was fantastic, though. What a thrill to see. You really can't appreciate the size and grandeur of it until you're standing right there. It's huge, ancient, magnificent. I am so glad I got to see it in person. Definitely a "bucket list" stop.

It wasn't just the rock, either. There were all these baboons all over the place, wild baboons. They picked up loose rocks and threw them at us, so we had a rock fight with these baboons. It was incredible. They would hide behind bigger rocks, and then they'd peek out and throw rocks at us; we'd pick up some small rocks and throw them back at the baboons. It was really good, fun stuff. For us and for the baboons.

There were a lot of little outdoor cafés too. We'd stop and have wine and flirt with the girls if we could find any. Most of them were Spanish girls, beautiful but very proper. They would flirt a little bit but nothing more than that—we didn't get anything serious going.

We spent a few days in Gibraltar, and then we headed off to Málaga, along the coast. The beautiful Spanish coast is called the Costa del Sol, and it's easy to understand why: the sun shines all the time along the beaches. I couldn't get over how beautiful that coastline was, and that's coming from someone who grew up in Southern California.

Málaga was our final destination, as I mentioned, but we were about to make a phenomenal detour. Unforgettable. We were about fifteen miles from Málaga when we passed through a small beachside town. It was absolutely gorgeous. I mean, fantastic. The road went right along the waterway. This little town had outdoor cafés and all the things that we'd wanted to see along the coast. It was just so cute and quaint. We all fell in love with it.

We grinned at each other, saying, "Whoa, man, what a beautiful town."

Then we started noticing something else to fall in love with: beautiful women. All of these gorgeous girls. We couldn't believe it; they were walking in groups of five or four or three. Many of them were Scandinavians, but there was pretty much every nationality from Europe you could imagine. Germans, Swedes, Finns; you name it. Beautiful girls. All of them suntanned, all of them heading for the beach or from the beach to the shops.

Immediately, I told the driver, "Stop! We want to stop here."

So he stopped, and we got out. We went to one of the outdoor cafés, said we wanted to order lunch, and sat down at a table to watch all these girls walking by. We were right on the beach, and it was just glorious.

I kept ordering vino *tinto* (red wine). I wanted a steak sandwich. After about four glasses of wine, I was getting pretty well ripped. The other guys kept drinking wine because I was drinking wine. All that wine seemed to have a negative effect on the skills of our "interpreter." He couldn't tell me how to say "steak sandwich" in Spanish.

Finally, I called the waiter over. "I wish somebody would speak English," I told him. "I'm starved, and I'm getting drunk."

And he said, "What would you like, sir?"

It just blew me away that he could speak English. "I want a steak sandwich," I told him.

"A *pepito*."

"Yes," I said, trusting that was what it was called in Spanish. The guy's English was too good for him to have misunderstood what I'd asked for.

Sure enough, I got a steak sandwich, perfectly done: warm roll, beautiful piece of steak. (And steak tastes so wonderful in Europe.)

The other guys had ordered too, and everything was perfect.

We discussed it over lunch, and then we told the driver, "We don't want to go to Málaga. We want to stay in this town."

So we sent him on a quest to find us hotel rooms, but he came back after a while and said he'd had no luck finding any. The place was booked solid. We told him to keep looking because we wanted to stay there no matter what.

In the meantime, we found out the town was called Torremolinos, and it was a huge tourist area, very famous in Europe because of the beautiful Spanish beaches and the supposedly "hot-blooded Spanish lovers." The beaches had a well-deserved reputation, but we found out later that there were very few available men in the area. We basically had everything to ourselves, our pick of women. For the next few days, we could be the hot-blooded lovers, not Spanish, but in Spain.

Our driver finally did find a place where we could stay; it was big, like a condominium complex or apartment complex. Very clean and nice. It was government-subsidized housing for widows and families that did not have a father to support them. These families were allowed to take in boarders. And that's what happened with us. We ended up staying with a widow and her family, and we paid them for our rooms. They loved it because they made extra money, and we just loved them. It worked out perfectly.

We would go out most of the time and not come home at night if we hooked up with girls. We would stay at their place or on the beach. So that's what we did. When I would go to my room to change clothes, I had to go through the complex, and all the families would just stare because they were very curious about the Americans staying there.

Some would yell, "El Rubio!" (the blond one). I was about twenty-one years old. What a fantastic experience.

We liked Torremolinos so much that I decided to come back when I had more leave time. The other guys agreed, so when we got more leave, we went back. I went back again later on too, on my own, and stayed for a couple of weeks. I had a blast every time.

When I went back alone, I met an English girl who fell in love with me. I fell in love with her too. In fact, when she had to leave to go back to Middlesex, I went with her to the airport, got on the plane with her and everything. The La Guardia (Spanish police) boarded the plane and escorted me off. She was clinging to me, and I was holding her tight. It was quite a scene, but we were madly in love. Plus, I was drunk and barefoot.

Torremolinos was a great place, a special place. There was an aura about me there. I could feel it. All our guys scored there. The girls were fantastic. Even the homeliest guys in our group had beautiful girls in Torremolinos. It was magical, a glorious, unforgettable place. James Michener, one of my favorite authors, wrote a book called *The Drifters,* set in Torremolinos. He described El Dorado, a club that the American expats loved; we liked to go there and to the other bars he described. Michener was a prolific author, and many of his books were extremely famous. He wrote about so many other places that I wound up going to: the South Pacific, Australia, all kinds of beautiful, exotic locales. But his description of that magical town will always be my favorite.

In any case, Torremolinos, like all good things, had to come to an end. When I finally got back to the base in Morón after my last leave in Torremolinos, we had orders to go to West Germany. Our whole fighter squadron would fly F-104s to Wiesbaden, West Germany.

I really didn't want to go to West Germany; I loved Spain. Well, my flight chief really liked me. He was my sergeant back in the States at George Air Force Base too, so he knew me. And he knew I was short-timer. (Meaning that I was getting ready to be discharged and finish my four years after this assignment.) He kind of kept me out of trouble. That was not an easy job, as I'm sure you realize.

Usually, I created the trouble, but not always. One of our guys on the alert pad sat in the seat of my airplane and accidentally shot off a rocket, a GAR-8, which went across the runway and knocked down a mobility shack. I already mentioned this briefly, but I didn't fill in the details or the outcome. The police (La Guardia) and the military police were on us like you couldn't believe. Threw us down to the ground because we could have been saboteurs; security was tight. And La Guardia was no joke; everyone said, "We're police," but the only real police were Franco's police, the La Guardia.

That was something that I didn't like about being in Spain. But the country and people were magnificent. The women were beautiful—so many wonderful girls there. And Torremolinos. Unforgettable, magical Torremolinos. I didn't want to go to West Germany in the worst way.

Mission to Wiesbaden, West Germany (1963)

Sitting right next to the historic city of Mainz, Wiesbaden was a twenty-five-minute car ride from the Frankfurt airport. We arrived from sunny Spain, landed in West Germany, and it was freezing. I was not going to like this. I hate the cold. Remember what I've said about not wanting to be there if you can't grow a coconut on it? Well, in this place, any coconuts would be frozen, just like I was.

We went to check out our surroundings. Our aircraft were in these big, covered, concrete hangars that were camouflaged. There were a lot of police dogs all over the place. They were real attack dogs, and every time we would ride in a weapons carrier, we'd have to ride with these dogs. They had no muzzles, which I guess was supposed to make them intimidating. It worked. They were beyond intimidating; they were downright scary and dangerous.

So we got all settled in, and there were plenty of crew chiefs and other personnel. That meant we'd get a lot of time off.

West Germany was like any other place. As soon as we got some time off, we went into town, and guess what we did! We looked for girls. Of course.

We all ended up with attractive German girls. There was one *fraulein* who worked in one of the pubs, and I schemed on her, flirting with her every chance I got. I did whatever I could to make her laugh. I thought she liked me, but all the other guys were hitting on her too.

After a couple of weeks, my scheming succeeded. She let me take her home and spend the night with her. It was a big deal. She was very sweet and loving, and I enjoyed our time together.

We were there in the fall, so we got to experience Oktoberfest. That was a lot of fun; great beer and a great time.

It wasn't all good, though. There was a race riot on the base between the blacks and the whites; I'll never forget that. Some guys came running through the barracks, blacks and whites, talking about this riot that had started. These guys I knew from Arkansas had started it all, it turned out: a race riot over a black guy taking out German girls.

It only got uglier from that point on. A big fight broke out in the chow hall, and I remember that this one black guy had an umbrella. Man, that guy was dangerous, crazy. He kept stabbing the ground underneath the table with the spoke at the bottom of the umbrella. I was the one he was trying to stab, by the way. He had gone completely nuts a minute or so before, and so I slid to the ground and attempted to crawl away, trying to get away from him because he was so crazy. Besides, I did not want to get caught up in a race riot. My tour was almost up. It didn't matter. As soon as I got up, I managed to get pulled into a slugfest.

The whole racial thing got out of control, and a whole lot of people got into trouble. It was worse than it would have been ordinarily because we were on alert. We were prepared to go to war with Russia (USSR). It was a very intense time, and the race issues didn't help.

Then we got orders to go back to Spain. Man, was I relieved. Sunshine and coastline. That's what I needed. I wanted to stay in Spain, preferably until my discharge, which was coming up soon. It was close to Christmas by that time, and all the married guys were happy because they were going to get Christmas leave before us single guys did. I didn't care about Christmas leave, anyway, because I wanted to stay in Spain.

Things got complicated, though, and deteriorated rapidly. What a mess it was. Here's what happened: I had been scratching for a couple of weeks, ever since spending time with my beautiful *fraulein*. I hadn't gone to the sick call right away, but the itching got so bad that I had to. Sure enough, I found out that I had crabs. That was it; the sick call had to report it, and all the guys flipped out because they put our squadron in quarantine, which meant their leave was canceled and they weren't going to get to go home for Christmas with their families.

Guess who was on the bad list? Yup. Broman. Again.

"Broman stopped everybody from going home because he didn't report that he had crabs when he was in Germany."

"He's got them now, so the whole barracks has to be quarantined. Everything's unpacked. Everything's got to be sprayed."

Those were the comments making the rounds. It was really getting nasty.

I knew what they were thinking because it was what I would have been thinking if someone else had done it: *Man, we're going to beat the holy crap out of Broman.*

A blanket party was planned, so my life was in danger. Sort of. My pride was definitely in danger. Plus, lots of guys got pretty badly roughed up during blanket parties.

Fortunately, after they sprayed and so forth, it turned out that the crabs could be contained. All the guys who were scheduled for leave to go home for Christmas were still able to go. And they were so happy that they forgot all about the blanket party.

The rest of us had to stay on base. I didn't mind. I was so relieved that everything turned out okay. Besides, I'd wanted to stay in Spain, anyway.

My discharge came soon after that. It was honorable, as I mentioned earlier, and my level 5 work as a crew chief would serve me well in civilian life. At the time, I didn't realize how much the skills I'd learned in the military would help me as a deep-water diver. I was just excited to start my so-called real life, the life I would be in total control of. I could hardly wait.

* * * * * *

So I was about to dive into a huge new moon pool, even though I didn't know it at the time, and even though I didn't think about my life in terms of moon pools at that time. But life *is* a series of moon pools, for each and every one of us, whether we realize it or not.

As I've said throughout this book, moon pools are all about reflection and the gifts that we gain from reflection—wisdom, clarity, insight, tranquility. They effortlessly flow into one another, each drop and ripple blending and enhancing the others. It is a beautiful, natural process, just as all life is. It only gets ugly when we get in the way. When we let things flow, it's all always natural and beautiful and filled with grace.

When I think about my life in terms of moon pools, I automatically see how my time in the military led me to my destiny as a deep-water diver and an entrepreneur, and how all of it led me to my time as a hippie, which was also part of my destiny, seeded in my adventures in the San Francisco counterculture of the 1960s and brought to fruition in the tropical rain forest of Australia. (Interestingly enough, Cape Tribulation was "discovered" by the hippies in the 1970s, and it became the end of the London-Kathmandu-Cape Tribulation overland trail. Amazing! Without even knowing it, I had traveled that very trail and landed at the end of it, right at Cape Trib.)

So now that I've shown you how I traveled up and down that wild and magnificent spiral to come full circle, as I promised I would do at the beginning of this section, let me take you forward in my life to the years following my time in Australia. I spent time in New Orleans, Louisiana, in various parts of Mexico, and, of course, in California. Ultimately, I found myself immersed in the biggest moon pool of my life: nearly dying and having to be put on life support. That moon pool wasn't one that I had dived into, though. It just opened and swallowed me up.

PART V
Biggest Moon Pool of All: The End (Almost)—Northern California

I've shared the many significant moon pools in my life, from my childhood through my coming full circle after the greatest events and most exciting adventures of my life. Now let me describe another extremely significant moon pool: the moment when my life almost ended, not in deep water, as you might expect, but on dry land. A twisting mountain road, to be precise. Yes, I'm starting and ending my story by telling you about two episodes in which I almost lost my life in dangerous situations. *Almost.* Remember, danger is part of me. I can't live without it. It's who I am, what I do, what I crave. It's why I was a deep-water diver, and it's why I was so good at it for so long. I felt the fear, and I respected it, but it never kept me from doing what I was put on this earth to do.

When I nearly drowned in Cyanide Creek, North Queensland, Australia, as I described in the opening of this book, nature was at the helm, even though I was the one driving the Land Cruiser that the floodwaters submerged. When I crashed my Mercedes in Placerville, California, nature wasn't doing anything. It was all me. I was the one at the wheel, driving way too fast, flirting with danger, and thinking I was in control.

It's always the Higher Power that's in control, though, never any single one of us. I already knew that—I'd seen it underwater countless times—but I still believed that I had more control than I did have, than any of us ever has.

For a while, it looked like the end for me was going to be "moon roof," not "moon pool," which would have been incredibly ironic for a lifelong deep-water man. But the universe had different plans for me.

Going Deep: From the Pacific to the Gulf and the Bayou—Long Beach, California, and New Orleans, Louisiana (1976)

I enjoyed my time in Long Beach after returning to the States from my years of living and working in Australia. The houseboat in Alamitos Bay was great, but after a while, I needed a change. Long Beach held too many memories, too many reminders of things I wanted to forget.

First and foremost were the reminders of Ali. It had ended between us, and that affected me deeply. Far more than I recognized at the time. It was a soul-level loss, the greatest loss of my life (as I've already shared). Added to that were all the memories of my childhood and adolescence, which became hard to take as well, especially because I was working for my dad at the time. I enjoyed the deep-water diving as much as ever; the day-to-day interactions with my dad, not so much. Actually, that was part of what had triggered my moon pools of recollecting childhood and adolescence in the first place. It was important for me to do, but it got to be too much after a while. Eventually, I just felt smothered, overwhelmed by the past that I couldn't escape from, much less change. The long and short of it was that I needed to move on.

But to *what,* and to *where?* After working with my dad, I knew I needed a break from diving. I was diving off the *Queen Mary,* which I had dived off years before, just prior to leaving for Port Moresby. A lot of hull cleaning. Not very interesting, but work was work. I always enjoyed telling every Englishman I met that I had "cleaned the *Queen Mary*'s bottom."

Actually, I guess I can say that the *Queen Mary* herself inspired my next choice. There I was, working away at the barnacles and other detritus clinging to the hull, and an image of ancient vines and tree roots came into my mind. Old banyans like in Southeast Asia. Or along the bayous in Louisiana. I'd always enjoyed Louisiana when visiting the operations of Broman International there.

Hmm, I thought. *Maybe New Orleans.* Even apart from Broman International's operations in Lafayette, the city of New Orleans had always intrigued me: dangerous yet charming, warm and muggy weather (kind of like the tropics but without coconuts), beautiful in a mysterious way (all those strangely magnificent old trees and vines in the bayous). The dichotomies that always resonated with me abounded there, and I decided it was the next place for me.

By that point in my life, though, I did a little planning before I just jumped in. As I said, I knew I didn't want to work as a deep-water diver, so what livelihood could I have in New Orleans? I really didn't want to be a shrimper. (You'll remember my Singapore business ventures from part III, and although they were profitable, the seafood industry wasn't one that I wanted to be in full-time.) I had picked New Orleans as my destination because of the local color and flavor, so I wanted to do something that would allow me to be in the center of it all the time. What is the center of every city? The bars of course! Everyone everywhere goes to bars, especially the most beautiful women. That was the answer: I would work as a bartender. The bottom of a glass could offer as much deep reflection as the bottom of the ocean. It all depended on where you placed your attention while looking. Depth without focus and clarity haven't ever meant much—didn't then and never will.

So I went to bartending school in Long Beach, and then I took a few local jobs tending bar to make sure I got the hang of it before I made the move to Louisiana. New Orleans. NOLA. The Big Easy. Crescent City. Any city with that many nicknames had to be a place for me. A place where I could lose myself for a while. My next moon pool. I'd had so many Pacific moon pools already. A moon pool in the Cajun bayous or along Lake Pontchartrain or in the Gulf of Mexico was very enticing. Intoxicating. That might be dangerous for a would-be bartender, but that was all the more reason to do it. At least for me. Danger was like that old coconut: if it wasn't there, I didn't want to be there, either.

Anyway, I had all my plans set, so the only stumbling block to surmount was my dad. Old Art didn't want me to be a bartender, and he didn't want me to go to New Orleans. It all came to a head at the end of one workday. I was sitting in my car and reading a letter, and he came up to the driver's side window.

"You do this, you change your name too. You're not a Broman any longer!" he yelled, even though he was just a few inches away from my ear.

I kept reading and just ignored him.

He stepped back, pulled a .38 pistol out of his boot, and held it on me. His having the gun didn't surprise me; his whole crew was always packing. They all carried guns in their boots. But his pulling a gun on me pissed me off.

As soon as my dad saw the look on my face, I could tell that he knew he'd made a mistake. I understood that he wanted me to stay in the diving business, but I had made a different choice, which was my right. I'd had it with his attitude by that point, and this was the last straw. I was really angry.

I slowly got out of my car, and he started to quickly back away toward his van. I rushed toward him, and he ran to his van, got in, and started the engine. I jumped on the passenger's side running board in the same instant that he started to drive off. I hung on for a good stretch, staring at him all the way.

"I'm going to New Orleans to tend bar!" I shouted over the motor.

He kept looking straight ahead, his hand on the gear shift. Before he could shift into a higher gear, I jumped off.

I won that battle, but neither one of us ever won the war. I owed a lot of my diving ability to my dad, and I never lost sight of that. But we had so much unfinished business, and my dad didn't want to ever get into that. So the only way for there to be peace was for me to put as much physical distance between us as I could. Asia, Europe, and Australia had provided that, and it worked for quite a while. But I wanted to be in the States now. So New Orleans, Louisiana, it would be.

It was time for my next moon pool. Time to take that deep breath, dive in, and go deep.

Learning to Fly—New Orleans, Louisiana (1976)

I finally left Southern California for New Orleans. My first order of business was visiting the wife of one of my most loyal employees who had since passed away. He had taken over part of the operations of Broman International after I sold it to Brambles, but then he'd subsequently been diagnosed with cancer, which proved a death sentence. He was kind of a father figure to me. I first met him in Houston, Texas, when I was buying equipment for Broman International. We hit it off immediately, and I made him the manager of my Lafayette, Louisiana, site. Eventually,

I moved him and his family to Australia. After he died, his wife returned to the States. I'd always liked her, so I was happy to see her, but it was so sad to see her without her husband. They had been so deeply in love. We reminisced about him and the fun times we'd had together. It was good to see her, and I hoped we would stay friends. As a native of New Orleans, she had a lot of tips to offer me. We both enjoyed our time together, and I think it helped ease her grief.

* * * * * *

I settled in to my new digs and established an agenda for myself. My plan was to get a job bartending and also to get my pilot's license. Thirteen years after my honorable discharge from the US Air Force, I was finally going to learn how to fly! My next adventure in the blue would be the sky, not the sea, although the ocean would always be my true home. Ultimately, I wanted to fly the Beaver seaplane so that I could work as a charter pilot on flights across the Gulf to Mexico. Flying lessons and a pilot's license were the necessary steps to reaching that goal, and bartending would pay the bills in the meantime. (I'll get to my bartending adventures in a bit.)

My flight lessons were pretty eventful, and I did well enough. Getting my pilot's license was a quite a different story. In the first place, it was rather humorous because I am afraid of heights. Clearly, that is an occupational hazard for an aspiring pilot, but I remained undeterred.

I have flown all over the world, on jets and helicopters, so I told myself I could handle it. My actual rationalization went something like this: *Damn it, Broman, you've jumped out of helicopters and rolled onto rigs in the midst of storms and sixty-foot seas! You can do this.*

And I did. I got my pilot's license in a Cessna 172, and that was another very exciting moon pool. I had never experienced what it felt like to go deep in the sky instead of the water, but I really enjoyed it. I found the two were closer than I'd expected: both were about taking a leap of faith and trusting in a Higher Power to protect me. Deep down, I would always be a diver; diving was in my blood, my body, and my soul. But I really did like flying.

Once I had my pilot's license, the next step was to check out the pontoons and floats. The Beaver would be quite a bit bigger, so I would need plenty of practice. I wanted to fly the de Havilland Canada DHC-2

Beaver, a single-engine, high-wing, propeller-driven aircraft primarily known as a bush plane. It is used for cargo and passenger hauling, as well as for aerial application (dusting and top dressing), and as such, it has been widely adopted by the military as a utility aircraft. In short, this was and still is one of the most successful and famous bush planes ever produced.

It would take some time until I was ready to fly the Beaver and work as a charter pilot. In the interim, I honed my bartending skills, and what a time I had working as a bartender in New Orleans.

Tending Bar at Bobby McGee's—New Orleans, Louisiana (1976–1978)

When I left California, I really didn't think that it would be hard to get a job bartending in Louisiana. Having never found it difficult to get a job, I kind of just took it for granted that it would be easy this time. So I started to look around the city. I went to the French Quarter first, but it didn't feel like the right place to me.

As I went around town, I heard about Fat City, the happening section of New Orleans. (Though technically in the suburb of Metairie, Fat City was treated as part of the city of New Orleans.) And that's where I landed. As soon as I arrived in Fat City, I knew immediately that this was the place for me. Filled with brand-new bars and hideaways, it was very different from the old French Quarter. Fat City was new and exciting, filled with bands playing cutting-edge music. I loved it. The French Quarter had its place and still does, but Fat City was the new, happening place. And that was where I belonged, where I wanted to be.

Bobby McGee's Lounge and Restaurant opened on the corner of Eighteenth Street and North Arnold Road, in the heart of Fat City. (It later had to change its name to Molly Maguire's because of franchise law.) I went in for a drink, and I knew that this was the place where I wanted to work. It was perfect for me: exciting and new, and always the spot where the cool crowds hung out. That was critical because New Orleans was a party town—in fact, it was *the* party town. I wanted to work in *the* place in *the* party town, but I quickly realized that it wasn't going to be as easy as I had anticipated.

Getting a bartending job in California and most other places was relatively easy; I'd managed to do it in Long Beach while still going to bartending school. Getting a bartending job in New Orleans was vastly different. It was more like running for governor: if you wanted to be elected, you needed contacts to help you. In New Orleans, it was not about what you knew, but who you knew. It's like that everywhere to a certain extent, but there it was extremely so.

I lived in an apartment close to the Playboy Club, and I pretty much made that the club my "office." I got to know the head bartender and manager, but I never hit on her. Instead, I made friends with her, and she liked me. She gave me the nickname "California."

"Hey, California," she would say as soon as she saw me. "What's going on?"

We would talk about all kinds of things, mostly my travels around the world. I told her I wanted to be a bartender at Bobby McGee's and asked her how I might do that. She was sweet and helpful, but she said it might be impossible. It was the top club at that time, as I knew. But she knew the bartenders who worked there, and she said she would introduce me to them so I could get to know them, see if I even had a chance before applying to the owners.

We made arrangements to meet at the International Hotel that Friday night (or Saturday morning!) at 3:00 a.m. That was when and where the bartenders and servers from the Fat City bars, restaurants, and clubs went after finishing their shifts.

We met in the hotel lobby at the appointed time, walked into the bar, and sure enough, there were all the Bobby McGee's bartenders. My friend from the Playboy Club introduced me.

I shouted, "A round of drinks!"

I talked, and they talked, and I told them that I wanted to work at Bobby Magee's.

"So, what are my chances?" I asked.

We laughed a lot.

I told them that I'd gone to bartending school in California and worked at the bar in an Italian restaurant. "I'd would work for free at Bobby McGee's, just to train in such a cool place," I said.

They didn't ever really tell me if they thought I'd stand a chance.

But I had fun, so I started hanging out with the Bobby McGee's bartenders after their shifts. We got along great, so I decided to go ahead and apply for the job with the owners.

I went to Bobby McGee's, met with the owners, and showed them my bartender's diploma. One of the owners liked me and wanted to give me a chance; the other one didn't. But the one who liked me won out: I was to start the next Saturday, early.

I showed up for my first shift on the job dressed in a white shirt, black tie, and tight, black dress pants. I looked good. I was eager to make a good impression and do good work, but that first Saturday was a joke. Up to that point, I'd really thought that I could bartend, but I soon found out that I was the worst bartender Bobby McGee's had ever had.

Let me not get ahead of the story. Here's how it went from the time I got to the bar my first day on the job:

I arrived at ten o'clock, as instructed, because we opened at eleven. I met with the owners. The one who liked me was going to oversee me until the other two bartenders came in for their shift.

My first customer wanted a mint julep. I had only tended bar in California! I had never made a mint julep in my life, and that was one they didn't teach us in bartending school.

Shit! I thought, pissed that my very first order would have to be a drink I'd never learned to make. But then I remembered that I had my little bartender's book. Well, it took me forever to make that damn drink, and it was so hokey to be reading my little book the whole time, trying to conceal it under the bar.

The owner knew how shaky I was, but he wanted me to stay on. He kept giving me encouraging nods and smiles. After a few customers, I was still slow, but I pulled it off, talking my way through it and schmoozing the customers. (Schmoozing is half the job of bartending, anyway.)

There was a couple sitting at one of the tables by the stage. They were drinking margaritas, chatting it up. All of a sudden, the women pitched her drink in the man's face, and he pitched his whole glass back at her. She ducked, and the glass hit the floor, shattering. There was glass all over, and the margarita was dripping off the wall and the furniture. This was a brand-new, beautiful bar! What kind of people would do that?

Well, I got pissed off, and I ran out from behind the bar and took charge of the situation. They were still in their seats, screaming at each other. I stood right in front of their table. "What the fuck are you doing?" I yelled over their screaming. "Look at the mess you guys have made. The upholstery is sopping wet, the wall is wet, there's glass all over. This fight might be your business, but it's mine while you're in here."

They stopped screaming, and I got them calmed down. The guy apologized and left a forty-dollar tip. While I was getting one of the servers to clean up the mess, the woman came up to the bar and asked me for another margarita. She sat on one of the stools to wait for her drink, and she apologized too. Then she gave me another forty dollars as a tip for the trouble they caused. That was eighty dollars in tips in two hours!

The owner was happy with the way I handled the situation, and he knew I would get faster as I went along. "I'm going to team you up with some of the other more experienced bartenders so you can learn. But, first, I'm going to start you out in the servers' bar, and that way you can learn to fix drinks fast."

That was fine with me. If I forgot anything, I would always have my little bartender's recipe book handy.

It wasn't quite that easy. The waiters gave me hell. The servers' bar was located out of sight by the kitchen, and if I was slow on a busy night, they would yell, "California, get those drinks a rolling!" ("California" was pretty much my nickname all the while I lived in Louisiana.)

I always had two blenders going, and I learned to mix drinks fast and furious. I couldn't blame the waiters for getting pissed; their tips were at risk if they were slow with the drinks. Eventually, I reached the point where I could smoke a joint and never miss a beat with the drinks. I was good.

After a while, I got put back on the front bar. It was so cool. I loved it. Man, what was not to love? The music was great, the women were beautiful, the cocktail waitresses were all sexy foxes. I would have three or four girls waiting for me at closing sometimes. Sometimes I wished I had been a bartender all my life. How I loved that bartending gig! (I still miss it.) I had been the chairman of the board of an international company, and sometimes I almost forgot that I had. This was too much fun.

One of the cocktail waitresses was named Brandy. (Pretty funny, right? She didn't even get the humor.) She was from New York, a real knockout, but she knew it, so I didn't bother with her. There were plenty of other women who were super cool, fun, and down-to-earth. And I had access to all of them.

One morning at about three, I had just gotten home after my shift and a stop at the International Hotel for a drink afterward. I was just getting ready to crash when my phone rang. I thought it might be one of the girls I was dating, so I answered. Who else would know my schedule and that I would be awake at 3:00 a.m.? Well, it was Brandy. Turned out, she'd had a change of heart. We wound up having a good time together. Like I said, she was a knockout, gorgeous and very sexy.

I really loved New Orleans.

I worked as a bartender at Bobby McGee's for some time, through changes of management and ownership and with many beautiful waitresses. It was the place where many of the political officials started gathering for lunch and partaking in after-dinner drinks. As I said, it was *the* place.

While Fat City was on the rise, more and more apartment complexes opened to appeal to the young, single crowd. I moved into one of the more popular complexes in Fat City. This place was singles only and totally wild. It had a clubhouse bar where everyone hung out. It was very cool, sometimes insane, with hundreds of singles around the bar. Although it was crazy, we kind of came to be like family to one another. There were old, young, and middle-aged people living there, every type of person and personality imaginable.

I've said it before, and I'll say it again, I loved New Orleans. In particular, I will never forget the fabulous times I had in Fat City, tending bar at Bobby McGee's and chasing women at every opportunity. (Of course!)

New Orleans was a fantastic moon pool, but you know me by now: once I've jumped in and gone deep, it doesn't take long for me to crave a new adventure. So before long, I was ready to jump in again. This time, it was Mexico. I did do some flying across the Gulf, and I traveled the country too (the eastern side on the Gulf and not the Pacific side or the northern or central parts). Cancún was the first place that I explored in Mexico, so let's start there.

Adventures in Mexico—Cancún, Mérida, Isla Mujeres, Tulum, Cozumel, and the Yucatán (1978–1979)

Cancún was, and still is, magnificent: fourteen miles of pristine white beaches shaped like the numeral 7, crystalline, turquoise waters. What could be better than spending sultry nights there, sipping on the perfect margarita? Well, not too much! Cancún is all that, clearly, but it is so much more.

The history of Cancún dates back to 1967, when the Mexican government, recognizing the importance of tourism to the country's economic future, began a detailed search to pinpoint ideal sites for tourism development. Resting on the northeast corner of the Yucatán Peninsula in the state of Quintana Roo, Cancún was a part of the ancient Mayan civilization and is still considered the gateway to El Mundo Maya (the Mayan World). Cancún has the distinction of being the one Caribbean destination with the infrastructure, modern amenities, and service philosophy to rival leisure destinations worldwide. In other words, unlike many other parts of the Caribbean and Mexico, Cancún was built for tourism, and it continues to meet the needs of its myriad pleasure-seeking visitors.

That pretty much sums up Cancún's modern identity. However, its ancient roots are no less spectacular than its current beauty, and its history is even more magnificent and more fascinating than its contemporary, picture-postcard splendor. Of course, that spectacular history is all part of the ancient Mayan civilization. The Mayans were mathematicians, astronomers, architects, philosophers, and priests (of their native religion, not Catholicism). While Europe was still in the dark ages, the Mayans invented a complex calendar similar to the one that we use today. (This was much in the news in recent years when many suspected that the world would end in 2012 because of their misinterpretation of the Mayan calendar.) Mayan astronomers mapped the stars and planets, and Mayan architects built some of the most magnificent structures in the world—and with no tools (to be more precise, there is no archaeological evidence that any tools were used). The astronomical precision of these structures is absolutely breathtaking, rivaling the pyramids of Giza in Egypt and Stonehenge on England's Salisbury Plain.

So, yes, I enjoyed the water and beaches in Cancún, but the history and culture were unforgettable, and that is what I most enjoyed about my visit to that part of Mexico.

Let me back up a bit to explain how I got to visit the Yucatán in the first place. I was offered an opportunity to go to Mexico's Yucatán Peninsula to open a hotel in Cancún. This hotel would sell duty-free goods as well, and it would be small, brand-new, and very quaint. Right off the beaches, it was to have just forty-two rooms and a nice, intimate restaurant. Patios and gardens would surround the building, creating a peaceful refuge from the big tourist hotels—and from the tourists.

That was a fantastic opportunity, and I enjoyed the time I spent on the Yucatán Peninsula, particularly exploring the Mayan ruins. And, of course, I loved the beaches and the tropical waters—the coast and the sea are always what I come back to, no matter how far I roam. I stayed for a while, and I was successful, but, eventually, I returned to my California roots. I'll get into all that later. First, let me tell you some more about the fabulous places in the Yucatán.

The first time I went to Mérida, I was very impressed. This city, the capital of the Mexican state of Yucatán, has strong Mayan roots, and its culture and civilization made it all the more fascinating to me.

The Yucatecans fascinated me too. As I've shared, I always enjoy meeting native peoples, and these were no exception. I particularly admired their fierce pride in their culture and history. This pride was evident everywhere. The Yucatecans sprinkled their Spanish with Mayan words and were quick to recount the stories of resistance and revolution that have set this region apart from the rest of Mexico for centuries. Granted, those tales seemed a little distant when I was in Yucatán and Mérida in the late 1970s, but I could still feel the presence of courage and pride that had led to the resistance in the first place.

I found Mérida to be a gracious capital, languid in the way that cities in the tropics always are. Filled with pastel-colored mansions and wide avenues, Mérida was and is an architectural jewel. Evenings were a time for promenades by locals and tourists alike. Now one of the safest cities in Mexico, it also has one of the country's largest historic centers outside Mexico City, allowing its cultural, dining, and entertainment scenes to flourish.

In the late afternoon, the whole city seemed to congregate in the leafy Plaza Grande, beneath the shade of the towers of Mérida's austere sixteenth-century Cathedral of San Ildefonso. All sorts of eateries, galleries, and museums abound in this part of the city, and the Governor's Palace is just a few steps away, where gigantic paintings depicting Yucatán's violent history fill the walls. Mérida-born twentieth-century artist Fernando Castro Pacheco created these canvases specifically for the building. The Casa Montejo, now a cultural center and museum, is the city's oldest building, erected in the 1540s by Don Francisco Montejo, Yucatán's conquistador. There was a carving of two Spanish conquistadors standing atop the heads of Indians on the building's facade. The four front rooms have been sumptuously restored to late-nineteenth-century splendor, and they are opulent indeed.

Moving from culture to nightlife, Mérida was particularly appealing on weekend nights when the narrow streets around its central plaza were closed to traffic, music flooded from the sidewalk cafés, and people of all ages went strolling in the warm evening air. I went too. Mayan girls from the state of Chiapas would carry armloads of embroidered shawls, hoping someone would buy them. Artists would have watercolors and beaded jewelry spread out for sale. Food-cart vendors would make cheese roll-ups to go. And the drivers of Mérida's romantic horse-drawn carriages, their white-painted rigs decorated with roses, would patiently wait for fares.

It was glorious. I loved being there. I knew this was the crowded center of a city of a million people, but it felt as sweet and safe as a village in the countryside. Geography had a lot to do with this: the Yucatán Peninsula lies too far east to be on the drug-smuggling routes running north through central Mexico.

Two major ancient Mayan sites are an hour's drive from the city: Uxmal, to the southeast, and Chichén Itzá, to the east. Visiting these sites was fabulous, and the step pyramids rival any of the pyramids in Giza in magnificence and innovation.

The charming, small, colonial town of Izamal is just forty miles from the city, while sixty miles to the southwest is the seaside community of Celestún, nesting ground for one of the world's largest flamingo flocks.

Last but not least is the island of Isla Mujeres (the island of women) located close to one of many coral reefs, which is an area popular for its snorkeling and scuba diving. Isla Mujeres is also home to a population of sea turtles, and you have the opportunity to ride them. Guess who rode one! What a blast to cruise turquoise waters aboard such a gentle, ancient creature.

Unlike the pyramids in other ancient Mayan sites, those of Tulum are small. Most of the monuments there had ceremonial functions, and traces of red paint are visible on some buildings, indicative of their Mayan origin.

One small structure is of particular interest to archaeologists, as they suspect it was part of some ancient fertility rite. Inside it is a figure thought to represent the male sexual organ.

And now, for the crowning touch of my time in the Yucatán: Cozumel, the Island of the Swallows. In the Caribbean just off the eastern coast of the Yucatán Peninsula, opposite the Playa del Carmen and close to the Yucatán Channel, is beautiful Cozumel. In the Mexican state of Quintana Roo, Cozumel is a tourist mecca for scuba diving and snorkeling. The main town on the island is San Miguel de Cozumel. With its Mexican heart and Caribbean soul.

The name Cozumel, which means the "Island of Swallows," was derived from the Mayan language. The island is about thirty miles long and nineteen miles wide and is Mexico's largest Caribbean island.

Cozumel has tropical savanna climate, which is very close to a tropical monsoon climate. As you can tell, I felt right at home!

Renowned for its incredible snorkeling and diving as a result of the sea's remarkable clarity, Cozumel is ideal for both professional divers and first-time snorkelers. The island has plenty of accessible sites for underwater exploration over one of the world's largest reef systems, teeming with tropical fish and various forms of marine life. Ever since 1961, when Jacques Cousteau declared Cozumel to be one of the most spectacular diving sites in the world, people have come from every corner of the planet to discover this underwater Caribbean biosphere. Now, you already know my opinion of Jacques Cousteau as a diver, but I agree with him as far as the spectacular quality of every dive off Cozumel.

* * * * * *

So that's the story of my adventures in Cancún, Cozumel, and other areas of the Yucatán Peninsula. It was an utterly unforgettable experience, and

I enjoyed every minute of it. But, as I said, the time came for me to return to California. I came full circle yet again, diving into a new moon pool. There would be a big spiral, and I would dive deeper than ever before, but I'm getting ahead of the story again.

For now, let's just go back to California for a bit. The moon pool was open, and I waited for the water to clear just a little before I jumped in. I could feel the danger; I just didn't realize how much danger there would actually be.

Going Deep, High in the Mountains—
Placerville, California (1981)

My next moon pool was to be on dry land, in the mountains, in fact. I went from living fifty feet above sea level to the foothills of the Sierras. My time in Placerville led me to the biggest moon pool of all, which I'll get to in a bit. First, let me tell you about Placerville.

Formerly known as Hangtown, Placerville is the county seat of El Dorado County in California. Its fascinating history dates back to the California Gold Rush in the mid-nineteenth century, and that explains the alternate names for the town. After the discovery of gold in nearby Coloma, California, in 1848, which sparked the Gold Rush, the small town known as Dry Diggings (also called Old Dry Diggings) was established, named after the manner in which the miners moved cartloads of dry soil to running water in order to separate the gold from the soil. Later, in 1849, the town earned its most common historical name, Hangtown, because of the numerous hangings that occurred there. By 1850, the Temperance League and a few local churches had begun to request that a friendlier name be bestowed upon the town. The name was officially changed in 1854, when the City of Placerville was incorporated.

It was renamed Placerville. It remains a historic community and reflects much of its Gold Rush roots. Many buildings date from this period, and a walk down Main Street Placerville was also on the line of the Pony Express mail carrier service that connected California to the Midwest and East (basically from Sacramento to St. Joseph, Missouri). The frequent hangings that occurred in the lawless area and that gave the place its name of Hangtown, the old hangman's platform used for public hangings is still accessible to visitors, and street markers in town still point the way to the hanging spot.

Moving out of the town proper will take you up the mountain toward Lake Tahoe. There are some beautiful little mountain towns, like Pollack Pines that have big ponderosa pines. Some serious snow starts along the ascent and goes right on up to Lake Tahoe and to some of the most beautiful ski areas in the world.

The combination of the magnificence of the natural landscape surrounding Placerville and the quaint small-town atmosphere of the city itself make it a very intriguing, little place. Nestled in the foothills of the Sierras, all the houses around the town are built on hills, creating a terraced effect. There is one bar called The Liar's Bench, where all the attorneys go; next to it is a bar called Hangman's Tree. There's even a dummy hanging from the second story. The Bell Tower has a working bell, and people listen for it. All the shops are close together, and all the owners know one another and help one another. The hardware store is so unique, selling everything imaginable, just like the general stores of the nineteenth century. You almost feel like you arrived in Placerville via time travel, not by airplane or car or other modern transportation.

Then, beyond the foothills (down 1,000 feet or so in elevation), the landscape changes very rapidly (areas like Rolling Oaks are here). These are cattle and horse properties, also beautiful.

As I've mentioned, I owned property in this area for some time. In fact, lots of different properties, from 5 acres to 650 acres, and from Lake Tahoe to the Sacramento County line on the Cosumnes River. One piece was 160 acres, with two miles of Cosumnes River frontage with the best native trout fishing in the area next to large parcels I sold to movie people. They built log homes there.

You'll remember my near-drowning in Cyanide Creek in North Queensland, Australia (in part I). I was traveling to Cairns because of a call regarding my Tahoe property. That magnificent piece of land was worth a lot of trouble. I'd made many dangerous dives to pay for it. All well worth it. Nearly losing my life. But life is so fragile. I knew that from diving. I knew it from rolling underwater as a five-year-old, and again in the undertow off Melbourne, Australia, and yet again in Cyanide Creek.

But I still didn't really know just how fragile it was. I was about to find out, but before I get to that story, indulge me in a brief recounting of my time in the entertainment industry.

Yes, I was in a movie! *The Shadow Riders,* a made-for-TV movie that aired in 1982. This classic American Western was based on Louis L'Amour's novel of the same name. Directed by Andrew V. McLaglen, it starred Tom Selleck, Sam Elliott, Dominique Dunne, Ben Johnson, and Katharine Ross. And then there was one small but key role, that of a deputy sheriff, played by—you guessed it—Jim Broman. By now, I'm sure you'd think that I would have adored acting, being in the spotlight, and so on. Truth is I hated it. And I was a complete flop. I learned a lot about the movie business, though.

The movie is about two brothers who meet up after fighting on opposite sides of the Civil War, return home, and find their siblings have been kidnapped by ruthless raiders. Together, they set out on an adventure to rescue their family. It was a good movie, but, to be honest, I experienced so much real drama throughout my life—both the drama that I created and the drama I always somehow found myself immersed in—that drama for entertainment purposes never did much for me. In any case, I decided to make my first screen role my last.

There were two small but embarrassing moments that I must relate. The first one happened when I was in wardrobe prior to shooting my scene. They brought me this awful hat. It was extremely demeaning and totally uncool (to my standards of a cool hat, anyway). I wanted a hat like the ones Tom Selleck and Sam Elliot wore. So I refused to wear this bozo-type hat. The head of CBS came into wardrobe to find out what was holding things up. He was pissed because this type of delay cost big money. (This was kind of like my diving days on the rigs, when the oilfield guys would flip out over delays because they usually cost a cool million.) The cast and crew were on the payroll, so we all had to answer to the head. He said something to the wardrobe people, and they gave me a better hat. (Well, it was better than bozo, but not as good as the stars' hats.) I made the best of it. The second embarrassing moment came as I finished my scene. I walked to wardrobe, and a little boy came running up to me with a pen and paper, wanting my autograph. I felt so phony. I was not a star, and I didn't want to deceive the kid. I started to explain to the parents who were a few steps behind the boy, but someone from CBS showed up, telling me, "Just sign it. You're working for us now." So I signed it, and the kid was happy, but I never really felt right about it.

By the way, I was only in one scene, but my face did appear in all the commercials for the movie. I only worked as an extra for one day on *Shadow Riders,* but I was also the film coordinator, so I was with the director and cameraman every day. The production work was more exciting and interesting to me than the acting. My friend was the cameraman for *Shadow Riders,* and he got me the gig. (He was one of the best, by the way—worked on the original *Hawaii Five-O* with Jack Lord.) Just as in diving and other team-oriented types of work, interacting with the crew was fantastic—we became good friends, almost like family. The cast were a good lot too, even the stars. It was a great experience—off screen.

Eventually, of course, filming wrapped up, and I was back to my workaday life. Little did I know another deep Moon Pool was waiting just on the horizon.

From Moon Pool to Moon Roof— Placerville, California (1983)

During my time in Northern California, I was highly successful in land development. Owning great properties has always been one of my loves, from the cove hideaway on Cape Tribulation, North Queensland, Australia, to my property in the mountains of Lake Tahoe in California. I loved the Sierras, and I loved Placerville, but I missed having excitement every day. I wasn't diving, I wasn't bartending, I wasn't running a beach resort. I needed to do something exciting.

So, one day on one of my projects, I got on a D8, the largest bulldozer made by Caterpillar, and I fell in love with this big machine. I had a blast riding it. Every day, I continued to watch the crew working on my development, and I decided I was going to buy some D8s and other equipment and start a construction company. I knew it was essential to learn the business from the ground up; I'd done that with diving, bartending, and everything I ever did to earn a living. The most important thing in construction is to learn how to operate the huge machines. I did that. I bought two Caterpillars and a water truck, and pretty soon, I was doing my own work. Later, I was offered to do the longest subdivision road (nine miles). I accepted and got the contract. I had a Class A contractor's license to do that work. Successfully completed it.

But, eventually, that excitement dwindled too. I sold that business and equipment, and I moved on.

The problem was that I had nothing to move on *to*. And whenever I had nothing to move on to, whenever I got bored, trouble always soon followed. This time was worse than any that preceded it.

Leaving Poor Reds, my favorite pub, I was driving my six-month-old Mercedes at 125 miles an hour on a mountain road. A winding, twisting, tortuous mountain road. Remember my description of going up and down a spiral? I lived that metaphor in that moment. Perhaps as one of my friends put it later, "I was out of control and having too much fun."

That is a gross simplification of what actually happened. My right tire hit a culvert and blew. My car spun off the cliff. It rolled seven times. The car was totaled, obviously. I almost died in the crash. The only reason I didn't was that the person who saw me go off the cliff called 911. This was nothing short of a miracle, as it was three o'clock in the morning.

As the vehicle was rolling end over end, the only thing I could focus on was a pencil knocked off the dash and hurtling toward the backseat, propelled by the impact that hurled the car through the air and down the mountainside. The seatbelt system didn't work, and my head went right through the windshield, shattering the entire sheet of glass. I was thrown about inside the car, breaking every bone on the left side of my body. I fractured my skull, and part of my ear was severed. One of my lungs collapsed.

When the rescue team arrived, they had to use the Jaws of Life through the car's moon roof.

The rescue chief leaned down through the moon roof. "Can you hear me?" he asked.

"Yes," I said in a feeble voice. "But I'm almost dead."

He asked me if I could give him a phone number to call family.

I said, "Yes."

He said, "What is it?"

"Give me another drink, and I'll give it to you."

He told me he couldn't do that, so I wouldn't give him the number.

When I got to the hospital, they put all kinds of tubes in me. I was on life support. They had to strap me down because I kept ripping the tubes out, and then the surgeon had to reinstall them. He said I would die if I kept doing that, so they strapped me down.

I did survive, but I was on life support for well over two weeks. My recuperation was even longer, and I had to use a walker for months. They said I cheated death.

Still, I was ready for another moon pool—but not another moon roof. Were there more moon pools after that? Of course! Do you even have to ask? I was still me, and I always will be. But what happened following my convalescence was a completely different moon pool from any I'd ever dived into before. And that moon pool is a story for another book altogether.

That pretty much covers all my moon pools from 1942 to 1983. I realize that these moon pools as I have presented them to you are all over the place—both all over the world and jumping back and forth in time too. But that's how life is. At least for me. I'd jump into one moon pool, and all of a sudden I'd find myself thinking about another one from years before. When I was younger, diving into a moon pool would lead to my dreaming about other moon pools that were yet to be ... that existed only in my imagination. I came to understand that actual ripples in the deep water of my dives reached out to the figurative ripples that only existed in my dreams. Until I made them reality through guts, grit, and hard work. That's the practical side of the moon pools in our minds: we can see our dreams in their crystal-clear reflections, but it's up to us to make them happen.

We can only grow wise through experience, through recollecting and reflecting. We understand what life is about, and what we ourselves are about, by means of this process. Going within—reaching our core— requires honesty, integrity, and courage. The moon pool reflects all this back to us; it is the serene center where we go to seek and find the truth. We find the truth there because the moon pool is a sacred space, at once tranquil and dangerous, beautiful and harsh, clear and treacherous. Every sacred space is a paradox because danger and tranquility always dwell together, and beauty and harshness and clarity and treachery do as well. Therein lie both the mystery and the mystique: is the water crystal-clear, or does danger lurk in murky depths? We never really know for sure, and superficial appearances can be deceiving, even deadly.

All this is what the wisdom of the moon pool taught me. So I learned to trust my gut, take a deep breath, jump in, and go deep. That's what we all must do, in diving and in living. The Higher Power is always there, always with us, and it will always catch us when we fall or get lost in the waves. But we have to *believe* that we are protected. That means believing in ourselves and the Higher Power at the same time. That kind of belief is easy to comprehend but challenging to practice; it is deceptively simple, and it takes a lifetime to master. And yet, it is the only way to live in truth and with faith, and that is the only way to live life to the fullest.

Thank you for indulging me in my favored style of recollecting my story and sharing it with you. I wish you success in your own journey, in whatever form it takes. Whatever you do, do it boldly and bravely. And always remember, you can't live from fear *and* faith. So trust your gut, take a deep breath, jump in, and go deep.

ACKNOWLEDGMENTS

Throughout my many moon pools in life, I always ran with the best, and I feel deeply grateful for that blessing.

I want to thank all the old-time, hard-hat deep-sea divers who took care of me when I was growing up, starting with Captain Bill Thompson and Otto Block.

Next was Bill Biller, who sent me on my first wet-suit dive to fix a broken oil pipe. I was covered in oil, and I experienced firsthand what those poor birds and sea life go through after an oil spill. It was awful.

Most of all, my thanks to Scotty Chisholm, my godfather, who taught me everything about the hard-hat diving gear, working underwater with no visibility, in the sledge of the muddy bottom, in the creepy currents of the San Francisco Bay. He taught me how to weld and burn underwater, got me into the union, and gave me the best diving job in the country at that time (Moss Landing, California).

I also thank Torrance Parker, who wrote the book *20,000 Jobs under the Sea*. He is a great friend who was a legend in the commercial diving industry and assisted me with my article in the *Journal of Diving History* (the official publication of the Historical Diving Societies of USA, Canada, and Mexico), volume 17, issue 4.

Many thanks to Fred Johnson, a true friend.

I will always be grateful to Pete Blommers and Woody Treen, the owners of International Divers, for giving me my first deep-water job and the opportunity of a lifetime: diving on the state-of-the-art drillship *Glomar Conception*, in Territory of Papua, New Guinea, my first international assignment.

Many thanks also to Bob Benton, the head diver of Associated Divers. I made my first deep helium dive because of Benton.

I give just as many thanks to Don Thompson and former US Navy Master Diver Paul Pettingill, who ran the chamber and treated me during that life-threatening bout with the bends.

It is difficult to express in my words my gratitude to Captain Sir John Williams. The man was my guardian angel. It was because of him that I was able to sell my company, Broman International, without a hostile takeover.

Outside of the diving world, my thanks go to my friend Colonel David Hackworth, who led the search party for me in North Queensland, Australia, when my Land Cruiser was totaled in the flooded Cyanide Creek. His prowess in battle puts him in the ranks of such American heroes as Sergeant Alvin York and Audie Murphy.

My thanks also to the Miltons of California's El Dorado County, especially Mike Milton, my loyal and wonderful friend.

And also thanks to Warren Moore, who awarded me the longest rural subdivision road-building contract in El Dorado County, California.

I especially thank Dianna, my love, who has been right there to encourage me all through writing this book.

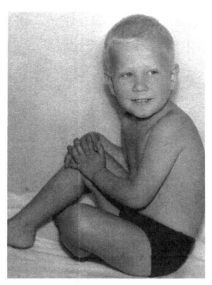

Growing up in Southern California, beach kid

High school

First hard-hat dive at sixteen years old

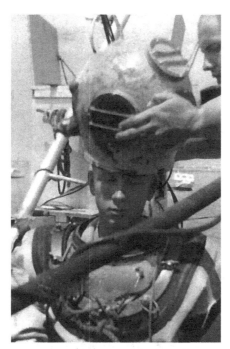

Putting helmet on for first dive

Ascending from Long Beach Harbor

Just breaking in and training with Scotty Chisolm

Getting ready to jump in

In the water

Scuba diving off Monterey, California

*Moss Landing, California, gantry in background
which holds the seventy-two-ton pipe*

*Seventy-two-ton pipe, twenty-four feet long and twelve feet
in diameter, which I inspected after installation under water*

*Divers and tenders in diver's shack, business
agent for the union to my left*

Taking a break after a long, hard dive

Dive in Oakland Harbor, California

PILE DRIVERS, BRIDGE, WHARF & DOCK BUILDER
457 BRYANT STREET   2315 VALDEZ STREET
SAN FRANCISCO   **UNION No. 34**   OAKLAND
DOuglas 2-2069   TWinoaks 3-5244
AFFILIATED WITH THE BAY COUNTIES DISTRICT COUNCIL OF CARPENTERS

FIRST QUARTER

NAME OF MEMBER   S.S. NO.

James Broman

JAN.

FEB.

1964   MAR. 3/20 *Mc Jennings*

HOLIDAYS THIS QUARTER — New Year's Day — Washington's Birthday

Union card as the youngest hard-hat diver in the union

First bell dive off Stearns Wharf,
Santa Barbara, California

Bell getting picked up to go into the water; I'm inside of it

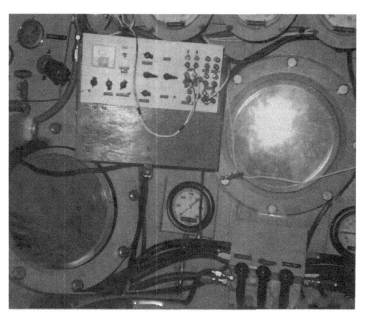

Inside the bell with control panel, telephones, submerged

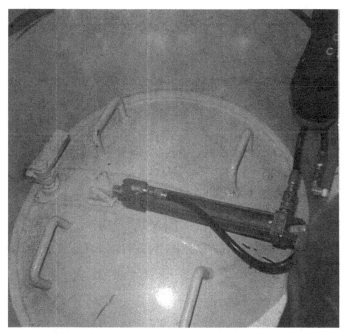

Hatch that opens to access ocean from bell

Log entry for first helium dive off the Cuss I at 263 feet
my deepest dive to that date, Santa Barbara, California

DIVCON

AUSTRALASIA PTY. LTD.
UNDERWATER CONTRACTORS
& ENGINEERS

JAMES BROMAN
DIVING SUPERINTENDENT

300 GEORGE STREET,
SYDNEY, AUSTRALIA 2000
TELEPHONE 28-8159

BOX 581,
PORT MORESBY
NEW GUINEA

International Diver, Inc. sold to Divcon, my new
business card, continued as diving superintendent

Going through the slalom course, practicing for the
Territory of Papua, New Guinea, Water-ski Championship

Port Moresby water skier, Jim Broman practising on Port Moresby harbor to-day. Jim is pictured executing some trick skiing manoeuvres. In the Port Moresby championships Jim was equal second in the trick skiing event. He tied with Evan Ives. Jim will be trying to defeat Ives at the Territory Championships in April.

Jim Broman trick skiing Port Moresby Harbour, Did finnally win the the tricks ski jump , 3rd the salom 1st overall

In Port Moresby Harbor trick skiing

317

*Making a 340-foot dive on air which is unheard of
and a record on air; helium had not arrived yet*

Started Broman International, logo designed by me

PROFESSIONAL UNDERWATER CONTRACTORS

BROMAN DIVERS INTERNATIONAL
PTY. LTD.

JAMES R. BROMAN
PRESIDENT AND MANAGING DIRECTOR

HEAD OFFICE:
P.O. BOX 509, SALE, VICTORIA. 3850, AUSTRALIA. TEL.: 44 2587. TELEX 51563
G.P.O. BOX S 1473; PERTH, WEST AUSTRALIA, 6001. TEL.: (092) 641318
P.O. BOX 52432, LAFAYETTE, LOUISIANA, 70501, U.S.A. TEL.: (318) 232 9313
P.O. BOX 1686, JOHANNESBURG, SOUTH AFRICA. TEL.: 8366059
C/O S.T.L., 2 SHENTON WAY, 2ND FLOOR, I.C.B. BLDG., SINGAPORE, TEL.: 981651-5

property of Jim Broman

*Broman International business card,
offices around the world*

Flying in by JetRanger helicopter to the
Glomar Conception *on the Bass Strait*

Making a dive off Mozambique, Africa, same
equipment used out of the diving bell

Trying new diving equipment, advanced hat

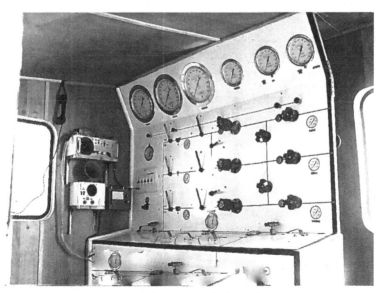

Broman Divers helium manifold on the Bass Strait

*My equipment after being awarded all the
platform work in the Bass Strait*

*First bell system ever built in Australia, built
by me, placed on the* Navigator drill ship

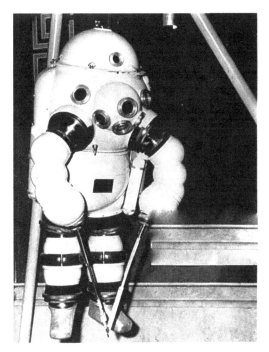

Galeazzi, one-atmosphere diving suit,
which hung in the shop for years

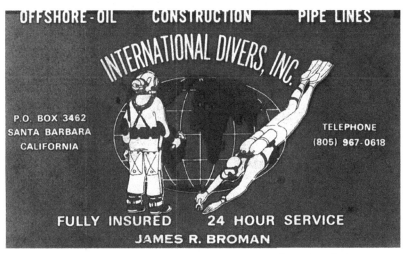

After successfully making deep-water dive, hired
by International Divers, Inc., business card

531st squadron patch in Masawa, Japan

I designed five thirsty-first patch for guys in the squadron

Crew chief on F104 Starfighter, Moron Airbase, Spain, during Cuba crisis

Sam Elliot and me on the set of the Shadow Riders *movie*

Tom Selleck and Sam Elliot on the set of Shadow Riders

Waiting for my scene, Shadow Riders